PHP Programming for Windows®

Contents At a Glance

PHP Programming for Windows®

Andrew Stopford

New Riders

www.newriders.com

201 West 103rd Street, Indianapolis, Indiana 46290
An Imprint of Pearson Education
Boston • Indianapolis • London • Munich • New York • San Francisco

PHP Programming for Windows®

Trademarks

Warning and Disclaimer

Publisher
David Dwyer

Associate Publisher
Stephanie Wall

Production Manager
Gina Kanouse

Managing Editor
Kristy Knoop

Acquisitions Editor
Deborah Hittel-Shoaf

Development Editor
Chris Zahn

Product Marketing Manager
Kathy Malmloff

Publicity Manager
Susan Nixon

Project Editor
Todd Zellers

Copy Editor
Gayle Johnson

Indexer
Cheryl Lenser

Manufacturing Coordinator
Jim Conway

Book Designer
Louisa Klucznik

Cover Designer
Brainstorm Design, Inc.

Cover Production
Aren Howell

Proofreader
Sossity Smith

Composition
Gloria Schurick

❖

This book is dedicated to Emma. For you, my love.

❖

TABLE OF CONTENTS

About the Author

Andrew Stopford has been developing web and software applications for the last seven years and is currently a web programmer with the major online retailer dabs.com. Andrew has written about various computing and web application subjects in magazines and websites worldwide, such as *Web Update, Macromedia Europe Developer's Journal, Internet.Works,* Zend.com, asptoday.com, and gendev.net. Andrew is also a member of various open source projects including XML-RPC for ASP Project and the NMatrix Project.

About the Technical Reviewers

These reviewers contributed their considerable hands-on expertise to the entire development process for this book. As this book was being written, these dedicated professionals reviewed all the material for technical content, organization, and flow. Their feedback was critical to ensuring that this book fits our readers' need for the highest-quality technical information.

Zak Greant is the lead developer for 51 Degrees North (http:// 51north.com) and is a proud member of the Foo & Associates (http://fooassociates.com) programmers' cooperative. He leads the PHP Quality Assurance Team (http://qa.php.net/) and is an active contributor to the PHP documentation, mailing lists, and source code.

Dan Hendricks has been involved with the design of dynamic web pages for seven years. After finishing his undergraduate degree at the University of Wisconsin, Eau Claire, he worked as a web-based learning specialist for the university. Currently, he is working as a consultant for a regional web design company in Wisconsin and is pursuing a master's degree in information systems.

Graeme Merrall is a senior developer for the Internet arm of a major television station in Sydney, Australia. Graeme has been developing in PHP since version 2 and has authored a number of tutorials on PHP as well as being the co-author of *PHP Functions Essential Reference,* also from New Riders.

Torben Wilson is a freelance developer, technical, writer, and contributing author of New Rider's *PHP Functions Essential Reference.* He has been programming professionally in PHP since 1996 and has been on the PHP Documentation Team since 1997.

Acknowledgments

The acknowledgments are perhaps the hardest thing to write in a book, because many people go into making a book happen. From an early age, I have wanted to write a book, and I want to thank the people who helped make it happen.

Let me begin with the staff at New Riders, particularly Theresa and Stephanie for getting the ball rolling. Thanks to Deborah for keeping the project moving along and for organizing me. Also thanks to Chris for catching my less-than-great English and for being patient with a first-time author. Also, thanks to my technical editors, Zak Daniel, Graeme, and Torben, for all their help in answering my questions and help in improving this book. My uttermost thanks to you all.

Thanks to all the people who along the way have given me a great deal of help and support. Thanks to Vernon Viehe, Billy Ray, Winson Cheung, Tim Slater, Colin Cherot, Wayne Smith, Chrissy Rey, Tim Goss, David Shumate, Elizabeth Cherry, Gordon Bell, and anyone else I might have forgotten. You know who you are.

No PHP book is complete without giving thanks to the community that helps develop PHP. Many thanks to Rasmus Lerdorf and the other PHP developers who continue to create and build PHP into one of the most astounding programming languages ever developed. Further thanks to Andres Otto and Daniel Bealshausen of the php4win project for all the work they do. Also, thanks to John Lim for taking the time to write the foreword and for all the help and information he provides. Also, thanks to Jim for creating and developing the great ADODB extension for PHP.

Writing a book tends to swallow your time whole, so my thanks go to all the people who suffered because I was writing. Thanks to my mum, dad (thanks for the office, Dad), and sisters (Suzannah and Hayley) for all the love and support they have given me. Also, my thanks to two of the greatest people I have ever met, Mary and Terry, for their warmth, love, and support (not to mention the coffee).

Finally, to the one person who has to suffer the most through my endeavors. This book is what it's all about, and it's all for you, my sweet. I love you with all my heart, Emma.

Tell Us What You Think

As a reader of this book, you are the most important critic and commentator. We value your opinion and want to know what we're doing right, what we could do better, what areas you'd like to see us publish in, and any other words of wisdom you're willing to pass our way.

As the Associate Publisher for New Riders Publishing, I welcome your comments. You can fax, email, or write me directly to let me know what you did or didn't like about this book--as well as what we can do to make our books stronger.

Please note that I cannot help you with technical problems related to the topic of this book, and that due to the high volume of mail I receive, I might not be able to reply to every message.

When you write, please be sure to include this book's title and author, as well as your name and phone or fax number. I will carefully review your comments and share them with the author and editors who worked on this book.

Fax: 317-581-4663

Email: nrfeedback@newriders.com

Mail: Stephanie Wall
          Associate Publisher
          New Riders Publishing
          201 West 103rd Street
          Indianapolis, IN 46290 USA

Foreword

In my life, I have known a lot of programming languages. Some have been great friendships all my life, such as C, and others, such as Prolog, were mere student flirtations.

I first met PHP in 1999 when I was still working with Active Server Pages, and I was immediately struck by its simplicity and elegance. PHP seems to combine some of the best features of JavaScript and Perl while avoiding many of their faults. In PHP, strings are just another data type (unlike JavaScript, where they are objects), and PHP uses a clean C-like syntax that is easy to read (thereby avoiding Perl's eccentricities).

As a Windows programmer, I was delighted by the large library of user-contributed extensions available for PHP. What would have required the purchase of commercial libraries in ASP was available for free in PHP, and with source code to boot. I felt that Windows programmers could gain a lot by using PHP, so in August 2000 I started one of the first web sites to cover cross-platform PHP scripting and using PHP on Windows—http://php.weblogs.com.

While using PHP, I started to port some of my ASP code to PHP. Since I programmed primarily in JScript, it was mostly a matter of putting $ signs in front of all the variables. However, I began to miss one of my favorite tools in Windows—ADO, Microsoft's set of objects for manipulating databases. So I developed the PHP database wrapper library called ADOdb, which provides functionality similar to that of ADO for PHP and runs on both Windows and UNIX. To my pleasant surprise, it seems that many PHP programmers are also Windows programmers, and thousands of people have downloaded and are using this open-source library.

I am very pleased to see that, in the same spirit of promoting cross-platform PHP, Andrew Stopford has spent a lot of time and effort coming up with this book on PHP for Windows. He even covers how PHP can work with the latest Microsoft technologies such as .NET, which is complementary to PHP because it is language-neutral. I hope this book proves useful, both in your home and as a reference at work.

—*John Lim*

Introduction

PHP is a word not commonly used in sentences that also have the word Windows. PHP is a very popular open-source programming language for the web. It is used with other open-source software, such as the Linux OS and the Apache web server (plus, it runs extremely well on these platforms). But Windows itself is often left out. You don't often find books or web sites that focus on Windows PHP development. Rather, the focus is largely on developing on Linux platforms.

Why should that be so? PHP is as capable of running both on a Windows desktop and in a Windows enterprise as any commonly used language, such as ASP and ColdFusion, to mention a couple. In addition, PHP can cope with all the features a Windows web developer needs, such as COM, LDAP, ODBC, and ADO.

You can successfully create solutions with other open-source technologies (the MySQL database, for example) that run on both platforms. However, sometimes a developer focuses on one platform and needs to take advantage of what that platform offers.

This book addresses these issues and shows you how to go about using PHP to take advantage of the Windows platform.

Who Should Read This Book

This book is aimed at developers who focus largely on Windows as their development platform and who want to take advantage of some of the features it offers. The book also appeals to developers who use Windows as a staging platform before they upload their solution to a Linux server. (If this is you, please read the next section.)

Who This Book Is Not For

This book is not for developers who use the Linux platform. This book aims to allow Linux developers to reuse some of the code on both platforms. However, most of the technologies covered in this book are not yet implemented on the Linux platform. I recommend New Riders' *Web Application Development with PHP 4.0,* by Tobias Ratschiller and Til Gerken, for developers who are developing PHP solutions for both platforms.

Prerequisites

This book assumes that you have a Windows OS, such as Windows 98. Most chapters will work with most Win32 OSs; however, you will need Windows 2000 for the Active Directory chapter. You will also need the database software described in this book and Microsoft Visual Basic 5.0 or 6.0 for the COM sections of the PHP, COM, and .NET chapter. For the .NET portions of the PHP, COM and .NET chapter you will need the .NET Framework 1.0. Please note that the ASP code that is presented throughout the book is ASP 3.0.

Overview

This book is divided into three main parts, plus appendixes. Each of these parts and the chapters within them are discussed next.

Part I: Getting Started with PHP

Part I is aimed at developers who might have little or no PHP development experience. If you are an ASP developer, you will find information on how PHP differs from what you know and how to apply what you know to learn PHP.

Chapter 1: Introduction to PHP

What PHP is and how it came about are both important and interesting to know. You will learn how PHP has developed, why it develops differently from the way most software develops, and what the future might hold for PHP on the Windows platform.

Chapter 2: Installation and Optimization

You'll learn how to install and optimize PHP on the various common Windows web servers.

Part II: Introduction to PHP Programming

Part II is aimed at developers who might have a moderate amount of PHP experience and who want to dig deeper into PHP syntax and functions.

Chapter 3: PHP Programming

If you are completely new to PHP, this chapter teaches you the language's syntax and functions.

Chapter 4: PHP and Files

Accessing files is an important part of the functionality of your applications. Here you'll learn how to access files using PHP.

Chapter 5: PHP and Sessions

Maintaining state in your web applications is often vital. Here you'll learn how to use PHP's built-in state management functions and how to use WDDX to transfer state between PHP applications and applications written in other languages, such as ASP.

Chapter 6: PHP and Databases

Databases are commonly used in your web applications. You'll learn how to use PHP with common Windows databases, such as Microsoft Access and Microsoft SQL Server, and other databases, such as Oracle and MySQL, using PHP's built-in functions and ODBC functions.

Part III: Advanced PHP Programming

Part III is aimed at experienced PHP developers who want to learn how to use some of the more advanced features of the Windows platform with PHP.

Chapter 7: PHP, COM, and .NET

COM is the cornerstone of the Windows platform. Here you'll learn how to create COM objects with Microsoft Visual Basic and use them in your PHP applications. You'll also learn about the future of the Windows platform with Microsoft .NET and how you can start working with .NET and PHP.

Chapter 8: PHP and XML

XML is fast becoming the standard language of the Internet. You'll use it more and more in your web applications. In this chapter you'll learn how to use PHP's built-in XML functions and how to use COM to access Microsoft's XML functions.

Chapter 9: PHP and Web Services

Web services are set to change how the web works. Here you'll learn what web services are and how you can create them using PHP and SOAP.

Chapter 10: PHP and ADO

ADO is a fast and powerful way to access databases. This chapter shows you how to use both COM and PHP functions to take advantage of ADO.

Chapter 11: PHP and Active Directory

An important part of a Windows 2000 network is its management and structure. The Windows Active Directory plays a vital part in this. You'll learn how to use PHP with Active Directory using both COM and PHP's LDAP functions.

Part IV: Appendixes

Part IV includes some useful appendixes that help you establish ODBC database connections and install a variety of web servers.

Appendix A: Creating an ODBC Connection

You'll learn how to install an ODBC database connection for Access and SQL Server databases on the Windows 9x, Windows 2000, and Windows NT platforms.

Appendix B: Installing a Web Server

You need a web server to start developing PHP applications. This appendix shows you how to obtain, install, and set up the most common Windows web servers, including Microsoft PWS, Microsoft IIS 4 and 5, and Apache.

Conventions

This book uses the following conventions:

Convention	Usage
Italic	New terms being defined. Also, in syntax statements, where you should substitute a value of your own choosing.
`Monospace`	Commands, syntax, options, and so on, as well as Internet addresses, such as `www.a-coda.com`.
➥	A code continuation character is inserted into code when a line shouldn't be broken, but we simply ran out of room on the page and had to continue the code to the next line.

I

Getting Started with PHP

1

Introduction to PHP

WHEN I FIRST STARTED USING PHP SOME three years ago, I came from an ASP background and started searching for information that would help me develop PHP solutions on a Windows platform.

PHP is available for the Windows and Linux platforms, but most of its developer audience consists of Linux developers. As such, most books, articles, and web sites show you how to use PHP on the Linux platform. Windows-specific information can often be hard to find.

This book addresses this issue and looks at how to install and start using PHP on the Windows platform. Along the way, we will look at technologies such as the Simple Object Access Protocol (SOAP) and Local Directory Application Protocol (LDAP) and see how to use them with PHP in a Windows environment.

Although this book focuses on the Windows platform, if you are a Linux developer, you still might find it useful. The PHP syntax is the same on both platforms, as are most of the functions. Some developers use Windows for prototyping before uploading their code to a Linux production server.

> **Note**
> There are some differences between various Win32 platforms in certain system-specific areas such
> as logging, file systems, and command execution. It is recommended that you check the PHP man-
> ual on the PHP web site for any details that relate to your platform if you are having trouble
> getting a function to work correctly.

The following chapters should be of interest to both Windows and Linux
users:

- Chapter 3, "PHP Programming"
- Chapter 4, "PHP and Files"
- Chapter 5, "PHP and Sessions"
- The MySQL section of Chapter 6, "PHP and Databases"

If your focus is Linux, the following web sites might help:

- http://www.php.net/manual/en/install.linux.php
- http://www.linuxfund.com
- http://www.phpbuilder.com (also features great resources for Windows
  PHP development)

What Is PHP?

What the acronym PHP stands for has always been a little unclear, but officially it stands for hypertext preprocessor.

If you have ever used ASP or ColdFusion, you are familiar with mixing
these languages with HTML to obtain database data, perform logic, and create
HTML pages on-the-fly. In essence, this is what PHP is: It's an open-source
server-side programming language that can be mixed with HTML in the same
way that ASP and ColdFusion can be. It runs on the Windows and Linux platforms.

How Did PHP Develop?

If you like to know how a technology has developed, this section is for you.
Here I cover how PHP has developed historically.

PHP 1.0

The story of how PHP was developed begins in 1994 with Rasmus Lerdorf.
At the time, Lerdorf had just graduated from college and wanted to track the

number of users visiting his online resume. He created Personal Home Page tools for this task, which were effectively a bunch of CGI scripts written in Perl.

PHP 2.0/FI

Lerdorf's friends were interested in these scripts, and at their request, he started adding more features. He decided to redevelop his PHP tools in C, and he added some programming features and an HTML Form Interpreter. This became known as PHP 2.0/FI and was a kind of semi-programming language that could be added to standard HTML code.

At this point, PHP 2.0/FI became *open source* (this topic is covered more in a moment), and a group of developers (Lerdorf, Andi Gutmans, Zeev Suraski, Stig Bakken, Shane Caraveo, and Jim Winstead—also covered more in a moment) gathered around PHP to create PHP 3.0.

PHP 3.0

While PHP 2.0/FI was still around, two university graduates, Andi Gutmans and Zeev Suraski, were using PHP for a university project and had created a new, much improved core scripting engine for PHP. Encouraged by their professor, Michael Rodeh, who also was head of IBM research in Haifa, Israel, they released the source code for the new engine to the PHP community. The community built on the new engine, and it quickly became the official next release of PHP—PHP 3.0.

With PHP 3.0, the Form Interpreter was added to the PHP core, and the programming language was built upon. What developed from PHP 2.0/FI was one of the first web programming languages of its kind—a server-side programming language mixed with HTML. Up to this point, most web-based applications had been built using CGI and Perl or C++. Along with ColdFusion and ASP, PHP helped introduce a new way to mix HTML and a programming language on the same page.

Even at that point, PHP was a powerful programming language. As an open-source language, it was growing in its functionality and features.

PHP was refined, and although it was based on C and C++, it also took features from languages such as Pascal, Basic, and Perl. PHP 3.0 also added an API so that developers could write PHP modules and further extend PHP without needing to change and compile the PHP core.

Gutmans and Suraski were looking to the future. They put the PHP core through another rewrite to help create PHP 4.0.

PHP 4.0

Of all the versions, PHP 4.0 is the most powerful and modular. It quickly helped PHP prove itself as an enterprise-wide contender comparable in might to ColdFusion and ASP.

PHP 4.0 is the most powerful version of PHP to date. Significant changes to PHP helped it grow past its roots as a collection of Perl CGI scripts to a full-fledged web programming language. PHP scripts are no longer run line by line; instead, they are compiled and then run. Object-oriented support was implemented, and important new types and strict type checking and matching features were added.

Suraski and Gutmans created the Zend Corporation. Half of the PHP core was under commercial license (called the Zend engine). Much of the PHP core and the PHP language itself remain open source. With the rewrite, PHP was even more modular than before.

As you will see later in this chapter, Zend has created many products that can be added to the PHP core to increase power and flexibility.

What Is Open Source?

Open source is often a topic of debate, and it is a strange way of working for most Windows developers, but as a Windows developer, I find it an inspiring development model.

I encourage you to visit the following web sites for more information:

- `http://www.opensource.com`
- `http://www.sourceforge.net`
- `http://www.gnu.org`

How Does PHP Development Differ from Developing in ASP or ColdFusion?

The most important distinction between PHP and ASP or ColdFusion is that it's free and open; both ASP and ColdFusion are commercial and closed products. Experienced PHP developers often look at PHP's source code to figure out what is going on when the going gets tough.

ASP is freely available with the Windows NT Option Pack and is a part of the Windows 2000 operating system, and it runs only on Microsoft web servers. For other web servers, you must purchase third-party commercial implementations. ASP can use any COM-compliant language, such as VBScript and JScript.

ColdFusion is available for other web servers (and other platforms, such as Windows and Linux) and has a free version available. However, most of the features you would want to use (such as accessing databases) are included only on the commercial version. ColdFusion differs quite a lot from PHP and ASP in that it uses a markup-like syntax called CFML. PHP and ASP use a more conventional programming-language-like syntax.

Interestingly, ColdFusion was developed much like PHP. In 1994, web developer Jeremy Allaire was using Perl and CGI for his web applications but saw the need for an easier way to do things. He joined forces with his brother, and they created ColdFusion.

At the time ColdFusion was released, another company called Aspect Software created a product called Hot Lava that was similar to ColdFusion but that used the Visual Basic scripting language as its programming language. Microsoft bought the company in early 1996 and later that year released Active Server Pages (ASP) as part of Internet Information Server (IIS) 3.0.

Who Is Responsible for Further Development of PHP?

The PHP core can be developed by anyone, but some of the main PHP developers are listed in this section:

Rasmus Lerdorf continues to contribute to the development of the PHP core. He has joined the advisory board of the ActiveState Corporation, which created the popular Windows ports of Perl, TCL, and Python and tools for Perl and PHP development, such as the Komodo IDE. Lerdorf is also a member of the Apache Software Foundation Group.

Andi Gutmans is partly responsible for the PHP 3.0 core and the Zend engine (which is a part of PHP 4.0). He is also one of the partners in the Zend Corporation.

Zeev Suraski is partly responsible for the PHP 3.0 core and the Zend engine (which is a part of PHP 4.0). He is also one of the partners in the Zend Corporation. He helped run PHP on web servers such as IIS and databases such as MySQL and Sybase.

Stig Bakken has been a part of PHP development since PHP 2.0/FI and continues to help develop the PHP core in his spare time.

Shane Caraveo has been helping with the development of the PHP core since PHP 2.0/FI. He helped port PHP 2.0/FI and PHP 3.0 to Windows and helped develop PHP to run on Windows web servers such as IIS and PWS.

Jim Winstead is one of the developers responsible for helping develop PHP since PHP 2.0/FI.

Sascha Schumann is a very active member of the PHP development group. He is responsible for several PHP SAPI modules for AOL Server, Apache 2.0, TUX, and HTTPd, to name a few. He also has made improvements to the PHP language, such as thread safety and `regex` cache.

Sam Ruby is a senior programmer at IBM and is a member of the PHP core group and the Apache Software Foundation group. He has done much work with PHP and Java and is responsible for the Servlet version of PHP. He also has done a lot of work on PHP and the Windows platform, creating the first set of instructions for installing PHP on the Windows platform and creating the .NET PHP module.

Theis C. Arntzen is a member of the PHP core group and is largely responsible for the Oracle PHP modules.

Andrei Zmievski is a member of both the PHP core group and the Apache Software Foundation group. He is responsible for the WDDX, session extension, and Perl-compatible regular-expression modules. He is also one of the folks behind the PHP-GTK project.

PHP Today

PHP is approaching its 4.1 landmark version. This section looks at the current state of PHP.

Applications Developed in PHP

For a complete list of PHP applications, go to `http://www.php.net/projects.php`. Here are a couple of PHP applications that stand out:

- Midguard: Midguard is a powerful database-driven content-management system for the web and WAP.

- Phorum: Phorum is a PHP-based discussion forum. PHP applications are popular, and although they are open-source, they tend to use the MySQL database as the supported database.

Products for PHP

The following is a list of products that are available from the Zend Corporation. You can download them from http://www.zend.com/zend/products.php.

- Zend Optimizer: The Zend Optimizer is a freely available extension to PHP that allows your code to be optimized before it is run by the PHP core. This improves your code's speed and efficiency. We will look at how to use the Zend Optimizer in Chapter 2, "Installation and Optimization."

- Zend Cache: The Zend Cache is a commercial add-on product for PHP that improves speed by optimizing code and caching repetitive code. The performance improvement can be huge if you are really crunching code. The cache also comes complete with a friendly GUI system so that you can control the cache and benchmark if you want to.

- Zend Encoder: The Zend Encoder is a commercial add-on product for PHP that allows you to encode your PHP scripts so that they can't be read by others but can still be run through PHP. If you want to protect your PHP code, this system is ideal.

- Zend IDE: A commercial Java-based IDE editor (thus, it runs on both Windows and Linux platforms), Zend IDE provides PHP syntax color coding, debugging, and more. Zend has said that it will add more to the editor over time.

The Future of PHP

No one really knows what PHP 5.0 will bring. However, a few interesting ongoing projects might suggest how PHP will develop in the future:

- PHP GTK: The PHP GTK project is a departure from most PHP projects in that it is aimed at creating client-side applications complete with a GTK GUI. You can learn more about this project and download the code at http://gtk.php.net.

- Zend: Zend will undoubtedly bring more commercial products to PHP. A PHP compiler is in the pipeline. This means that PHP will be able to compete with the new breed of compiled web applications, such as Microsoft's ASP.NET. See the Zend web site at http://www.zend.com.

- ActiveState: As I mentioned, ActiveState has Rasmus Lerdorf on its advisory board. It has added support for PHP development and debugging to its Komodo IDE editor. Although this is sheer speculation on my part,

I hope ActiveState will produce a PHP distribution/installer and bring to PHP what it has brought to Perl and Python—its expertise in Microsoft .NET and SOAP. Visit ActiveState at `http://www.activestate.com`.

Summary

This chapter looked at who invented PHP and how it has developed as open-source technology. I also introduced you to a few of the key people involved in the development of PHP and showed you what the future holds for its development. In the next chapter, I will show you how to install PHP and create a sample page to test your installation.

Installation and Optimization

THIS CHAPTER SHOWS YOU HOW TO DOWNLOAD, install, and optimize PHP on your computer. The steps vary slightly depending on what version of Microsoft Windows you have, but I will show you the differences as you proceed through this chapter. By the end of this chapter, you should have a working, optimized version of PHP ready to start using.

Planning Your Installation of PHP

The first step in installing PHP is to download it. PHP is open-source software and thus is ever-changing. Every day/week/month the software is improving, so I encourage you to look only to the Internet for PHP. The versions of PHP distributed on CDs are often out of date.

What to Download

Unlike software such as ASP or ColdFusion (but like the early days of Perl), you need to manually install PHP. You can download an automatic Windows installer for PHP, but it's often better to install PHP manually. The automatic installer does not include all PHP modules and is limited to IIS, PWS, Xitami, and Apache web servers, whereas you have full flexibility with a manual installation. This chapter covers the steps for installing PHP both manually and using the installer. As we run through these methods, I will explore the pros and cons of each.

Optimization Considerations

You can optimize PHP with a product from Zend called the Zend Optimizer (covered in the section "Zend Optimizer"). Before downloading PHP, you should consider whether you want to optimize PHP with this product. If you do, you should first check the Zend Technologies Ltd. web site (`http://www.zend.com`) to see what version of PHP the Zend Optimizer supports, and then download that version of PHP. In considering whether you want to use Zend Optimizer, be aware of what web server you are using. The gain in speed from the optimizer might not be more than what you would get from simply running PHP as an Apache module. Although no actual benchmarks on this are available, it's worth considering which speed-gain method works best for you.

Compiling PHP

PHP can be compiled from its source code. Sadly, most of the documentation for this is aimed at the Linux community, because you must compile PHP for this OS. It is quite rare to compile PHP on the Windows OS. Unless you want to stay on the cutting edge of PHP and want to compile PHP every time its source changes, you won't need to compile it. You can find further information on compiling PHP at `http://www.php.net/manual/en/install.windows.php`.

Downloading PHP

You have two options when downloading PHP for Windows: go to the official PHP web site, or go to the PHP for Windows project site. Both approaches are explored in the next sections.

Option One: The Official PHP Web Site

PHP's home and the place where PHP is developed and updated by its open-source community is `http://www.php.net/downloads.php`, shown in Figure 2.1. You can download PHP for Windows and Linux here. For Windows, you can download the manual and automatic installations.

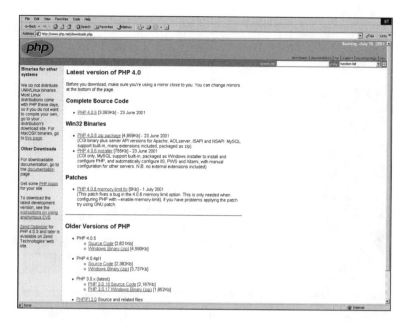

Figure 2.1   The official PHP web site.

Downloading the Manual Installation

Under the Win32 Binaries heading, click PHP *x.x.x* zip package to download (this was the PHP 4.0.6 zip package at the time this book was written). Save this file to a convenient place on your hard drive. Manual installation instructions are covered in the section "Installing PHP."

Downloading the Automatic Installer

Under the Win32 Binaries heading, click PHP *x.x.x* installer to download (this was the PHP 4.0.6 installer at the time this book was written). Save this file to a convenient place on your hard drive. Instructions on using the automatic installer are covered in the section "Installing PHP."

Option Two: The php4win Project Site

A great resource site for PHP programmers on the Windows platform is the site www.php4win.com, shown in Figure 2.2.

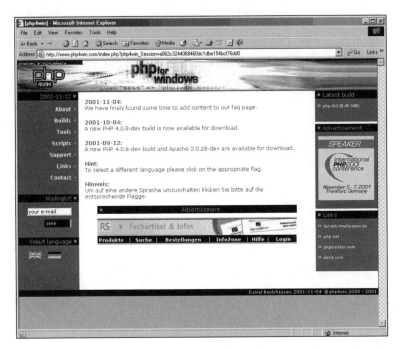

Figure 2.2   The php4win web site.

It's worth noting that you can use installers taken from either site. The steps remain the same.

Downloading the Manual Installer

Although I call this the manual installer, it is not really what you might expect from a manual installer. It's more a collection of compiled files. The fact that you have to manually install these files is why this method is called a manual installation.

From the home page, select the latest build. From there, you are presented with the manual installer file to download. It is packaged as an .exe file, as shown in Figure 2.3.

Figure 2.3   The latest PHP build from the php4win web site.

Installing PHP

Now that you have an installer, it is time to install PHP. The installation process
is different for Windows than for Linux. For Linux instructions, I recommend
that you visit `http://www.php.net/manual/en/install.linux.php`.

I will begin the process with the manual installer and then will cover the
automatic installer.

Manual Installer

The manual installer is the more difficult installation method. However, it is
also more flexible.

Creating a PHP Directory

The first step is to create a directory into which you will install PHP. Figure 2.4
shows how I created a directory called PHP in the root of my C drive.
You might want to add security features to this directory. I recommend adding
at least Read & Execute permissions to the IIS guest account.

As shown in Figure 2.5, my Internet guest account is ANDREW\
IUSR_ANDREW, with Read & Execute permissions added. (Note that
the permissions dialog box truncates the Internet guest account name
when displaying the account name. For example, Figure 2.5 shows the
IUSR_ANDREW account name as ANDREW\IUSR.)

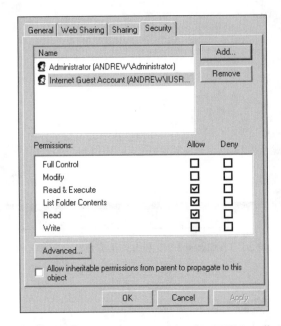

Figure 2.5   NTFS file permission options for the PHP installation folder.

How you add NTFS file permissions to an account name depends on what
type of Windows OS you have. In most cases you can right click the folder
and select properties, then select security, but please consult the documentation
for your version of the Windows OS for more information. Figure 2.5 shows
the Windows 2000 NTFS file permissions.

Unzipping the PHP Files

Next you need to unzip the manual installer file in your PHP directory.
   If you used the official PHP site download, double-click the zip file. The
WinZip application should open (see Figure 2.6). Click Extract, and enter
the path to your PHP directory, such as C:\PHP. (Note that if you don't have
WinZip installed, you can download it from http://www.winzip.com.)

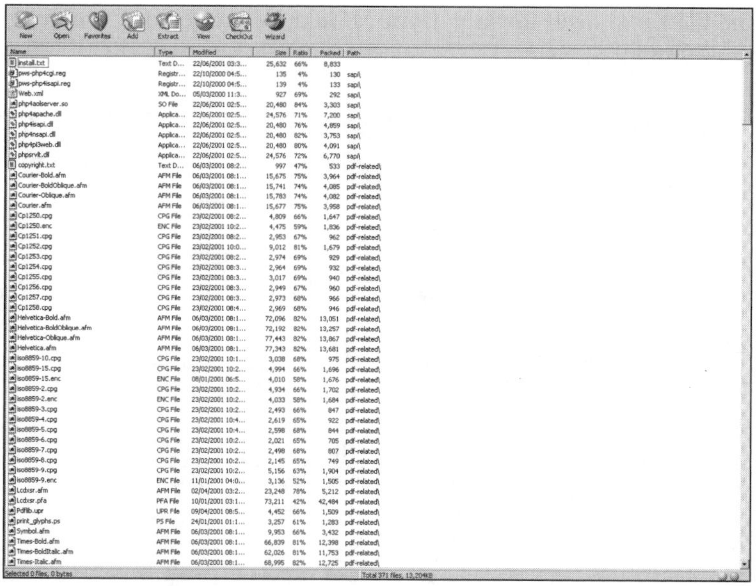

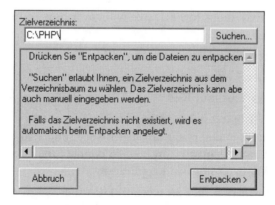

Figure 2.6   The PHP manual installer contents shown in WinZip.

If you downloaded the PHP binaries from the php4win project site, double-click the .exe file. In the dialog box shown in Figure 2.7, enter the path to your PHP directory, such as C:\PHP\. Then click the Entpacken (Unpack) button.

Figure 2.7   The manual PHP installer from the php4win web site.

After the files have been unzipped, you should see a directory structure, as shown in Figure 2.8.

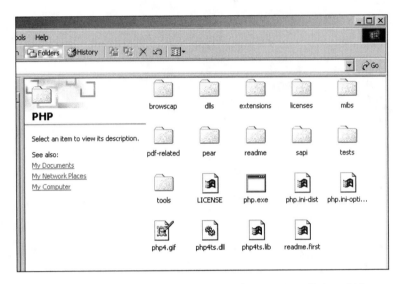

Figure 2.8 PHP manually installed into the PHP installation folder.

The directories in this directory structure include the following:

- browscap: Files for browser detection.
- dlls: Installation files (these are discussed in a moment).
- extensions: Extensions to PHP (we will cover how to install these later in this chapter).
- licenses: Licensing information for PHP.
- mibs: High-level information about some of the protocols used in PHP.
- pdf-related: Various font files.
- pear: The PHP Extension and Application Repository—a collection of PHP extensions and applications that is very similar to Perl's CPAN. This folder contains information on how to connect to and use PEAR, as well as PEAR extensions and applications.
- readme: Information files on several PHP issues. Be sure to read these files so that you are aware of any installation and other issues relating to your PHP release.

- sapi: Files that are used to install PHP to your web server (these are covered later in this chapter). This files represent the Server API (Application Programming Interface). The libraries contain the code that allows PHP to natively interface with a variety of web servers.

- tests: A PHP file that can be used to test PHP (this is covered later in this chapter).

- tools: Various open-source programs that are used by certain PHP extensions (such as MING).

Installing the PHP System DLL File

The first step to installing PHP is to place the PHP DLLs and support files in the Windows System directory. You need to move the php4ts.dll and php4ts.lib files, as well as all the files in the C:\PHP\dlls\ folder, from the C:\PHP\ folder. Move these files to the C:\WINDOWS\System\ folder (if you're running Windows 95/98/ME) or the C:\WINNT\System32\ folder (if you're running Windows NT/2000).

While moving the files, you might see one or more error messages. You can safely ignore messages stating that the msvcrt file is in use. Click the OK button to continue.

If you see a dialog box that asks whether you want to copy older files over newer files, click No to continue. Copying older files over newer files might have negative effects on your system.

Installing Other PHP DLL Files

The next stage is to add DLL files that PHP needs in order to run. You must add these to your system path.

From the dlls folder (in our example, this is C:\PHP\dlls\), copy all the DLL files to your system path.

If you receive a "file in use" error message, as shown in Figure 2.9, you can ignore it. Go ahead and click OK.

Figure 2.9 File copy error message.

If you receive a file copy message that warns of copying older files over newer files (see Figure 2.10), click No. As mentioned earlier, copying over newer files with older files can cause chaos.

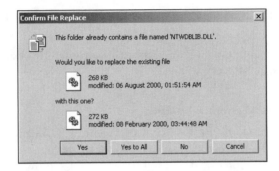

Figure 2.10 File replace warning message.

Installing the php.ini File

The next stage is to locate and install the php.ini file. This file is where you set up all the options that PHP needs, such as where the PHP extensions are located, what extensions to use, and so on.

The php.ini file actually starts life as two files called php.ini-dst and php.ini-optimized. You can use either of these files to create the php.ini file. You would normally use php.ini-dst. However, if you would like fewer options to choose from, a simpler layout, and more preselected options to help PHP run faster and more securely, use the php.ini-optimized file. In these examples, I use the php.ini-dst file, but the installation technique is the same for both files.

Rename the file php.ini and then copy it to the Windows directory (usually C:\WINDOWS\ or C:\WINNT\). Next, open the php.ini file in an editor such as Notepad, as shown in Figure 2.11, and locate the following text:

```
extension_dir = ./
```

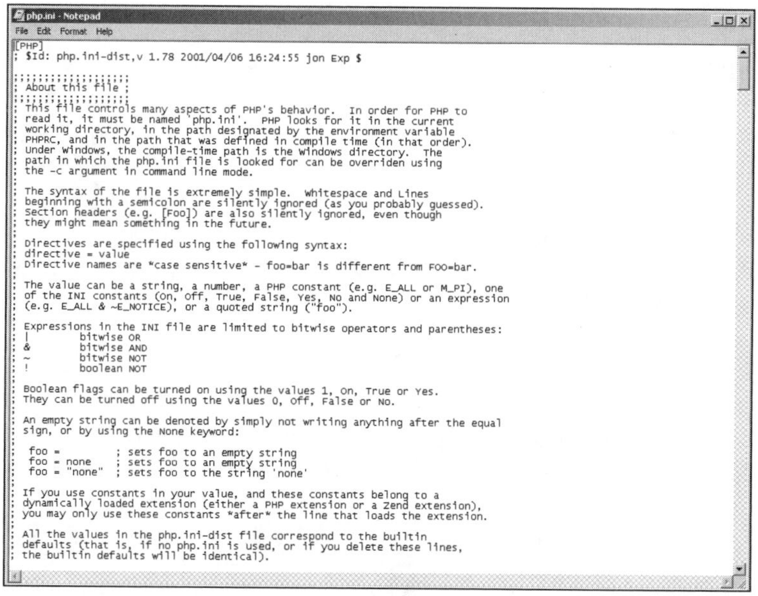

Figure 2.11   The PHP.ini file.

You need to enter the path of the PHP extensions, so change the line

```
extension_dir = ./
```

to

```
extension_dir = C:\PHP\extensions\
```

Next, locate the following line:

```
;extension=php_domxml.dll
```

This is the DOMXML extension for PHP. Note that all extensions that were installed when you installed PHP are listed here. To use any extension, you simply uncomment it by removing the leading semicolon (;):

```
extension=php_domxml.dll
```

Finally, save the php.ini file.

Setting Up Your Web Server

In order to use PHP, you need a web server. If you don't already have one set up, refer to Appendix B, "Installing a Web Server," for setup information.

Installing PHP on Your Web Server

To complete the installation, you must tell your web server where PHP is and what to do when it encounters a PHP file. This section covers how to set up PHP on a web server as a CGI application. The later section "Optimizing Your Installation" covers how to set PHP as an ISAPI filter on Microsoft web servers and php4apache as an Apache module on Apache web servers.

Note that the PHP ISAPI filter is considered unstable and might have odd interactions with other ISAPI filters. As such, it's not considered a good choice for a production site.

Microsoft Internet Information Server (IIS) 5.0

To begin, select Start, Programs, Administrative Tools, Internet Services Manager (ISM). The ISM is the administrative interface for IIS 5.0. (Note that the ISM shown in Figure 2.12 is titled Internet Information Services.)

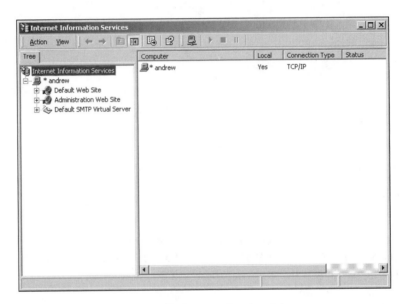

Figure 2.12   The Internet Services Manager.

Right-click Default Web Site and select Properties. Then select the Home Directory tab, as shown in Figure 2.13.

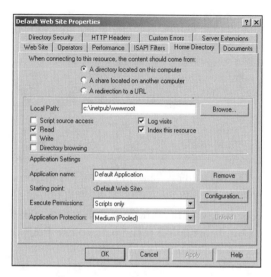

Figure 2.13   The Default Web Site Properties dialog box.

Click the Configuration button. You see the Application Configuration dialog box, shown in Figure 2.14.

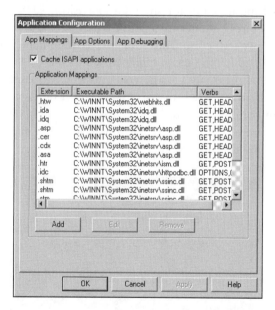

Figure 2.14   The Application Configuration dialog box.

Click the Add button. You see the Add/Edit Application Extension Mapping dialog box, shown in Figure 2.15.

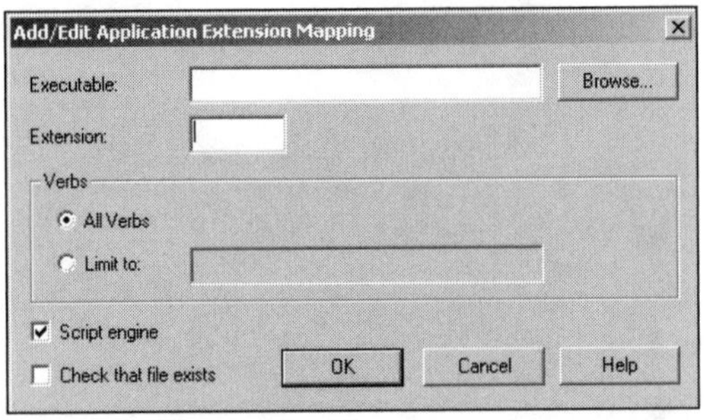

Figure 2.15   The Add/Edit Application Extension Mapping dialog box.

In the Executable section, you need to specify how IIS will find PHP to
process PHP files. This information is the path to the PHP directory and the
PHP executable, plus some system commands:

```
C:\PHP\PHP.exe %s %s
```

You also need to add some extension information so that IIS will know what
file extension PHP files end in. This book assumes that you have used the
.php extension (such as myfile.php), but the final choice is up to you.

IIS requires the %s %s symbols (called system commands) at the end of
PHP.exe when setting up paths for any CGI extensions, such as the PHP
executable. IIS requires certain information when passing a script to a CGI
extension, and the system commands meet this requirement. The first %s
symbol is the full path to the script being passed to the CGI extension. The
second %s symbol is any script parameters that the CGI extension might need.
System commands are case-sensitive, so C:\PHP\PHP.exe %S %S would not
work; the system commands must be lowercase.

When you have everything entered, it should look like Figure 2.16. Click
OK to finish the installation, and then close the ISM.

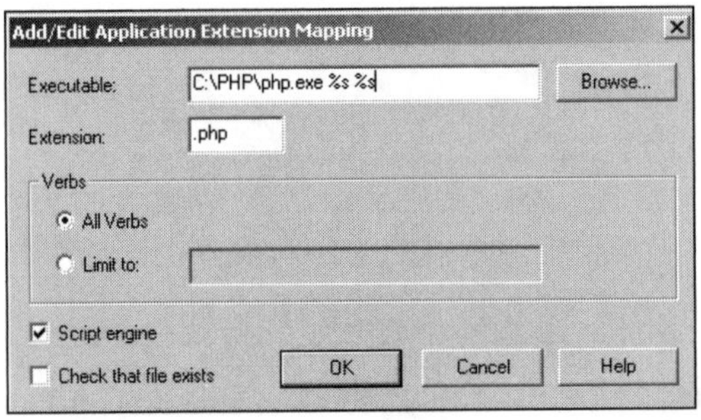

Figure 2.16   The Add/Edit Application Extension Mapping dialog box with
completed PHP installation information.

You now need to stop and restart IIS. At the command line, type

```
Net stop w3svc
```

This stops IIS. To restart IIS, type

```
Net start w3svc
```

Microsoft Internet Information Server (IIS) 4.0

To begin, select Start, Programs, Windows NT 4.0 Option Pack, Microsoft Internet Information Server, Internet Service Manager (when IIS 4.0 actually loads it is displayed as Internet Information Server in the Microsoft Management Console the generic name of all NT 4.0 Administration GUI applications), as shown in Figure 2.17.

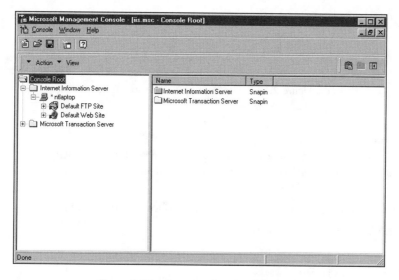

Figure 2.17   Internet Service Manager.

From this point on, the process is essentially the same as that just described for IIS 5.0. Follow the same steps as you would for installing IIS 5.0.

Microsoft Personal Web Server (PWS) 4.0

For this installation, you need to edit the Windows Registry. Select Start, Run and type `regedit`. The Windows Registry Editor appears, as shown in Figure 2.18.

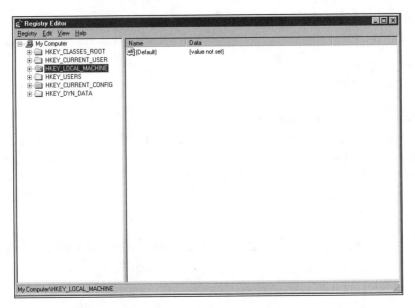

Figure 2.18 The Windows Registry Editor.

Caution

Be aware that altering the Registry can lead to a damaged Windows system. It is advised that for all Registry work, you back up the Registry before you continue.

In the Windows Registry Editor, open the following folders:

HKEY_LOCAL_MACHINE

System

CurrentControlSet

Services

W3SVC

Parameters

Script Map

Your screen should look like Figure 2.19.

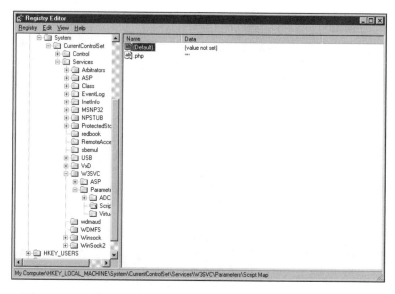

Figure 2.19   The Windows Registry Editor displaying the PHP key.

Right-click the Script Map value. Select New, String Value, and type .php in the Name box. Double-click the .php value. The Edit String utility appears, as shown in Figure 2.20.

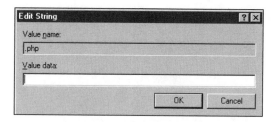

Figure 2.20   The Edit String utility.

In the Value data field, type C:\PHP\PHP.exe, and then click OK to add the value. You can now close Regedit.

You need to make sure that PWS is set up to process PHP files correctly. To do this, select Start, Programs, Microsoft Personal Web Server, Personal Web Manager. In Personal Web Manager, click the Advanced button at the bottom of the toolbar on the left. You see the dialog box shown in Figure 2.21.

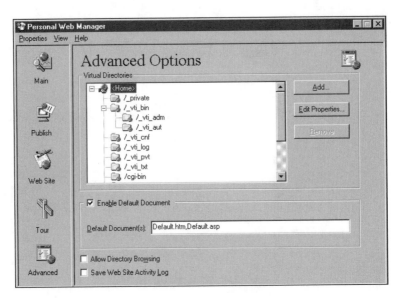

Figure 2.21   Personal Web Manager showing advanced options.

Click the Edit Properties button. You see the dialog box shown in Figure 2.22. Make sure that the Execute option is selected. If it isn't, choose it. Click OK, and exit Personal Web Manager.

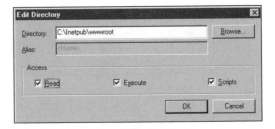

Figure 2.22   The Edit Directory dialog box.

Reboot your computer to complete the installation.

Apache

Installation on Apache is done via the httpd.conf file. You can open this file by selecting Start, Programs, Apache httpd server, Configure Apache Server, and then select Edit the Apache httpd.conf Configuration File. This opens the file in Notepad, as shown in Figure 2.23.

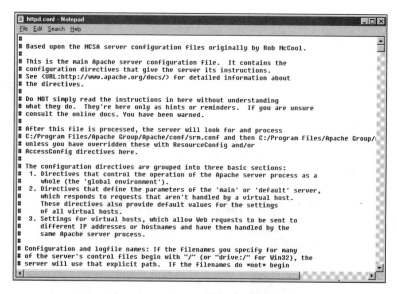

Figure 2.23   The Apache httpd.conf file shown in Notepad.

Add the following lines to the end of this file:

```
ScriptAlias /php/ "c:/php/"
AddType application/x-httpd-php .php .phtml
Action application/x-httpd-php "/php/php.exe"
```

Note that pathnames are case-sensitive.

After making these changes, you need to restart Apache. The simplest way to do this is to select Start, Programs, Apache http server, Control Apache Server, and then select Restart. Apache restarts. If no problems have been reported, you are ready to test your installation.

Other Web Servers

Here is a list of links for installation instructions for other web servers:

- Netscape: http://www.php.net/manual/en/install.netscape-enterprise.php

- OmniHTTPd: http://www.php.net/manual/en/install.omnihttpd.php

- O'Reilly: http://www.php.net/manual/en/install.oreilly.php

- Other: http://www.php.net/manual/en/install.otherhttpd.php

Note

Further manual instructions are also included in the manual installer files from both www.php.net and www.php4win.com.

Automatic Installer

To run the automatic installer, you need one of the following web servers:

- IIS
- PWS
- Apache
- Xitami

When you run the automatic installer, you see the Welcome dialog box, as shown in Figure 2.24.

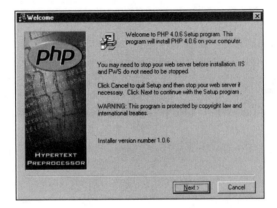

Figure 2.24   The automatic installer Welcome dialog box.

As noted in the Welcome dialog box, you should stop your web server if it is other than IIS or PWS. Click Next to continue. You see the licensing information dialog box. Click the I agree button to continue.

In the Installation Type dialog box, choose the Advanced method, and click Next to continue. In the Choose Destination Location dialog box, shown in Figure 2.25, you are asked which folder you want to install PHP in.

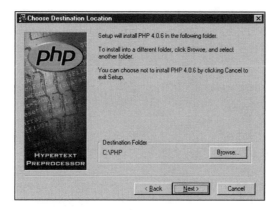

Figure 2.25   The Choose Destination Location dialog box.

In the next two dialog boxes, accept the defaults. You then see the Mail Configuration dialog box, shown in Figure 2.26. Enter your mail details, and then click Next to continue.

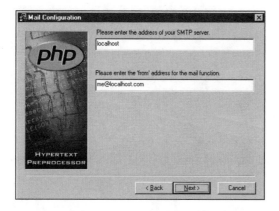

Figure 2.26   The Mail Configuration dialog box.

In the Error Reporting Level dialog box, shown in Figure 2.27, you are presented with a selection of choices concerning the level of error reporting you would like. Accept the default of Display all errors, warnings and notices, and click Next to continue.

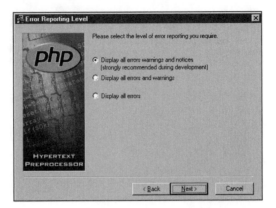

Figure 2.27   The Error Reporting Level dialog box.

In the Server Type dialog box, shown in Figure 2.28, select the web server you will be installing PHP to (I have selected the Xitami web server for this example). Click the Next button to continue.

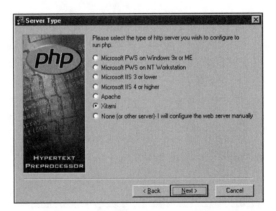

Figure 2.28   The Server Type dialog box.

In the File Extensions dialog box, shown in Figure 2.29, you select the file extension of your PHP files so that the web server knows that they are PHP files and can process them accordingly. The .php file extension is selected for you, but if necessary, you can use other file extensions, such as .phtml and .php3. Click Next to continue, and the installation finishes.

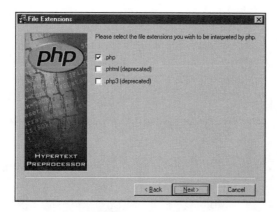

Figure 2.29   The File Extensions dialog box.

Testing the Installation

Now that you have installed PHP, you can test your installation. To do so, you need to know your document root. Here are the default document roots for various servers:

- PWS: C:\Inetpub\wwwroot\
- IIS 4: C:\Inetpub\wwwroot
- IIS 5: C:\Inetpub\wwwroot
- Apache: C:\Program Files\Apache Group\htdocs\
- Xitami: C:\Xitami\webpages\

Copy the file extensions.php from C:\PHP\test\ to your document root, and launch your web browser with `http://localhost/extensions.php`, as shown in Figure 2.30.

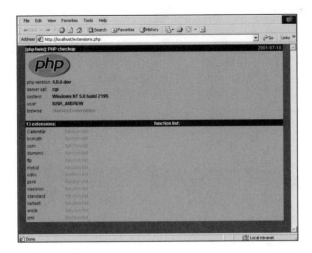

Figure 2.30 The extensions.php test file being successfully run.

You can also create your own test PHP script. In Notepad, type the following commands:

```
<?php
phpinfo();
?>
```

Save this file as testinstall.php to your document root. It's worth noting that Notepad sometimes adds .txt file extensions to files, so be sure that when you save your file you select Save As type as All Files.

You can then test the script using http://localhost/testinstall.php, as shown in Figure 2.31.

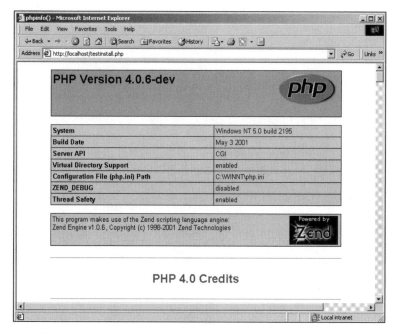

Figure 2.31   The testinstall.php test file being successfully run.

Optimizing Your Installation

Now that you have PHP installed and running, it's worth considering how you can optimize your installation.

CGI

During the installation process, I showed you how to install PHP as a CGI application. CGI, however, has its limitations.

CGI was developed as web pages began to make the transformation from static HTML pages to dynamic pages built from programming languages or database data. At the time, Perl and C were popular programming languages, but there was no easy way of linking these to a web server so that web pages could be created using a programming language.

CGI was developed as a common way of allowing the web server to pass requests for certain file types (such as C and Perl files) to external applications (such as a gateway). For example, Perl files end with the .pl extension, so all requests for .pl files from the web server are passed to the Perl interpeter. The same is done with PHP if you use CGI mode—in other words, all requests for .php files from the web server are passed to the PHP interpreter. See Figure 2.32.

Figure 2.32   The CGI process.

> **Note**
> CGI and Perl are often confused because of the early relationship they had. However, CGI is not Perl, and Perl is not CGI. They are two different things.

I showed you how requests for PHP files are passed to the PHP interpreter when you mapped the .PHP file extension to PHP via the PHP.exe program in the "Microsoft Internet Information Server (IIS) 5.0" section earlier in this chapter.

Overcoming CGI Limitations

CGI can place great demands on resources. Every time the web server passes a file to an application via CGI, it must invoke that application for every request. The result is that each application needs memory and processor time to run. Therefore, a web server that is passing tens of thousands of CGI requests a day can quickly become overloaded.

UNIX/Linux systems have a way to deal with this problem. Instead of compiling the application (such as PHP) as a CGI module, you can compile it right into the web server. This is a common approach for Apache web servers, where, instead of suffering the overhead of CGI, Apache's own code can easily manage and handle requests within its own memory space.

This is not a viable solution for most Windows web servers (although it is possible with the Apache web server on both UNIX and Windows systems). However, there is a mechanism for accomplishing something very similar— SAPI (Server Application Programming Interface).

A SAPI basically gives you the same effect as compiling a module directly into the web server. When creating a SAPI filter, the web server vendor gives you access to certain APIs so that the vendor's web server can run requests to your SAPI filter in managed memory space. In other words, a SAPI filter does not give you the large memory and processor overheads of a CGI application.

SAPI and PHP

PHP for Windows is available as both a CGI application and a SAPI application.

SAPI is a generic term. Just as there are different web servers, so there are different SAPI applications.

Note

The extension list provided is missing the phpsrvlt extension, which is the Java servlet version of PHP. Although it's not a SAPI extension, if you run Java servlets, it's well worth a look. However, note that it has known instabilities under Windows, so check the release notes before you install it.

The extension list includes the following:

- Php4isapi: Internet Server Application Programming Interface (ISAPI), Netscape Server Application Programming Interface (NSAPI), the SAPI for IIS
- Php4nsapi: NSAPI, the SAPI for Netscape web servers
- Php4apache: Apache module SAPI
- Php4aolserverL AOL server SAPI

PHP ISAPI

I will only cover how to install the PHP ISAPI extension here. The PHP documentation covers how to install the other SAPI extensions.

Note that Personal Web Server does not support ISAPI. ISAPI is for IIS 4 and IIS 5 web servers only. Also note that running PHP as an ISAPI filter is not as stable as running it as a module integrated into Apache, so it is not recommended for production environments.

To begin installing the PHP ISAPI extension for IIS 5.0, you must first load the Internet Services Manager as you did in the CGI installation. Select Start, Programs, Administrative Tools, Internet Services Manager (ISM).

Right-click Default Web Site and select Properties. Then select the ISAPI Filters tab, as shown in Figure 2.33.

Figure 2.33 The Default Web Site Properties dialog box.

Click the Add button. You see the Filter Properties dialog box, shown in Figure 2.34. In the Filter Name field, type `PHP`, and in the Executable section, type the path to the ISAPI directory (or click Browse). If you have been following the CGI installation, the path is `C:\PHP\sapi\php4sapi.dll`.

Figure 2.34 The Filter Properties dialog box.

The installation at this point is like the CGI installation. Click OK to close the Filter Properties dialog box, and then click the Home Directory tab, as shown in Figure 2.35.

Figure 2.35   The Default Web Site Properties dialog box.

Click Configuration. You see the Application Configuration dialog box, shown in Figure 2.36.

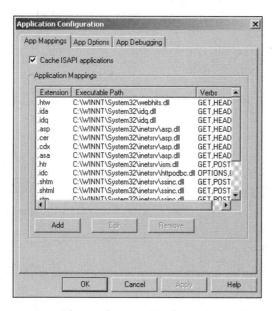

Figure 2.36   The Application Configuration dialog box.

Click the Add button. You see the Add/Edit Application Extension Mapping dialog box, shown in Figure 2.37.

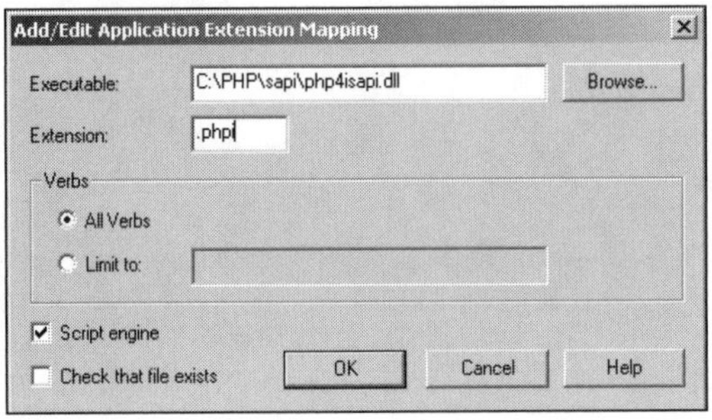

Figure 2.37 The Add/Edit Application Extension Mapping dialog box, showing the mapping for .phpi extensions.

In the Executable field, select the path to the ISAPI extension you specified previously. You can also click Browse, but be sure to change the Files of type setting to Dynamic Link Libraries (*.dll).

In the Extension field, type the file extension you want PHP files to have. This can be .php, but if you want to run PHP files in both CGI and ISAPI modes, you must use a different file extension. For ISAPI files, I have typed .phpi.

To complete the installation, close the ISM and stop and then restart IIS. To do this, from the command line type

```
Net stop w3svc
```

This stops IIS. To restart it, type

```
Net start w3svc
```

Testing PHP ISAPI

You can test the PHP ISAPI extension using the test page you created earlier. Just rename the file so that its file extension matches the one you used for PHP CGI:

```
testinstall.phpi
```

If you run this script in your web browser, you should see that the Server API section reads ISAPI, as shown in Figure 2.38.

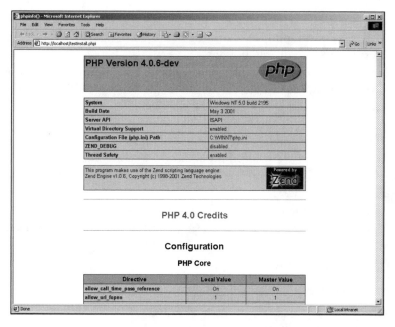

Figure 2.38   The testinstall.phpi script, showing that
the ISAPI filter for PHP is working correctly.

Zend Optimizer

The Zend Optimizer is a free add-on product from Zend Technologies Ltd. that optimizes the code that the Zend compiler generates for faster execution. This lets you run your PHP code more quickly than normal without needing to change the code.

The Zend Optimizer currently is for PHP 4.0.6 running in CGI mode only. It is worth noting that the Zend Optimizer can be used across several OSs, including Windows, Linux, and Solaris. However, the installation steps covered here are for the Windows version of the Zend Optimizer. (Other OS procedures can be found on the Zend Technologies Ltd. web site at http://www.zend.com.)

Downloading the Zend Optimizer

To download the Zend Optimizer, first visit http://www.zend.com/store/products/zend-optimizer.php.

You need to register with the Zend Technologies web site before you can download the Zend Optimizer. Creating login details for the web site gives you access to other resources and downloads.

When you are presented with the download page, you must download the version of the Zend Optimizer that supports the version of PHP that you have installed.

Installing the Zend Optimizer

The Zend Optimizer is packaged for Windows as a zip file. Unzip this file to a directory of your choice (I recommend the C:\PHP\ directory that you set up earlier in this chapter.)

The directory name that the zip file creates contains the Zend Optimizer version, the version of PHP the Zend Optimizer is for, and the OS the Zend Optimizer is for. In our example, this is as follows:

```
C:\PHP\ZendOptimizer-1.1.0-4.0.5-Windows-i386\
```

Please note that this will vary depending on what version of PHP you intend to target with the Zend Optimizer. I suggest that you rename this directory with a simpler name, such as

```
C:\PHP\ZendOptimizer\
```

as shown in Figure 2.39. This simplifies the installation process.

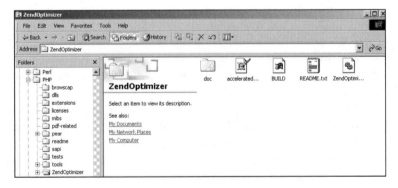

Figure 2.39   The Zend Optimizer installation directory.

To complete the installation, you will need to alter the php.ini file. Open the php.ini file and add the following lines to the end of the file:

```
zend_optimizer.optimization_level=15
zend_extension_ts="C:\PHP\ZendOptimizer\ZendOptimizer.dll"
```

`zend_extension` should be set equal to the Zend Optimizer directory (such as C:\PHP\ZendOptimizer\ZendOptimizer.dll).

Unless you are using another of Zend Technologies' products, the Zend Encoder, you can add another line to your PHP file that helps you run your PHP files faster via the Zend Optimizer:

```
zend__optimizer.enable_loader = 0
```

Testing the Zend Optimizer

If you run the PHP test script you developed earlier in this chapter, you will see that Zend Optimizer information is displayed in your browser, as shown in Figure 2.40.

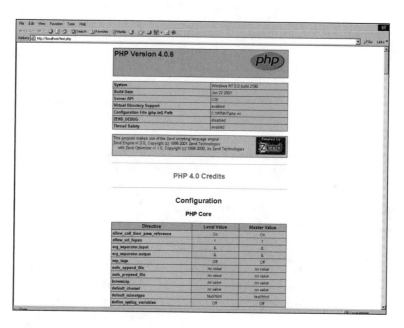

Figure 2.40   A test script showing that the Zend Optimizer is working correctly.

Installation Troubleshooting

Table 2.1 summarizes some of the problems you might run into when installing PHP and shows you how you might troubleshoot them.

Table 2.1   **Potential Installation Issues**

Problem Type	Nature of the Problem	Solution or Item to Check
General	The load PHP test script works, but if I change the php.ini file to load PHP extensions, the load test script fails.	Make sure that you set the extension_directory path to the correct path.
CGI	When I try to load the PHP test script, all I see is the PHP code.	Your web server is not correctly set up to pass PHP files to PHP. If you are using PHP in CGI mode, make sure that you include the %s %s information after the path information. (See the CGI installation steps for further information.)
ISAPI	When restarting my web server after installing PHP in ISAPI mode, I get an error.	If you have enabled any PHP extensions, make sure that the extension_dir path is set to the correct path.
Zend Optimizer	The Zend Optimizer information does not display in the load PHP test script. I get errors when I attempt to load the PHP test script when the Zend Optimizer is installed.	Make sure that the zend_extensions path is set to the correct path. Make sure that your version of the Zend Optimizer is compatible with your version of PHP. If you compile PHP, be sure to do so with debugging disabled.
	Zend Optimizer information does not show up, or I get random problems when I try to load the PHP test script.	The Zend Optimizer works only with PHP in CGI mode. Make sure you are not attempting to run PHP in ISAPI mode with the Zend Optimizer enabled.

Other Problems

If you still can't solve your installation problems, the folks on the php-install mailing list should be able to help. You can find out how to subscribe to this mailing list by visiting `http://www.php.net/support.php`.

Summary

This chapter covered where and how to download PHP, how to install PHP to your file system, and how to set it up for your web server. We then looked at how to install PHP using ISAPI or the Zend Optimizer. You should now have a fully functional version of PHP installed on your system, ready for use so that you can begin coding.

II

Introduction to
PHP Programming

3

PHP Programming

NOW THAT YOU HAVE PHP INSTALLED AND working on your system, you can begin looking at how to develop web applications with PHP. This chapter discusses how to start developing PHP web applications and the various data types, structures, and controls that make up the language.

PHP Coding Tools

Before you start coding PHP, you need an editor to write, edit, and save your scripts. You could use Notepad, but other editors are available, with features such as syntax color coding and debugging. These are discussed in the following sections.

PHP Edit

An open-source editor, PHP Edit features PHP syntax color coding, debugging, function and object reference, and much more.

Further information and downloads for PHP Edit are available at
`http://www.phpedit.com/`.

Macromedia HomeSite

Macromedia HomeSite is an HTML editor that has support for ASP, ColdFusion, and PHP. Color coding support is native to HomeSite, but other features, such as syntax reference, are available only from third parties.

Further information and a trial download are available at `http://www.macromedia.com/software/homesite/`.

Macromedia HomeSite third-party PHP add-ons are available at `http://www.wilk4.com/asp4hs/php4hs.htm`.

ActiveState Komodo

Available for both Windows and Linux systems, ActiveState Komodo is a commonly used editor. Support for PHP is provided directly from within the product via syntax color coding and remote debugging.

Further information and downloads for ActiveState Komodo are available at `http://www.activestate.com/Products/Komodo/`.

Zend IDE

A Java-based IDE, this tool features syntax color coding as well as powerful remote debugging features. Further information and a trial download for Zend IDE are available at `http://www.zend.com/store/products/zend-ide.php`.

Basic PHP Syntax

Like ASP, PHP uses what I call "open–close bracket" syntax. In a classic ASP program, the syntax starts with an open bracket (<%) and ends with a close bracket (%>):

```
<%

Response.write("A classic ASP program")

%>
```

Much the same is done in PHP. The open–close bracket syntax starts with <?php and ends with ?>:

```
<?php

print("A PHP program");

?>
```

PHP also allows a style of syntax that is familiar to client-side script developers. This style of syntax starts with `<SCRIPT LANGUAGE="php">` and ends with `</SCRIPT>`:

```
<SCRIPT LANGUAGE="php">

print("test");

</SCRIPT>
```

If you have a background in ASP, never fear. PHP also lets you use ASP-style open-close bracket syntax:

```
<%

print("A PHP program")

%>
```

However, for this style of open-close bracket syntax to work, you must edit the php.ini file:

```
asp_tags = On
```

This is set to `Off` by default.

Multiline Programs

Multiline PHP programs have additional syntax:

```
<?php

print("This is your first");

print(" PHP Program");

?>
```

Note that PHP requires an end-of-line character—the semicolon (;). If you run the program with no end-of-line character, as in the following code, you will receive a `Parse error` message:

```
<?php

print("This is your first")

print(" PHP Program")

?>
```

If you have never used end-of-line characters, they can often trip you up. If you receive a `Parse error` message when writing your web applications, check for an end-of-line character at the line number given in the error message, as shown in Figure 3.1.

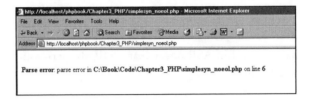

Figure 3.1   A `Parse error` message.

Variables

PHP is described as a loosely typed language. That is, you don't need to declare the type of variables before you can use them. PHP sets out variable types for you. To see this, look at the following code:

```
<?php

//our data types
$intdata = 1;

$doubledata = 5.00;

$stringdata = "Andrew";

$booldata = TRUE;


//list data types
$IntType = gettype($intdata);
print("$intdata is a $IntType data type<BR>");

$DoubleType = gettype($doubledata);
print("$doubledata is a $DoubleType data type<BR>");

$StringType = gettype($stringdata);
print("$stringdata is a $StringType data type<BR>");

$BoolType = gettype($booldata);
print("$booldata is a $BoolType data type<BR>");


?>
```

When you store data in a variable, PHP sets the type of variable according to the type of data you are storing. First, you specify what data your variables will hold:

```
$intdatavar = 1;

$doubledatavar = 5.00;

$stringvar = "Andrew";

$boolvar = TRUE;
```

PHP sets each variable to the type of data you are storing. For example, because you are storing the string "Andrew" in the $stringvar variable, PHP sets the variable to a string type. You can see this by showing what type of data your variables are using through the GetType function:

```
$IntType = GetType($intdatavar);
```

You then display the variable and its type:

```
print("$intdatavar is a $IntType data type<BR>");
```

If you run the script, you will see this working, as shown in Figure 3.2.

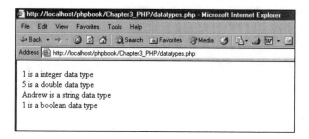

Figure 3.2   PHP data types.

Note that the Boolean type is shown as a 1. PHP displays Boolean values as a 1 for true and null (empty value) for false. We will explore this further in the next section.

Setting Data Types

Although loosely typed variables can be useful, it is sometimes necessary to set types explicitly (loosely typed variables can be described as implicitly typed), such as when handling data that has been input from a database. To do this, you use the SetType method:

```php
<?php

//our data types
$intdata = 300;

$doubledata = 5.00;

$string = "False";

$bool = TRUE;

//list data types
$IntType = GetType($intdata);
Print("$intdata is a $IntType data type<BR>");

$DoubleType = GetType($doubledata);
Print("$doubledata is a $DoubleType data type<BR>");

$StringType = GetType($string);
Print("$string is a $StringType data type<BR>");

$BoolType = GetType($bool);
Print("$bool is a $BoolType data type<BR>");

//change data types

SetType($doubledata, "integer");

SetType($intdata, "double");

SetType($bool, "string");

SetType($string, "boolean");

//display new types

$IntType = GetType($intdata);
Print("$intdata is now a $IntType data type<BR>");

$DoubleType = GetType($doubledata);
Print("$doubledata is now a $DoubleType data type<BR>");

$StringType = GetType($string);
Print("$string is now a $StringType data type<BR>");

$BoolType = GetType($bool);
Print("$bool is now a $BoolType data type<BR>");


?>
```

As in your first script, you add some content to the variables and display that content and the variables' types:

```
$intdata = 300;

$doubledata = 5.00;

$string = "False";

$bool = TRUE;

$IntType = GetType($intdata);
Print("$intdata is a $IntType data type<BR>");

$DoubleType = GetType($doubledata);
Print("$doubledata is a $DoubleType data type<BR>");

$StringType = GetType($string);
Print("$string is a $StringType data type<BR>");

$BoolType = GetType($bool);
Print("$bool is a $BoolType data type<BR>");
```

You can then change the type of each variable using the SetType function:

```
SetType($doubledata, "integer");

SetType($intdata, "double");

SetType($bool, "string");

SetType($string, "Boolean");
```

Within the SetType function, you first state what variable you want to change (such as $doubledata) and then what type you want to change the variable to (such as integer). To complete the script, you display the variable contents and type:

```
$IntType = GetType($intdata);
Print("$intdata is now a $IntType data type<BR>");

$DoubleType = GetType($doubledata);
Print("$doubledata is now a $DoubleType data type<BR>");

$StringType = GetType($string);
Print("$string is now a $StringType data type<BR>");

$BoolType = GetType($bool);
Print("$bool is now a $BoolType data type<BR>");
```

If you run the script, you should see that the data types have been altered as you set them in the script, as shown in Figure 3.3.

Figure 3.3   Using the SetType function to change variable types.

Although changing integer and double types is no problem, converting Boolean and string data types presents a bigger challenge. In the script output, you can see that the string output is displayed as a 1. According to the rules of how PHP displays Boolean values, this is correct, because PHP displays true values as 1, so this converts directly into a string as a value of 1.

Also in the script output, you can see that the Boolean output is displayed as a 1. You converted the False string to Boolean, so, according to PHP, the Boolean output should be empty. This is sadly not the case; PHP in fact sees anything other than a null string or 0 value as being a true Boolean value. You can show this by setting the string in the script to a value of 0:

```
$string = "0";
```

If you run the script (see Figure 3.4), you can see that the Boolean value is now displayed as an empty value. Remember that PHP sees a 0 value as a Boolean false value, so when you convert a 0 value set as a string to a Boolean, that value becomes a Boolean false value. Also remember that PHP displays Boolean false values as null values, so you get an empty value displayed when you run the script.

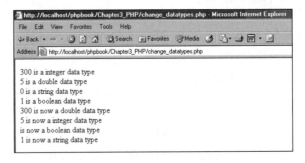

Figure 3.4   Data with a false Boolean value.

Typecasting

Typecasting gives you another method of setting variable types.

```php
<?php


$somedata = 6.23;

$newtype = GetType($somedata);

Print("$somedata is set by PHP to be a $newtype data type with the value of
➥ $somedata<BR><BR>");

//change to string
$changetype = (string) $somedata;

$newtype = GetType($changetype);

Print("$somedata is now a $newtype data type with the value of
➥ $changetype<BR>");

//change to int
$changetype = (integer) $somedata;

$newtype = GetType($changetype);

Print("$somedata is now a $newtype data type with the value of
➥ $changetype<BR>");

//change to double
$changetype = (double) $somedata;

$newtype = GetType($changetype);

Print("$somedata is now a $NewType data type with the value of
➥ $ChangeType<BR>");

//change to boolean
$changetype = (boolean) $somedata;

$newtype = GetType($changetype);

Print("$somedata is now a $newtype data type with the value of
➥ $changetype<BR>");


?>
```

First, you give a variable a value:

```php
$somedata = 6.23;
```

You know that, given this value, PHP will set its type for you to a double. You can, however, change it at will. If you want to set it to a string, you can use the following:

```
$changetype = (string) $somedata;
```

Here the variable `$changetype` takes the value of the data variable `$somedata` but assumes string as its data type. You can do this with all the PHP data types, as the script shows. If you run the script, you can see typecasting at work, as shown in Figure 3.5.

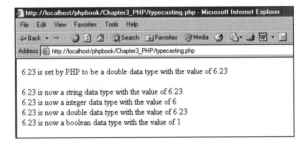

Figure 3.5 Using the `ChangeType` function for typecasting.

In the script, you can see that the data value of 6.23 has been set by PHP to be a double data type. As you typecast the variable to each of the PHP data types, you can see how the variable value changes in accordance.

Arithmetic Operators

PHP lets you use arithmetic operators on compatible variable types. What variable types are these? Any variable type that can hold data in a numeric form; this means any variable type other than Boolean. The following example also uses string concatenation (joining strings). Don't worry if you are unfamiliar with this. We will look at it in further detail in a moment.

```php
<?php

//numbers to use

$num1 = 10;
$num2 = 20;

//addition

$add_sum = $num1 + $num2;

Print($num1 . " + " . $num2 . " = " . $add_sum);

print("<BR>");
```

```
//subtraction

$sub_sum = $num2 - $num1;

Print($num2 . " - " . $num1 . " = " . $sub_sum);

print("<BR>");

//division

$div_sum = $num2 / $num1;

Print($num2 . " / " . $num1 . " = " . $div_sum);

print("<BR>");

//multiplication

$mup_sum = $num2 * $num1;

Print($num2 . " * " . $num1 . " = " . $mup_sum);

print("<BR>");

//modulus

$mod_sum = $num2 % $num1;

Print($num2 . " % " . $num1 . " = " . $mod_sum);

print("<BR>");


?>
```

First, you set two variables that will hold values for you to perform arithmetic operations on:

```
$num1 = 10;
$num2 = 20;
```

Next, you perform an arithmetic operation on the two variables:

```
$add_sum = $num1 + $num2;
```

Finally, you display the result of the arithmetic operation:

```
Print("$num1 + $num2 = $add_sum");
```

If you run this script, you can see the result of the various arithmetic operations, as shown in Figure 3.6.

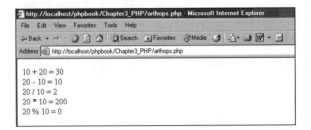

Figure 3.6   Arithmetic operators.

It is interesting to note that the following also works in this script:

```
$num1 = 10;
$num2 = "20";
```

Here you make each variable a mixed type. $num1 is an integer type, and $num2 is a string type. If you change the variables to the following, the script still works:

```
$num1 = 10;
$num2 = "aa20";
```

The script still runs, but the arithmetic operators fail to work. If PHP sees data other than numeric data in a variable, it ignores that variable.

String Operators and Functions

PHP provides you with several methods for working with string variables. Quite often you use string variables from sources such as HTML forms, files, and databases, so PHP provides many methods for manipulating this kind of data.

We will begin our look at string methods by defining some strings to work with:

```
$first_name = "Fox";
$space = " ";
$last_name = "Mulder";
```

Joining Strings

To join these strings, you use PHP's concatenation operator:

```
$name = $first_name . $space . $last_name;
```

Here you create a new string by joining the three original strings. Note that you use a dot character to join strings.

Length of a String

You can find out the length of the new string using the `strlen` function:

```
$string_length = strlen($name);
```

Trailing Space

PHP lets you remove a trailing space (often called white space) from either the start and end of a string or just the start of a string. Because the new string has no trailing space, you must add it to be able to apply these functions:

```
$space_name = " $name ";
```

You can then remove it from the start of the string using the `ltrim` function:

```
$ltrim_name = ltrim($space_name);
```

You can remove the trailing space from both the start and the end of the string using the `trim` function:

```
$trim_name = trim($space_name);
```

String Case

PHP lets you change a string's case to either all uppercase or all lowercase. To change the string to uppercase, you use the `strtoupper` function:

```
$uppercase_name = strtoupper($name);
```

To change the string to lowercase, you use the `strtolower` function:

```
$lowercase_name = strtolower($name);
```

Substrings

PHP lets you find the position of a substring, create a substring, and add substrings to a string. To create a substring, you use the `substr` function:

```
$sub_string = substr($name, 3);
```

Here you specify the string you want to create the substring from (in this case, the string $name) and the position within the string to create the substring from (in this case, from the third character to the end of the string).

You can find the position of a substring using the `strops` function:

```
$substr_position = strpos($name, $sub_string);
```

Here you specify the string in which to locate the substring's position (in this case, the string $name) and the substring whose position is to be located (in this case, the substring you created earlier: $sub_string).

Finally, you can add a substring to a string using the `str_replace` function:

```
$sub_name = str_replace("Fox", "Scully", $name);
```

In the `str_replace` function, you first specify which string is to be found (in this case, `"Fox"`). What string you will replace it with (in this case, `"Scully"`) and what string you will be working on (in this case, $name) come next.

Testing String Methods

You can test all these methods using the following script:

```php
<?php
//strings

$first_name = "Fox";
$space = " ";
$last_name = "Mulder";

//joining

$name = $first_name . $space . $last_name;

print("$name is our joined string");

print("<BR>");

//length

$string_length = strlen($name);

print("The length of the joined string is $string_length");

print("<BR>");

//trailing space

$space_name = " $name ";

print("A string trailing space is *$space_name*");

print("<BR>");

$ltrim_name = ltrim($space_name);

print("A string with leading trailing space removed is *$ltrim_name*");

print("<BR>");

$trim_name = trim($space_name);

print("A string with trailing space removed is *$trim_name*");
```

```
print("<BR>");

//case

$uppercase_name = strtoupper($name);

print("An uppercase string is $uppercase_name");

print("<BR>");

$lowercase_name = strtolower($name);

print("A lowercase string is $lowercase_name");

print("<BR>");

//substrings

//substring

$sub_string = substr($name, 3);

print("A substring is $sub_string");

print("<BR>");

//substr position

$substr_position = strpos($name, $sub_string);

print("The substring position is $substr_position");

print("<BR>");

//replace substr

$sub_name = str_replace("Fox", "Scully", $name);

print("An inserted substring is $sub_name");

print("<BR>");


?>
```

If you run this script, you can see how all the string methods work, as shown in Figure 3.7. Note that when showing the concatenation method, I have surrounded the string with a * character. This is to show the trailing space between that character and the string.

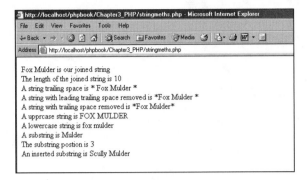

Figure 3.7 String methods.

Logic and Loops

Controlling a program's flow is vitally important. You might need to test some logic conditions (is the value true or false?) or loop through some values. Such elements have always been present in programming languages, and PHP is no exception.

Logic

PHP gives you several means of testing logic. When you test logic, you look at a value and ask if a condition of the value is or is not equal to a value:

```php
<?php

$password = "a12b";

if($password == "a12b") {

    print("Password found");

}


?>
```

This code uses the PHP `if` statement. Its syntax is straightforward. If a value equals the value you want, PHP returns a true value. This code asks if the variable `$password` is equal to `a12b`. If it is, a message is displayed, as shown in Figure 3.8.

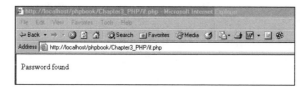

Figure 3.8 Testing true logic with the `if` statement.

What would happen if the variable `$password` were not equal to the value you are looking for? Using the preceding example, it would not display anything. However, PHP lets you handle false logic conditions as well:

```php
<?php

$password = "3333";

if($password == "a12b") {

    print("Password found");

} else {

    print("Password not found");

}

?>
```

If the value you are looking for is not found, you resort to the `else` condition. If the variable `$password` has the value you are looking for, the `Password found` message is displayed. However, if the value you are looking for is not found, the `Password not found` message is displayed. Setting the variable `$password` to something that is not found triggers the `Password not found` message, as shown in Figure 3.9.

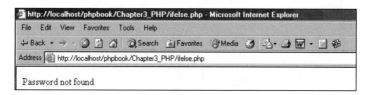

Figure 3.9 Testing false logic with the `if else` statement.

If you have lots of `if` statements to test, you could use the following:

```php
<?php

$password = "bb22";
```

```
if($password == "aa11") {
    Print("Password for user Joe found");
}

if($password == "bb22") {
    Print("Password for user Fred found");
}

if($password == "cc33") {
    Print("Password for user Jack found");
}


?>
```

The biggest problem with this approach is that PHP executes all the if statements even when a true condition is returned. To get around this, you can use
nested if statements:

```
<?php
$password = "bb22";
If($password == "aa11") {
    Print("Password for user Joe found");
} elseIf($password == "bb22") {
    Print("Password for user Fred found");
} elseIf($password == "cc33") {
    Print("Password for user Jack found");
}
?>
```

However, if you have a lot of nested if statements, your code can quickly become unreadable. A better approach is to use the switch and case statements:

```
<?php

$password = "bb22";

switch($password) {

    case "aa11":
    Print("Password for user Joe found");
    break;

    case "bb22":
    Print("Password for user Fred found");
    break;

    case "cc33":
    Print("Password for user Jack found");
    break;

}

?>
```

Here you test each value of the variable $password in a case statement. If a matching value is found, the Password found message is displayed.

Note that I used a break statement so that when a true condition is returned, it stops executing the switch statement. Without it, the switch statement would behave like our original if statements and continue to search all the way through.

Iteration

PHP lets you loop through conditions using several means. All loop conditions let you loop through the code until a condition is met, such as until a count reaches a certain value. The first method you can use is the for loop:

```php
<?php

for ($count = 1; $count <= 10; $count++) {

    print("$count");
    print("<BR>");

}

?>
```

The for loop breaks up into the following:

1. What value to start the loop from—in this case, 1 ($count = 1).
2. How the value is tested. In this case, if the value reaches 10, the loop stops ($count <= 10).
3. How the value is altered as it loops. In this case, the value is incremented in each loop ($count++).

So this loop counts from 1 to 10 and then stops (see Figure 3.10).

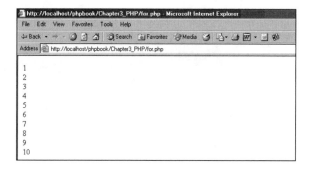

Figure 3.10 An incrementing for loop counting from 1 to 10.

A few important elements occur within the for loop. The first is the testing of logic. The preceding example sees whether the value is equal to or less than 10. You can, however, test for other conditions, as shown in Table 3.1.

Table 3.1   **Other Conditions**

Condition	Meaning
==	Equal to
!=	Not equal to
<	Less than
>	Greater than
>=	Greater than or equal to
<=	Less than or equal to
===	Equal to and of the same data type

You can use these conditions not only with the for statement but with any statement that can test logic, such as the if statement. In the preceding for statement, note the way in which the loop is altered as it loops. You can either increment or decrement the loop. You decrement it using the following:

```
$count--
```

Thus, you can alter the example as follows:

```
<?php

for ($count = 10; $count >= 1; $count--) {

    print("$count");
    print("<BR>");

}

?>
```

If you run the script, you can see that it now counts from 10 to 1, as shown in Figure 3.11.

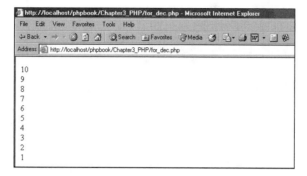

Figure 3.11   A decrementing for loop counting from 10 to 1.

PHP gives you another way to loop through code—the while statement:

```php
<?php

$count = 1;

while ($count <= 10) {

    print("$count");
    print("<BR>");

    $count++;


}


?>
```

First, you set the count to a starting value—in this case, 1:

```php
$count = 1;
```

Next you loop until the count reaches 10:

```php
while ($count <= 10) {
```

As with the for loop, you can use various forms of logic testing. Inside the loop of the while statement, the count is incremented:

```php
$count++;
```

Of course, you can decrement the code in the same way you would with the for loop. If you run the script, you can see that the while loop counts from 1 to 10 before stopping, as shown in Figure 3.12.

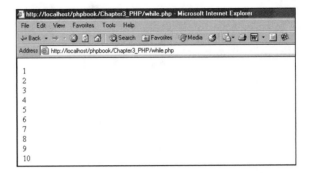

Figure 3.12   An incrementing `while` loop counting from 1 to 10.

PHP lets you determine how the loop is controlled through the use of the `do while` statement:

```php
<?php

$count = 1;

do {

    print("$count");
    print("<BR>");
    $count++;


} while ($count <= 10);


?>
```

This looks similar to the `while` loop. If you run this script, it will count from 1 to 10 before stopping. So why use this script instead of the `while` loop? The difference between the two statements is in the placement of the `while` statement. With `do while` loops, the value is altered (in this case, incremented), and then the value is tested. With the `while` statement, the loop's value is tested and then altered. It is important to note when a loop's value is tested and when it is altered. In the preceding `do while` loop, value 1 is never tested, because it is incremented to 2 before it can be tested.

Arrays

An array is a great way to store data in an organized way that can be referenced for later use. In Figure 3.13, you can see that an array looks very much like a set of numbered cards; on each card is printed a value. Card 3 would have the value L printed on it.

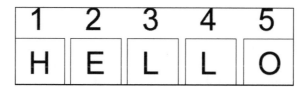

Figure 3.13   An array structure.

Arrays have precise terms for these kinds of things; each card is called an array element. Each value in an array element is called an array value, and each array element is referenced by its array key. PHP lets you use several methods when working with arrays.

```php
<?php

$message[0] = "H";
$message[1] = "E";
$message[2] = "L";
$message[3] = "L";
$message[4] = "O";


while (list ($key, $val) = each ($message)) {

    print("$val");
    print("array key $key equals value $val");
    print("<BR>");

}


?>
```

First, the array is created:

```php
$message[0] = "H";
$message[1] = "E";
$message[2] = "L";
$message[3] = "L";
$message[4] = "O";
```

The array variable type is used here. This is marked by the array element at the end of the variable. Note that the array starts at 0; in PHP, all arrays start at 0. In this example, $message[1] equals E. Of course, now that you have an array, you must be able to work with it. PHP lets you run through the contents of an array as follows:

```php
while (list ($key, $val) = each ($message)) {
```

```
print("$val");
print("<BR>");

}
```

A while loop loops through the array. The array is broken into its element key and element value using the list statement and the each statement to work through each element in the array in turn. Looping through the array, each element value is displayed:

```
print("array key $key equals value $val");
```

If you run the script, you can see that the element values are displayed.

When setting element keys, you don't have to use numbers. You can use any value you like. You can change the preceding script to use letters instead of numbers as follows:

```
<?php

$message["A"] = "H";
$message["B"] = "E";
$message["C"] = "L";
$message["D"] = "L";
$message["E"] = "O";


while (list ($key, $val) = each ($message)) {

    Print("$val");
    Print("<BR>");

}


?>
```

You can also look up values in an array using the element key:

```
<?php

$message["A"] = "H";
$message["B"] = "E";
$message["C"] = "L";
$message["D"] = "L";
$message["E"] = "O";


while (list ($key, $val) = each ($message)) {

    if($key == B) {

        Print("The array key is $key and its value is $val");

    }
```

```
    }

?>
```

This code looks up an element key called B and displays its value, as shown in
Figure 3.14.

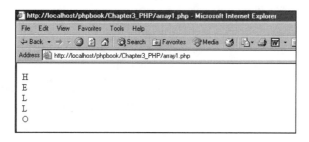

Figure 3.14   An array element value found through its element key.

PHP gives you another syntax for creating arrays using the array statement:

```php
<?php

$message = array ("A"=>"H", "B"=>"E", "C"=>"L", "D"=>"L", "E"=>"O");

while (list ($key, $val) = each ($message)) {

    Print("The array key is $key and its value is $val");
    Print("<BR>");

}

?>
```

The variable $message contains the array that is created using the array state-
ment. The array statement lets you create arrays by defining first the element
key and then the related element value. If you run the script, you can see the
structure the array statement has created, as shown in Figure 3.15.

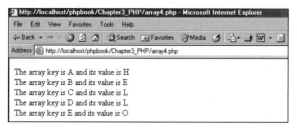

Figure 3.15   Array element keys and related values created with the array statement.

The array statement can also add element key values for you:

```php
<?php

$message = array ("H", "E", "L", "L", "O");

while (list ($key, $val) = each ($message)) {

    Print("The array key is $key and its value is $val");
    Print("<BR>");

}

?>
```

Here, only array element values within the array statement are defined. If you run the script, you can see that the array statement adds the element keys for you, as shown in Figure 3.16.

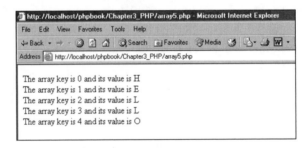

Figure 3.16   Array element keys created automatically by the array statement.

Sorting Arrays

Sometimes arrays can be messy; the element keys and values can be in a mixed order, and sometimes it's necessary to put them in order. Writing code to sort them can be time-consuming (even when you're adapting scripts from others). PHP thankfully provides a collection of statements to let you do this.

The following sections discuss four common sort statements for sorting an array by its element values or by its element keys. However, note that PHP also has other sort statements that you can use.

The *sort* Function

The sort statement lets you sort array values from the lowest to the highest value:

```php
<?php
//sort array from lowest value to highest
```

```php
$numbers = array (5, 2, 3, 1, 4);

//unsorted
print("unsorted array<BR>");

while (list ($key, $val) = each ($numbers)) {

    print("array key $key has value $val");
    print("<BR>");

}

Print("<BR>");

//sorted
print("sorted array<BR>");

sort($message);

while (list ($key, $val) = each ($message)) {

    print("array key $key has value $val");
    print("<BR>");
}


?>
```

This code creates an array and allows the `array` statement to create the element keys for you. The script then displays the unsorted array, sorts the array using the `sort` statement, and displays the sorted array.

The *asort* Function

When using the `sort` statement, note how the array keys change. Before the sort element key, 0 held the element value of 5, and after the sort, it contained the element value of 1. You can keep element key and value pairs related but at the same time sort the element values from highest to lowest. How? You use the asort function:

```php
<?php
//sort array from lowest value to highest but maintain key

$message = array ("A"=>"1", "B"=>"5", "C"=>"2", "D"=>"3", "E"=>"4");

//unsorted
print("unsorted array<BR>");

while (list ($key, $val) = each ($message)) {
```

```
        Print("The array key is $key and its value is $val");
        Print("<BR>");

    }

    Print("<BR>");

    //sorted
    print("sorted array<BR>");

    asort($message);

    while (list ($key, $val) = each ($message)) {

        Print("The array key is $key and its value is $val");
        Print("<BR>");

    }


    ?>
```

This code creates an array. Note that this example specifies element keys and values but, like the sort statement, you can allow the array statement to create element keys for you. The script then displays the unsorted array, sorts the array using the asort function, and displays the sorted array, as shown in Figure 3.17.

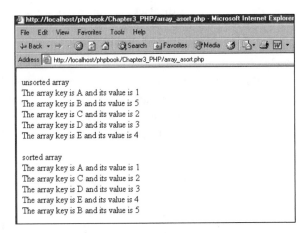

Figure 3.17   An array sorted from lowest element value to highest but with relative element keys using the asort statement.

The array element values have been sorted, but they relate to the same element keys before and after the sort. For example, element key E contains the value 4 before and after the sort.

The *rsort* Function

You can also sort array element values from the highest value to the lowest value using the rsort function:

```php
<?php
//sort array from highest value to lowest

$message = array (5, 2, 3, 1, 4);

//unsorted
print("unsorted array<BR>");

while (list ($key, $val) = each ($message)) {

    print("array key $key has value $val");
    print("<BR>");
}

Print("<BR>");

//sorted
print("sorted array<BR>");

rsort($message);

while (list ($key, $val) = each ($message)) {

    print("array key $key has value $val");
print("<BR>");
}


?>
```

This script is the same as the sort script, except that it uses the rsort function to sort the array from highest to lowest.

The *ksort* Function

PHP lets you sort an array by its element keys from the lowest value to the highest using the ksort function:

```php
<?php
//sort array from lowest key to highest

$message = array ("B"=>"1", "C"=>"5", "D"=>"2", "A"=>"3", "E"=>"4");

//unsorted
print("unsorted array<BR>");

while (list ($key, $val) = each ($message)) {
```

```
            Print("The array key is $key and its value is $val");
            Print("<BR>");

    }

    Print("<BR>");

    //sorted

    ksort($message);

    print("sorted array<BR>");

    while (list ($key, $val) = each ($message)) {

            Print("The array key is $key and its value is $val");
            Print("<BR>");

    }


    ?>
```

This script is the same as the previous examples, but it uses the ksort statement to sort the array.

In the script, note that I have kept the original element keys of letters.
When sorted using the ksort statement, the keys are placed in alphabetical
order. PHP sorts alphabetical element keys or values in the same way.

Structured and Reusable Code

My first experience with programming was in college. My teacher was
Chris Pickford, and he was one of the most patient people I have ever met.
Chris did his best to teach my class of novice but very keen programmers the
concepts and benefits of structuring and reusing our code. It was only when I
programmed for a living that I was thankful for what Chris taught me. This
section is for you, Chris.

Structured and reusable code allows you to break your code into ordered
pieces so that you can effectively and efficiently reuse pieces of your code
within your application. It makes sense to do this, because your application
might do certain things repeatedly, such as connect to a database, query a database, and display the database data. By breaking your application into pieces,
you reduce the number of errors that might occur and reduce the amount of
time it takes you to write an application (and saving time is always a good
thing). PHP lets you break up code using several methods, functions, classes,
and includes.

Using Functions

Functions are one of the easiest methods of breaking code into reusable pieces.

```php
<?php

function HelloName($namearg) {

return "Hello " . $namearg;

}

$phrase = HelloName("Andrew");

print("$phrase");


?>
```

This code creates a function that displays a message. You pass a name to the function, and it uses that name to display a message. First, you must create the function:

```php
function HelloName($namearg) {

return "Hello " . $namearg;

}
```

Note that you send the result of calling this function using the following:

```php
return "Hello " . $namearg;
```

In other words, the return statement sends back a result when the function is called. Therefore, to accept the result of the function, you must store the result as you call the function:

```php
$phrase = HelloName("Andrew");
```

Finally, you display the function's result:

```php
print("$phrase");
```

If you run the script, you can see the result of the function call.

Passing Data by Reference or by Value

Functions also let you modify the data you pass to them. Used in this context, you can either keep the data unchanged when it returns from the function (called *passing by value*) or change the data (called *passing by reference*).

```php
<?php

function WhoIsCool($namearg) {
```

```
    $namearg .= ' are cool';

    }

    $name = "PHP programmers";

    //by value
    WhoIsCool($name);
    print("$name");

    //break lines
    print("<BR>");

    //by reference
    WhoIsCool(&$name);
    print("$name");

    ?>
```

This code modifies a string variable called $name. You first apply some data to
the variable:

```
    $name = "PHP programmers";
```

The function you use appends a string of data to the string variable you pass
to the function:

```
    function WhoIsCool($namearg) {

    $namearg .= ' are cool';

    }
```

Next you call the function by value and display the result. Note that PHP
does this by default.

```
    WhoIsCool($name);
    print("$name");
```

You then call the function by reference and display the result:

```
    WhoIsCool(&$name);
    print("$name");
```

To call the function by reference, you append an ampersand (&) to the start of
any data you pass to the function (such as &$name). If you run the script, you
can see that when you call by value, the string variable is not changed by the
function (see Figure 3.18). However, when you call by reference, the value is
changed.

Figure 3.18 The result of passing by value and by reference.

Using Objects

PHP lets you extend and reuse your code in the form of objects. PHP objects let you break code into reusable segments, which PHP calls *classes*. This takes code structuring and reuse one step further from functions, because it lets you completely separate the different parts of an application. In other words, a class can hold its own variables and functions. By separating the code in this way, you can be sure that when you maintain and debug a segment of code, all the code you need to look at is held within that class. So how do you use objects in PHP?

```php
<?php

class myclass {

    function HelloName($namearg) {

return "Hello " . $namearg;

    }
}

//create new instance of class
$myobject = new myclass();

//call HelloName function of class and store result
$phrase = $myobject->HelloName("Andrew");

//display result
print("$phrase");

?>
```

First, you need to define a PHP class to create your object:

```php
class myclass {

    function HelloName($namearg) {
```

```
    return "Hello " . $namearg;

  }
}
```

A couple things are worth noting. First, all code in a class is held within the brackets of a class function. Second, note that the HelloName function from earlier in the chapter reappears here. You don't strictly need to contain your functions within a class, but it makes sense to do so when structuring your code. As before, the HelloName function accepts a variable as an argument, appends some data to the variable, and returns the variable as a result.

```
$myobject = new myclass();
```

In the rest of the PHP code, you can make use of the object. To do this, you must first create an instance of the object and store it in a variable. Why do this? This step is yet another method of code reuse. You can use the same object repeatedly to take different data and obtain different results. You can't reuse the object at the same time though, so you must create a different mirror image of the object each time you use it. In this example, you use the object only once, but the syntax rules remain the same. PHP provides you with the new function for creating mirror images of objects. You store the mirror image of the object in the variable $myobject:

```
$phrase = $myobject->HelloName("Andrew");
```

Now you can use the object. PHP breaks this down into the following:

ObjectInstance->FunctionName

In the example, you are calling the HelloName function of the myclass object. If you run the script, you can see the result of calling the function within the object. This example is quite simple. To show what other objects in PHP can do, we must build on it:

```
<?php

class myclass {

    var $nametoshow = "Everyone";

    function AddName($namearg) {

$this->nametoshow = $namearg;

    }

    function HelloName() {
```

```
        return "Hello " . $this->nametoshow;

    }
}

//create first instance of class
$myobject1 = new myclass();

//call HelloName function of class and store result
$phrase = $myobject1->HelloName();

//display result
print("$phrase");

print("<BR>");

//create second instance of class
$myobject2 = new myclass();

$myobject2->AddName("Andrew");

$phrase = $myobject2->HelloName();

//display result
print("$phrase");


?>
```

The class is made up of several things:

```
class myclass {

    var $nametoshow = "Everyone";

    function AddName($namearg) {

$this->nametoshow = $namearg;

    }

    function HelloName() {

    return "Hello " . $this->nametoshow;

    }
}
```

First, the class has a variable within it. Remember that this variable is available only to code within the class and thus is called a class variable.

```
var $nametoshow = "Everyone";
```

Note that you must declare the class variable using the var statement. This is so that PHP knows what is a variable and what is a function (called *declare code*).

Next, the object has two functions:

```php
function AddName($namearg) {

$this->nametoshow = $namearg;

}

function HelloName() {

    return "Hello " . $this->nametoshow;

}
```

The first function takes a variable as an argument and sets a class variable to the value of that argument:

```php
function AddName($namearg) {

$this->nametoshow = $namearg;

}
```

Note the PHP syntax for setting class variables:

```php
$this->nametoshow = $namearg;
```

This code line refers to the nametoshow variable within the current class. This syntax is used so that you can be sure that the variable is indeed a class variable and that PHP won't confuse it with another variable outside the class. Note that you can only set class variables in this manner with a function; as before, PHP expects declared code outside a function.

```php
function HelloName() {

    return "Hello " . $this->nametoshow;

}
```

The second function returns the class variable to code outside the class. The code to call on your class does two things. First, it creates an instance of the class and shows the result of the class variable:

```php
$myobject1 = new myclass();

$phrase = $myobject1->HelloName();

print("$phrase");
```

Next, it creates another instance of the class and passes a value to the AddName function, so the class variable takes that value. It then displays the new class variable value:

```
$myobject2 = new myclass();

$myobject2->AddName("Andrew");

$phrase = $myobject2->HelloName();

print("$phrase");
```

If you run the script, you can see that the value of the class variable is unchanged and also see the new value of the class variable, as shown in Figure 3.19.

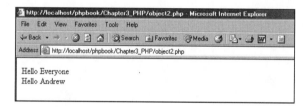

Figure 3.19   Changing the value of a class variable.

Summary

This chapter briefly looked at the various types of editors for Windows that you can use to create PHP scripts. We also took a broad look at the PHP language, including its basic syntax, variables, arrays, logic, loops, functions, and objects. Chapter 4, "PHP and Files," discusses how PHP interacts with files and the Windows file system.

4

PHP and Files

THIS CHAPTER COVERS THE USE OF FILES and directories through PHP. Both files and directories are an important part of application programming for the web on any platform. This chapter explores how to access and manipulate these essential system elements.

PHP's File and Directory Functions

As you learned in Chapter 3 "PHP Programming," versions of ASP prior to .NET (hereby referred to as classic ASP) differs from PHP in many ways. Classic ASP has a high reliance on its COM containers, and the file functions for classic ASP are provided via the scripting runtime COM container. This means that any classic ASP language using the file functions must first call on the file system object of the scripting runtime COM container before it can make use of those functions.

PHP, meanwhile, uses file functions that are compiled into the Zend engine. However, it is possible to call on the same scripting runtime via PHP's support for COM (see Chapter 7, "PHP, COM, and .NET").

PHP and Files

Using the PHP functions for files and directories does not vary much from either Linux or Windows, but there are some issues you must be aware of when you use files.

File Pointers

When an application (such as PHP or Microsoft Word) opens a file, the file's contents are made ready to be either read, written, or deleted. As soon as the file is open, the application keeps track of where it is reading or writing data within the file by using a file pointer.

NTFS and File Permissions

PHP has a host of file functions, which we'll look at later in this chapter. Among them are functions for checking and setting file permissions. If you use an NTFS file system, these functions won't work correctly. The NTFS file system uses a role-based method (share-level access is the analog in Windows 95/98/ME) to set file permissions, such as for Administrators. PHP's file permission functions don't pick up such permissions and in turn can't set them. Note that FAT32/16 has no role-based file permission system like NTFS. Although it's still possible to set file permissions on a per-file basis (such as setting a Word document to read-only) with FAT32/16, PHP cannot pick up or set such permissions.

To illustrate these principles, I have created a simple file called filecheck.txt (but you could use any file).

If you right-click the file, select Properties, and select the Security tab, you can see its permissions, as shown in Figure 4.1. As you can see, the file is both readable and writeable. You can test the file with the code shown in Listing 4.1. (Don't worry too much about what's going on here; I will cover the functions later in this chapter.)

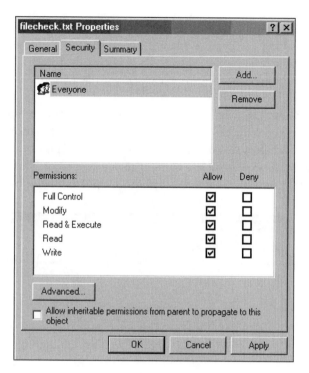

Figure 4.1   NTFS file permissions.

Listing 4.1   **fileperm.php**

```php
<?php

//open the file
$myfile = @fopen("weblangs.txt", "r") or die ("file does not exist
 or could not open file");

//is the file writeable
if (!is_writeable ($myfile)) {
print "not writeable";
}

//close the file
@fclose($myfile);

?>
```

If you inspect the results of running this code (see Figure 4.2), you see that the code reports that the file is not writeable, when the NTFS file permissions tell you that it is. As we mentioned above as a general rule, the PHP file permission checker and setter functions don't work with NTFS. You must set them manually.

Note that when using the fopen function we call it using @fopen. The @ symbol prevents the reporting of any errors; all of PHP's functions can be called in this manner. When is this of any use? Well we can display our own error messages, one method of which is to use the die statement. The die statement displays the error message and then stops the script from running any further.

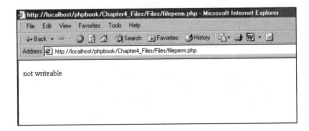

Figure 4.2   PHP displaying incorrect file permissions.

The first line of the code is shown in Listing 4.2.

Listing 4.2   **openclosefile_error.php**

```
$myfile = @fopen("weblangs.txt", "r") or die ("file does not exist
 or could not open file");
```

It reports an error if a file on a FAT32/16 or NTFS file system is not set to readable.

Opening and Closing Files

With these issues in mind, you can start looking at how to use PHP with files. First you must open a file, as shown in Listing 4.3.

Listing 4.3   **openfile.php**

```
<?php

//open file
$myfile = @fopen("weblangs.txt", "r") or die ("file does not exist
 or could not open file");

?>
```

In this script if the file does not exist, or a problem is encountered when opening the file (such as those described in the preceding section), the script reports an error (as shown in Figure 4.3).

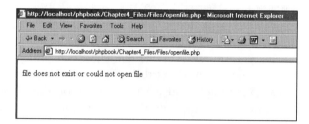

Figure 4.3   Displaying a file not found error message.

If you create a simple text file called weblangs.txt (the content can be anything you like; in this case I have used a selection of names of web scripting languages) in the same directory as the script, the script will not return a file not found error.

One more thing you must add to the script is to close the file when you have finished using it (see Listing 4.4). Using this function is good housekeeping; however, note that PHP closes files for you when the script ends.

Listing 4.4   **openclosefile.php**

```php
<?php

//open file
$myfile = @fopen("weblangs.txt", "r") or die ("file does not exist
 or could not open file");

//close file
@fclose($myfile);

?>
```

Creating Files

Often you might need to temporarily create a file to store data in. PHP gives you a quick way to create these temporary files. You use the `tempnam` function, as shown in Listing 4.5.

Listing 4.5   **createtempfile.php**

```php
<?php

//create temp file
$tempfile = tempnam ("C:\\temp\\", "tmp");

?>
```

The `tempnam` function allows you to set the path of where you will create your PHP file (in this case, C:\temp\) and what file extension the file will have (in this case, .tmp). Because you can specify the file extension, you can create text files, XML files, and so on.

Any temporary files you create will persist, so you need to remove them from your system to preserve resources. Be sure you delete all temporary files when you have finished with them.

Also note that you could not type `C:\temp\` in your script, because the `\` character is seen as an escape character within strings in PHP. You must provide a character to escape this behavior, as in the following:

```
C:\\temp\\
```

If you check your destination directory after running this script (in this case, C:\temp\), you should see that a .tmp file has been created (see Figure 4.4). PHP names these files for you, such as temp12.tmp.

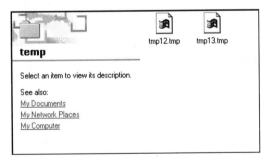

Figure 4.4   The contents of a directory after PHP has created temp files in it.

The second method you can use is to create files when attempting to open them. (You get to name files you create yourself.) PHP has some handy flags that the `fopen` function uses (which you saw earlier)—namely, the `w+` flag (see Listing 4.6).

Listing 4.6   **createfile.php**

```php
<?php

//open file
$myfile = fopen("tempfile.txt", "w+") or die ("file does not exist
 or could not open file");

//close file
@fclose($myfile);

?>
```

This creates tempfile.txt as a readable and writeable file. The `fopen` function
has several flags of this type, as shown in Table 4.1.

Table 4.1   *@fopen* **Flags and Results**

Flag	Result
r	Read only. A file pointer is placed at the start of the file.
r+	Read and write.
w	Write only. If the file exists, the contents are deleted. If it does not exist, it is created. A file pointer is placed at the start of the file.
w+	Read and write. If the file exists, the contents are deleted. If it does not exist, it is created. A file pointer is placed at the start of the file.
a	Write only (a stands for append). If the file does not exist, it is created. A file pointer is placed at the end of the file.
a+	Read and write. If the file does not exist, it is created.

You can also add what's known as the b modifier, in which you add a b to end
of the flags listed in Table 4.1 (with no space between the modifier and the
flag). The b modifier is for OSs (such as Windows) that differentiate between
binary and text files. If you are working with a binary file in your PHP script,
add the b modifier to your `fopen` flags, for example, `fopen("weblangs.txt",
"rb")`.

Writing a Line to a File

Let's next look at how to add a line to a file. We'll start with a file that has the
lines shown in Figure 4.5.

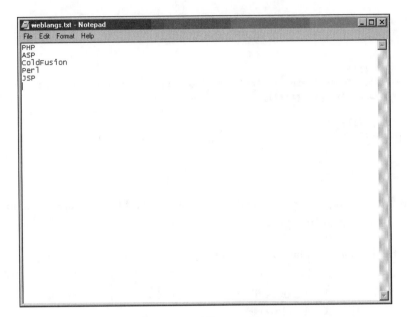

Figure 4.5   The test file.

To create a new line in this file, you would use the code shown in Listing 4.7.

Listing 4.7   **writeline.php**

```php
<?php

//open file
$myfile = @fopen("weblangs.txt", "a") or die ("file does not exist
 or could not open file");

//insert line
fputs($myfile, "Python\r\n");

//close file
@fclose($myfile);

?>
```

This code uses the fputs function to insert a new line (in this case, the word Python). If you compare Figure 4.5 to Figure 4.6, you can see that a new line has been inserted.

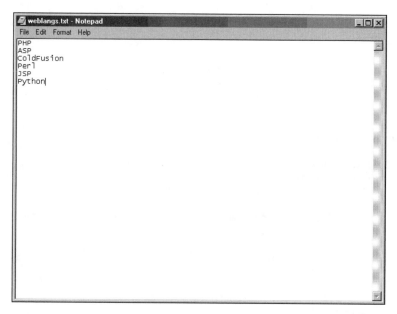

Figure 4.6 The test file with a new line added by your PHP script.

The fputs function adds a string of data to your file. This data will always have a size in bytes. The fputs function adds data according to its size in bytes. You can control this in the fputs function by setting the maximum number of bytes you want to pass. When working with strings you will very rarely need to set the maximum number of bytes you want to read into a file as strings are often small in size. However sometimes strings can be large (for example, a string containing data from a database table and so on), in this case you may wish to break the data in the string up into smaller chunks and add each chunk at a time, the fputs function lets us do both.

Reading a Line from a File

Reading a line from a file is pretty straightforward. You cycle through the file's contents and read it line by line using the fgets function. The fgets function does not strictly read files line by line; it reads a string's bytes from a file until it reaches a line-end sequence. Listing 4.8 shows you how the fgets function works.

Listing 4.8   **readline.php**

```php
<?php

$line_count = 1; // starting value of file count
$line_num = 0; //line number to search for

//open file
$file_to_read = @fopen("weblangs.txt", "r") or die ("file does not exist
 or could not open file");

while (!feof($file_to_read)) {
        //get file line
        $file_line = fgets($file_to_read , 50);

        //see if current line number in file equals desired file number
        if ($line_count == $line_num) {

                //display file line
                print("$file_line");
                break;
        }
        $line_count++;
}

//close file
@fclose($file_to_read);

?>
```

This example cycles through a file and reads it line by line until the desired line number is reached. You start by specifying the line you want to find:

```php
$line_num = 1; //line number to search for
```

As the code runs through the file, it counts the lines in the file. Because the search begins at the start of the file, you set the counter to 0. Each time the code goes through a line in the file, the counter is incremented:

```php
$line_count = 0; // starting value of file count
```

Running through the file is accomplished with the while statement and the fgets function. In the while statement, the while loop runs until the end of the file is reached. The feof function is used to indicate to the while loop that the end of the file has been reached:

```php
while (!feof($file_to_read)) {
```

You need to obtain each line number and see if it matches the line number you want:

```
//get file line
$file_line = fgets($file_to_read , 50);

//see if current line number in file equals desired file number
if ($line_count == $line_num) {
```

When the desired line number is reached, it is printed, and the search stops:

```
//display file line
print($file_line);
break;
```

If you run the script, you see line one of the file, as shown in Figure 4.7.

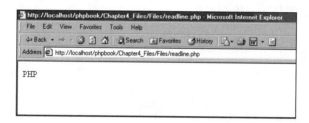

Figure 4.7   The contents of the test file displayed line by line.

Reading All Lines from a File

You can also read all the lines from a file using the script shown in Listing 4.9.

Listing 4.9   **readall.php**

```
<?php

print (readfile("weblangs.txt"));

?>
```

Here, the `readfile` function simply reads a file's contents. You can either store the result to a variable or display it. The readfile function can also read files from HTTP and FTP sources.

Reading Characters from a File

You can read characters from a file using the same methods used to read lines from a file: Open the file, iterate through it, and then close it (see Listing 4.10):

Listing 4.10   **readchars.php**

```php
<?php

//open file
$file_to_read = @fopen("weblangs.txt", "r") or die ("file does not exist
 or could not open file");

//cycle through file contents
do {
      //obtain each character in file
      $file_char = fgetc($file_to_read);

      //print each character in file
      print("$file_char<BR>");

} while (!feof($file_to_read));

//close file
@fclose($file_to_read);

?>
```

Instead of reading lines, this script reads characters using the `fgetc` function:

```php
//obtain each character in file
$file_char = fgetc($file_to_read);
```

You can then print each character as you obtain it:

```php
//print each character in file
print("$file_char<BR>");
```

If you run the script, you should see the contents of the file broken up by character, as shown in Figure 4.8. Note that obtaining characters one by one can introduce a lot of overhead when you're working with large files. In such cases, other means should be considered.

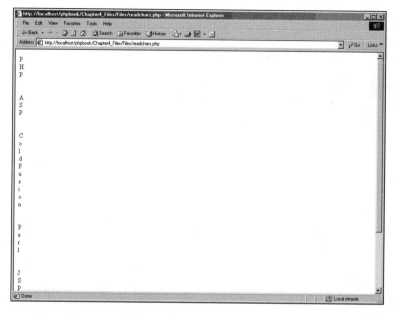

Figure 4.8   The test file read character by character.

PHP and Directories

PHP also gives you the power to work with your file directories.

Opening and Closing a Directory

You can open a directory using the `opendir` function:

```php
<?php

//directory to read
$directoryinfo = "C:\\temp\\";

//open directory for reading
$dirtoread = opendir($directoryinfo);

?>
```

As with files, PHP uses a pointer to indicate its position in a directory. To do this, PHP must first open a directory. In order to preserve system resources, you must ensure that your directory is closed when your script is finished. As with files, PHP automatically closes a directory at the end of the script. You can also set this in your code:

```php
<?php

//directory to read
$directoryinfo = "C:\\temp\\";

//open directory for reading
$dirtoread = opendir($directoryinfo);

//close directory
closedir($dirtoread);

?>
```

Listing Directory Contents

You can list a directory's contents by looping through them and printing what you find, as shown in Listing 4.11.

Listing 4.11 **dircontents.php**

```php
<?php

//directory to read
$directoryinfo = "C:\\temp\\";

//open directory for reading
$dirtoread = opendir($directoryinfo);

//loop through directory contents
while (false !== ($info = readdir($dirtoread))) {

        //print directory contents
        print("$info<br>");

}

//close directory
closedir($dirtoread);

?>
```

PHP lets you read entries from the directory opened with opendir using the readdir function:

```php
while (false !== ($info = readdir($dirtoread))) {
```

This function reads a directory line by line. You can then store each line it returns in a variable for further processing (in this case, displaying).

If you run the script, you should see the contents of the C:\temp\ directory printed to the browser, as shown in Figure 4.9.

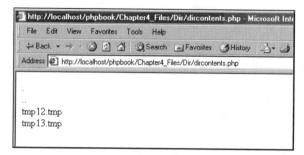

Figure 4.9   The contents of the C:\temp\ directory.

Creating and Deleting Directories

You can easily add and delete directories in PHP, as shown in Listing 4.12. Adding and deleting use a single PHP function for each action.

Listing 4.12   **deletingdirectories.php**

```php
<?php

//directory to read
$directoryinfo = "C:\\temp\\";

//directory to create
$directorytomake = "C:\\temp\\temp2\\";

//create directory
mkdir($directorytomake, 0700);

//open directory for reading
$dirtoread = opendir($directoryinfo);

//loop through directory contents
while ($info = readdir($dirtoread)) {

    //print directory contents
    print("$info<br>");

}

//close directory
closedir($dirtoread);
```

continues

Listing 4.12 **Continued**

```
//remove directory
rmdir($directorytomake);

?>
```

This script first sets the directory you will list and the directory you will create:

```
//directory to read
$directoryinfo = "C:\\temp\\";

//directory to create
$directorytomake = "C:\\temp\\temp2\\";
```

You then create the directory using the mkdir function (the same command that DOS uses):

```
//create directory
mkdir($directorytomake, 0700);
```

Note that this function does not apply permissions to Windows directories. If you run the script, it creates your directory and then lists the directory contents (using the same method as the previous script):

```
//loop through directory contents
while ($info = readdir($dirtoread)) {

        //print directory contents
        print("$info<br>");

}
```

You then close the directory you are searching and delete the directory you created. To delete a directory, you use the rmdir function (also the same command that DOS uses):

```
//remove directory
rmdir($directorytomake);
```

If you run this script, you should see the directory listed in the browser, as shown in Figure 4.10.

Figure 4.10   The contents of the C:\temp\
directory before the temp2 directory is deleted.

If you check your file system, you will see that the directory has been deleted, as shown in Figure 4.11.

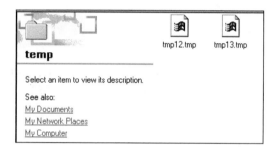

Figure 4.11   The C:\temp\ directory with the temp2 directory deleted.

File Work and Directories

PHP lets you work easily with the files in your directories, allowing you to easily copy, move, rename, and delete files.

Moving and copying might sound like similar operations, but moving moves a file to another directory, and copying creates a copy of the file.

To copy a file, use the code shown in Listing 4.13.

Listing 4.13   **copyingfiles.php**

```php
<?php

//directory to work from
$sourcedirectory = "C:\\temp\\";

$filetocopy = "tmp12.tmp";

$copyoffile = "tmp12_COPY.tmp";
```

continues

Listing 4.13   **Continued**

```
$fullname_filetocopy = $sourcedirectory . $filetocopy;
$fullname_copyfile = $sourcedirectory . $copyoffile;

copy($fullname_filetocopy, $fullname_copyfile);

 ?>
```

This script sets the directory where your files are located:

```
//directory to work from
$sourcedirectory = "C:\\temp\\";
```

You then set the filename you want to copy and the name of the copy of that file:

```
$filetocopy = "tmp12.tmp";

$copyoffile = "tmp12_COPY.tmp";
```

Here you set up in your script variables to hold the name of the file to be copied (such as C:\temp\tmp12.tmp) and the name of the file that you will copy to (C:\temp\tmp12_COPY.tmp).

```
$fullname_filetocopy = $sourcedirectory . $filetocopy;
$fullname_copyfile = $sourcedirectory . $copyoffile;
```

You then copy the file:

```
copy($fullname_filetocopy, $fullname_copyfile);
```

You can also copy a file to a new location using the code shown in Listing 4.14.

Listing 4.14   **copyfiles_newdir.php**

```
<?php

//directory to copy from
$sourcediectory = "C:\\temp\\";

$copydirectory = "C:\\temp\\copydir\\";

$filetocopy = "tmp12.tmp";

$fullname_filetocopy = $sourcediectory . $filetocopy;
$fullname_copyfile = $copydirectory . $filetocopy;

copy($fullname_filetocopy, $fullname_copyfile);

 ?>
```

Here you set the directory that contains the file you want to copy:

```
//directory to copy from
$sourcediectory = "C:\\temp\\";
```

The directory that you want to copy the file to is set in the next line:

```
$copydirectory = "C:\\temp\\copydir\\";
```

The file you want to copy comes next:

```
$filetocopy = "tmp12.tmp";
```

Here you set up in your script variables to hold the name of the file to be copied (such as C:\temp\tmp12.tmp) and the name of the file you will copy to (C:\temp\tmp12_COPY.tmp).

Note that you are using the copy command again, but instead of setting a new filename to copy the file, you set a new directory name to copy the file.

If you run the script, you see that the file has been copied to another directory, as shown in Figure 4.12.

Figure 4.12 The file copied to the copydir directory.

You can also rename files using the code shown in Listing 4.15.

Listing 4.15 **renamingfiles.php**

```
<?php

//directory we are working from
$workdir = "C:\\temp\\";

//create temp file
$filetorenam = tempnam ($workdir, "tmp");
```

continues

Listing 4.15   **Continued**

```
//newfile name
$newfilename = $workdir . "copyofile.tmp";

//print file message
print("File created: $filetorenam <BR>");

//rename file
rename($filetorenam, $newfilename) or die ("unable to rename file
 or file has not been created");

//print file message
print ("file renamed: $newfilename");

?>
```

Here you set the directory you are working from:

```
//directory we are working from
$workdir = "C:\\temp\\";
```

You then create a temporary file in that directory:

```
//create temp file
$filetorenam = tempnam ($workdir, "tmp");
```

You then set the filename of the renamed file:

```
//newfile name
$newfilename = $workdir . "copyofile.tmp";
```

You then rename the file using the rename function:

```
rename($filetorenam, $newfilename) or die ("unable to rename file
 or file has not been created");
```

Again, the rename function is very much like the rename command in DOS.

If you run this script, you see that the file has been renamed, as shown in Figure 4.13.

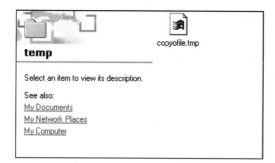

Figure 4.13 Renaming a file.

You use the `rename` function to move files:

```php
<?php

//directory we are working from
$workdir = "C:\\temp\\";

//directory to move to
$copydir = "C:\\temp\\spare\\";

//create temp file
$filetorenam = tempnam ($workdir, "tmp");

//new filename and path
$newfilename = $copydir . "copyofile.tmp";

//print file message
print("File created: $filetorenam <BR>");

//rename file
rename($filetorenam, $newfilename) or die ("unable to rename file
 or file has not been created");

//print file message
print ("file moved: $newfilename");

?>
```

This code does the same as the `rename` code in Listing 4.15. However, when you rename the file, you set its directory path to the directory you are moving the file to.

Last, you can delete files using PHP's `unlink` function, as shown in Listing 4.16.

Listing 4.16 **deletingfiles.php**

```php
<?php

//create temp file
$filetodel = tempnam ("C:\\temp\\", "tmp");

//print file message
print("File created: $filetodel");

//delete file
unlink($filetodel) or die ("unable to delete file
 or file has not been created");

?>
```

Here you create a temp file:

```php
//create temp file
$filetodel = tempnam ("C:\\temp\\", "tmp");
```

You then delete the temp file:

```php
//delete file
unlink($filetodel) or die ("unable to delete file
 or file has not been created");
```

Summary

This chapter looked at how to use PHP to interact with files and directories.
You saw that PHP's functions for checking file permissions are geared toward
UNIX systems, not Windows file systems (FAT32 or NTFS). We looked at
how you can create, delete, and rename files. We also looked at how to insert,
delete, and modify data in those files. We then covered how to create, delete,
and rename directories.

5

PHP and Sessions

Sessions or state control are an important part of most web applications. Often you want to pass some information around during the life of a web application, such as a user ID. Many different PHP scripts in your web application might need that information. Such information is called *session* or *state* information. PHP also lets you pass such information back and forth to other web scripting languages such as ASP using a protocol called Web-Distributed Data eXchange (WDDX) if your web application is made up of different web scripting languages. WDDX is not limited to sharing session data. It can share any data between applications. This chapter looks first at how PHP handles session data and then at how PHP handles WDDX session data with ASP.

PHP Sessions

Let's first look at what session data is and how it is handled.

What Is Session Data?

Session data is data that can be stored for later use in a web application. Note that session data is ASCII data only (such as letters and numbers). It is saved to a standard ASCII text file in a temporary location on your web server's hard drive. Sessions can contain binary data and therefore can include malicious or harmful code or information such a virus. However, most modern browsers have built-in security features, so the risk is small (and can be reduced further with antivirus software).

When a session is created, PHP creates a temporary file (known as a session file) on the web server's hard drive and creates a unique random ID for that file. So that it knows which user using the web application (using a web browser) created that session ID, PHP also creates a temporary file known as a cookie on the user's computer.

When a user visits another PHP page that needs that session data, the PHP page first looks at the ID from the user's cookie and then loads the correct session data from the session file on the web server using that ID (see Figure 5.1).

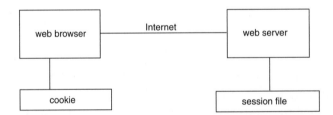

Figure 5.1   How PHP creates session data.

Sharing Session Data in a Stateless Environment

A stateless environment is when a computer cannot hold the information it has been sent (in a cookie). Therefore, it must request the data it needs from the server rather than hold a copy itself.

This might be because the user's browser does not support cookies, in which a copy of the data is stored (although this is rare), or because, for security or other reasons, a user's browser has been set to reject cookies being set. PHP can still maintain state in this circumstance by passing the session ID in the URL instead of using cookies. If you disable cookies in the browser and run any of the scripts that we develop later in the chapter, you can see the session ID in the URL. For example:

```
http://localhost/setsession.php?PHPSESSID=627f11bb2d08cc8bffcac28e2cdacd2f
```

Note that the session ID is referenced using a special parameter called PHPSESSID. PHP uses this parameter to recall data from the session that references this session ID within the session file. Also note that PHP can share session data in HTML forms. Switching between using URL and hidden form fields is left to PHP's automatic transparent URL/Form rewriter.

Sharing Session Data Between PHP Scripts

To show you how you can share session data across two PHP scripts, I have created a script (which saves the session data) to load another PHP script as follows.

Listing 5.1 **The Set Session PHP Script**

```
<?php

//data to save
$sessdata="Andrew";

//start session
session_start();

//save data to session
session_register("sessdata");

?>

<A HREF="setsession2.php">Next -></A>
```

You first define the data you save to a session:

```
$sessdata="Andrew";
```

Next you start a session:

```
session_start();
```

You then save your data to a session:

```
session_register("sessdata");
```

I have also added an HTML hyperlink that points to another PHP script that displays data within our session:

```
<A HREF="setsession2.php">Next -></A>
```

The PHP script that displays the data is as follows.

Listing 5.2 **The Load Session PHP Script**

```php
<?php

//start session
session_start();

//print session data
print("$sessdata");

//remove session
session_destroy();

?>
```

First, a session is started:

```php
session_start();
```

PHP references items in a session by the name of the variable that was stored in the session. In this example, the variable is called $sessdata, so you reference $sessdata to recall any data from it:

```php
print("$sessdata");
```

Note that you tell PHP that $sessdata is a PHP variable simply by starting a session. If you don't do this, PHP assumes that $sessdata is a variable local to the script and not a session variable. To complete the script, you can remove the session:

```php
session_destroy();
```

If you run the first script and click the hyperlink to load the second script, you should see the session data displayed.

Storing Multiple Items in a Session

PHP lets you store multiple items in single session.

```php
<?php

//data to save
$sessdata1="Andrew";
$sessdata2="Emma";

//start session
session_start();

//save item 1 to session
session_register("sessdata1");
```

```
//save item 2 to session
session_register("sessdata2");

?>

<A HREF="setsession_mutp2.php">Next -></A>
```

First, you define two sets of the data you want to save to a session:

```
$sessdata1="Andrew";
$sessdata2="Emma";
```

Next, you start a session:

```
session_start();
```

You then save both sets of the session:

```
session_register("sessdata1");

session_register("sessdata2");
```

To view the session, I have created another script. You link to that page using an HTML link:

```
<A HREF="setsession_mutp2.php">Next -></A>
```

This script looks like the following:

```
<?php

//start session
session_start();

//print item1 from session
print("$sessdata1");

print("<BR>");

//print item2 from session
print("$sessdata2");

//remove session
session_destroy();

?>
```

You first start the session:

```
session_start();
```

You then recall and display each item with the session. (Remember the script early in the session where you recall items from the session using the name of the variable that was stored to the session.)

```
print("$sessdata1");

print("$sessdata2");
```

Finally, you delete the session:

```
session_destroy();
```

Changing the Directory Where PHP Saves Session Files

By default, PHP saves session files to your system's temp directory. However, PHP lets you alter this location through the PHP.ini file or directly in your code. In both of the following examples, I have created a sample directory in my C:\WINNT\Temp\directory called phpsess, so my target directory is C:\WINNT\Temp\phpsess\. Of course, you can use any directory you choose. In most cases, you won't need to alter the location of the directory where PHP saves session files. However, should you ever need to, PHP does provide the functionality to do so.

Using the PHP.ini File

PHP saves session files using the `session.save_path` directive within the PHP.ini file. If I set mine to our target directory and run a PHP session script (anything we developed earlier will work), the session file is created in the target directory, as shown in Figure 5.2.

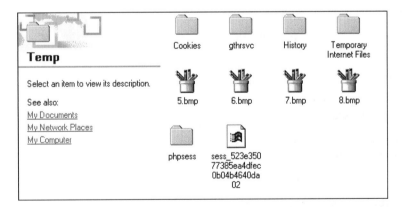

Figure 5.2   A PHP session file stored to the hard drive.

Using PHP Directly

Using PHP, you can use the `session_save_path` function to set the session file path:

```php
<?php

session_save_path("C:\WINNT\Temp\phpsess");

//data to save
$sessdata1="Andrew";

//start session
session_start();

//save data to session
session_register("sessdata1");

?>
```

Here I have set `session_save_path` to the target directory:

```php
session_save_path("C:\WINNT\Temp\phpsess");
```

Note that you must always use this function *before* you set or get session data in your PHP code.

PHP and WDDX Sessions

Using sessions is a powerful way to share data between PHP scripts. However, if you want to communicate with PHP scripts on another web server or with other web scripting languages (such as ASP) or web-aware applications, you quickly run out of options with sessions. Facilitating such communication requires other methods. This has been long addressed using special wire protocols such as RMI (Java), DCOM, and IIOP (CORBA).

Using such protocols can, however, be a problem. More often than not, such protocols are used within components of the web scripting language. For example, ASP uses COM components that communicate via DCOM. The wire protocols support a wide range of functions that for simple information exchange between web scripting languages are really just too complicated. Also, such wire protocols require their own network ports. This can cause security concerns at locations in your network, such as your firewall.

Several different companies have been aware of such shortcomings for a long time and have created several protocols to address these problems. It began with Dave Winer of UserLand software, who proposed a way of using XML to exchange data between applications (including web scripting languages) over HTTP. This solved all the problems faced by the wire protocols. HTTP was a standard wire protocol and didn't need a special port on the firewall. It was simple, and using XML meant it was text-based (thus small in size and easy to communicate). XML as a standard in its own right was widely understood by most applications.

Winer joined forces with Microsoft and eventually other companies to create what became known as the Simple Object Access Protocol (SOAP). (SOAP and PHP are discussed in Chapter 9, "PHP and Web Services.") A protocol also forked off from Winer's original idea to create XML-RPC (XML Remote Procedure Call). However, although both protocols were XML over HTTP protocols, they allowed for not only data exchange between applications, but also the capability to call functions on those applications. For just passing data between applications, SOAP and XML-RPC could be overkill.

Aside from the emergence of SOAP and XML-RPC, a third project was in development. Simeon Simeonov of the Allaire Corporation (now Macromedia) proposed a way of passing data between applications using XML over HTTP. Unlike the RPC capabilities of SOAP and XML-RPC, Simeonov proposed that his idea would only facilitate the passing of data between applications and nothing more. His idea became known as Web-Distributed Data eXchange (WDDX). WDDX development was sponsored by Allaire, which worked with third-party developer Nate Weiss to create an SDK to allow the exchange of WDDX data using Java, JavaScript, and COM.

Third parties added WDDX support to PHP, Perl, and Python. PHP support for WDDX was added to PHP and is maintained by Andrei Zmievski.

With WDDX, an application's variable types are converted (often referred to as *serialized*) into a WDDX variable type. WDDX packets are the resulting XML file that WDDX creates to pass WDDX variable types between applications.

WDDX can convert most variable types that applications use, such as strings, integers, and arrays. After a variable has been converted to a WDDX variable type, it is ready for another application to pick up. In this case, the process works in reverse—the application can convert a WDDX packet into a variable type that is native to it. This lets you share data types between applications without needing to worry about data type incompatibilities. WDDX handles it for you. You can see this by looking at a sample WDDX packet:

```
<wddxPacket version='1.0'>
<header></header>
<data>
<string>Andrew</string>
</data>
</wddxPacket>
```

Here you can see that WDDX has converted a string variable type containing the value Andrew into the following WDDX variable type:

```
<string>Andrew</string>
```

PHP's WDDX Functions

As mentioned earlier in this chapter, PHP has WDDX support built in, so you don't need to modify your PHP.ini file to start using WDDX.

PHP to ASP

Let's first look at how you can pass data from PHP to ASP using WDDX.

You create a WDDX packet by first serializing data into a WDDX packet and then presenting it.

A PHP Script to Serialize WDDX

```php
<?php

//define PHP data to send
$ValueToSend = "Andrew";

//convert PHP data to WDDX data
$wddxvar = wddx_serialize_value("$ValueToSend");

//output WDDX data
print("$wddxvar");

?>
```

You first set the data you want to serialize into a WDDX packet:

```php
$ValueToSend = "Andrew";
```

You then serialize that data:

```php
$wddxvar = wddx_serialize_value("$ValueToSend");
```

Finally, you present that data (see Figure 5.3):

```php
print("$wddxvar");
```

Figure 5.3   A WDDX packet created by PHP displayed in Internet Explorer.

Internet Explorer just shows the data within the WDDX packet. It doesn't show the surrounding XML structures. However, if you choose the view source option, you can see the WDDX packet's XML structures, as shown in Figure 5.4.

Figure 5.4   The XML structure of a WDDX packet created by a PHP script.

ASP Script to Deserialize WDDX Data

To receive the WDDX packet from the PHP script, you must load the packet into a variable within the receiving ASP script. None of the WDDX implementations (the WDDX COM component or PHP's WDDX functions) provides native ways of doing this. You must add this functionality using separate code. After you receive the WDDX packet, you can convert it into a data type native to the receiving application. This is called deserializing.

Using ASP, you can use a third-party COM component. A free COM component that allows such functionality is ASP Tear from `http://www.alphasier-rapapa.com/IisDev/Components/` (also included with the WDDX SDK). However, you can use any COM component that has similar functionality.

```
<%

set aspget = Server.CreateObject("SOFTWING.AspTear")
set wddxob = Server.CreateObject("WDDX.Deserializer.1")

'get WDDX data
wddxdata = aspget.Retrieve("http://localhost/phpbook/Chapter5
➥_Sessions/WDDX/PHP/two_wddxserver.php", Request_POST, "", "", "")

'convert WDDX data to ASP data
wddxvar = wddxob.deserialize(wddxdata)

'output ASP data
response.write "Hello " & wddxvar

set wddxob = nothing
set aspget = nothing

%>
```

First, you must load the WDDX and ASP Tear COM objects into memory for use by ASP. Don't worry too much if you are not familiar with using COM objects. They are discussed in Chapter 7, "PHP, COM, and .NET."

```
set aspget = Server.CreateObject("SOFTWING.AspTear")
set wddxob = Server.CreateObject("WDDX.Deserializer.1")
```

Next you use ASP Tear to obtain the WDDX packet produced by the PHP server and load it into a variable:

```
'get WDDX data
wddxdata = aspget.Retrieve("http://localhost/phpbook/Chapter5
➥_Sessions/WDDX/PHP/two_wddxserver.php", Request_POST, "", "", "")
```

You deserialize the WDDX packet into a native data type for ASP:

```
'convert WDDX data to ASP data
wddxvar = wddxob.deserialize(wddxdata)
```

You then output the value:

```
'output ASP data
response.write "Hello " & wddxvar
```

Finally, you unload the COM objects from memory:

```
set wddxob = nothing
set aspget = nothing
```

ASP to PHP

PHP can also receive WDDX packets. Here you will see a PHP script obtaining a WDDX packet from an ASP script.

An ASP Script to Serialize WDDX

```
<%

'define ASP data to send
ValueToSend = "Andrew"

set wddxob = Server.CreateObject("WDDX.Serializer.1")

'convert ASP data to WDDX data
wddxvar = wddxob.serialize(ValueToSend)

'output WDDX data
response.write wddxvar

set wddxob = nothing

%>
```

This is very much the same as the serializing PHP script. First, you define the value you want to serialize in WDDX:

```
'define ASP data to send
ValueToSend = "Andrew"
```

You then load the WDDX COM object into memory, ready for use by ASP:

```
set wddxob = Server.CreateObject("WDDX.Serializer.1")
```

You then serialize the value into a WDDX packet:

```
'convert ASP data to WDDX data
wddxvar = wddxob.serialize(ValueToSend)
```

You then display the WDDX packet:

```
'output WDDX data
response.write wddxvar
```

Finally, you unload the WDDX COM object from memory:

```
set wddxob = nothing
```

If you look at the WDDX packet created by the serializing ASP script, you can see that it is no different from the WDDX packet created by the serializing PHP script (see Figure 5.5).

Figure 5.5 The WDDX packet created by an ASP script.

A PHP Script to Deserialize WDDX Data

The deserialize PHP script needs to do the same as the deserialize ASP script: It must convert the WDDX packet back into a native variable type for our script (in this case, a native variable type for PHP):

```php
<?php

//get WDDX data
$wddxdata = join ('', file
('http://localhost/phpbook/Chapter5_Sessions/WDDX/ASP/one_wddxserver.asp'));

//convert WDDX data to PHP data
$wddxvar = wddx_deserialize("$wddxdata");
```

```
//output PHP data
print("Hello " . $wddxvar);

?>
```

You can obtain the WDDX packet from the ASP script using the PHP `join` function. To use the function in this manner, you must make sure that HTTP transparency is enabled in the PHP.ini settings file (the `allow_url_fopen` setting is enabled). (Note that HTTP transparency is enabled by default.)

```
$wddxdata = join ('', file
('http://localhost/phpbook/Chapter5_Sessions/WDDX/ASP/one_wddxserver.asp'));
```

As before, you deserialize the WDDX packet into a native variable type:

```
$wddxvar = wddx_deserialize("$wddxdata");
```

You then display the WDDX packet:

```
print("Hello " . $wddxvar);
```

ASP Arrays to PHP

WDDX also allows more-complicated data structures to be passed between applications. Here we will pass an array from an ASP WDDX script to a PHP script.

An ASP Script to Serialize an Array into a WDDX Packet

```
<%

'define data as ASP array
dim names
names = Array("Andrew", "Emma", "Terry", "Mary", "Thomas")

set wddxob = Server.CreateObject("WDDX.Serializer.1")

'convert ASP array to WDDX array
wddxvar = wddxob.serialize(names)

'output WDDX array
response.write wddxvar

set wddxob = nothing

%>
```

First, you create the array that you will convert to WDDX:

```
dim names
names = Array("Andrew", "Emma", "Terry", "Mary", "Thomas")
```

Note that currently, the WDDX COM object accepts only this definition of an array in ASP. The other definition, shown here, won't work:

```
'dim names(5)
'names(1) = "Andrew"
```

Next, you load the WDDX COM object into memory:

```
set wddxob = Server.CreateObject("WDDX.Serializer.1")
```

Then you convert the ASP array into WDDX:

```
wddxvar = wddxob.serialize(names)
```

Finally, you display the WDDX and unload the WDDX COM object from memory:

```
response.write wddxvar

set wddxob = nothing
```

As with all WDDX data, if you display the result of the ASP script, the WDDX packet is displayed, but with no surrounding XML structures (see Figure 5.6).

Figure 5.6   The array displayed as a WDDX packet.

However, if you view the content script's output, you can see the WDDX packet's XML structures, as shown in Figure 5.7.

Figure 5.7   The array displayed as a WDDX packet with surrounding XML structures.

It is interesting to note that it changes from the packets that you created previously and adds the following elements:

```
<array length="5">
```

This indicates the size of the array and that you are passing an array between applications. Within the array element, you list all the elements in the array:

```
<string>Andrew</string> etc.
```

Therefore, the array structure within the WDDX packet is as follows:

```
<array length='5'>
<string>Andrew</string>
<string>Emma</string>
<string>Terry</string>
<string>Mary</string>
<string>Thomas</string>
</array>
```

A PHP Script to Deserialize an Array from a WDDX Packet

As with the previous examples, this PHP script obtains the WDDX packet from the ASP script and converts it into a native variable type. However, this time the PHP variable type you must obtain from the WDDX packet is an array.

```
<?php

//get WDDX array
$wddxdata = join ('', file
('http://localhost/phpbook/Chapter5_Sessions/WDDX/ASP/asparrays_server.asp'))
;

//put WDDX array into PHP array
$wddxvar = wddx_deserialize("$wddxdata");

//iterate through PHP array
for ($arraycount=0; $arraycount<5; $arraycount++) {
print("$wddxvar[$arraycount]\n\r<BR>");
}

?>
```

As in the previous example, you use the PHP join function to obtain the WDDX packet from the ASP script:

```
$wddxdata = join ('', file
('http://localhost/phpbook/Chapter5_Sessions/WDDX/ASP/asparrays_server.asp'))
;
```

You then deserialize the WDDX packet into a PHP array:

```
$wddxvar = wddx_deserialize("$wddxdata");
```

To display the contents of the array, you loop through and display each item in the array:

```
for ($arraycount=0; $arraycount<5; $arraycount++) {
print("$wddxvar[$arraycount]\n\r<BR>");
}
```

If you run this script, you see the displayed array, as shown in Figure 5.8.

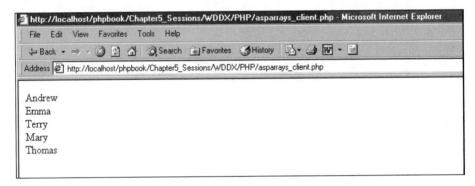

Figure 5.8   The contents of an array converted from a WDDX packet.

PHP Arrays to ASP

Currently, it's not possible to use the script in reverse (PHP array to ASP via WDDX). The reason for this is that PHP uses a more recent version of the WDDX specification to represent arrays in WDDX. When it is deserialized, the array becomes represented in the application as a list of variables. You can show this by creating a WDDX packet from a PHP array:

```
<?php

//create PHP array
$names = array("Andrew", "Emma", "Terry", "Mary", "Thomas");

//convert PHP data to WDDX data
$wddxvar = wddx_serialize_vars("names");

//output WDDX data
print("$wddxvar");

?>
```

If you run this script, you can see the WDDX packet it creates:

```
<wddxPacket version='1.0'>
<header/>
<data>
<struct>
<var name='names'>
<array length='5'>
<string>Andrew</string>
<string>Emma</string>
<string>Terry</string>
<string>Mary</string>
<string>Thomas</string>
</array>
</var>
</struct>
</data>
</wddxPacket>
```

You can obtain this packet using the following PHP script. Note that the array is named "names" in the WDDX packet. PHP uses this to reference the list of data when deserialized.

```php
<?php

$wddxdata = join ('', file
('http://localhost/phpbook/Chapter5_Sessions/WDDX/PHP/phparrays_server.php'))
;

$wddxvar = wddx_deserialize("$wddxdata");

while (list($key, $val) = each($wddxvar["names"])) {
print "$key = $val\n<BR>";
}

?>
```

However, the WDDX COM object fails to load the WDDX packet when presented in this way by the PHP script.

Other PHP Functions for WDDX

PHP has a few other functions that can be useful when you're working with WDDX:

```php
<?php

$names = array("Andrew", "Emma");
$name2 = "Terry";
$name3 = "Mary";
$name4 = "Thomas";
```

```
$wddxpack = wddx_packet_start("PHP-WDDX");

wddx_add_vars($wddxpack, "names");

wddx_add_vars($wddxpack, "name2");
wddx_add_vars($wddxpack, "name3");
wddx_add_vars($wddxpack, "name4");

$wddxvar = wddx_packet_end($wddxpack);

//output WDDX data
$wddx_out = wddx_deserialize($wddxvar);

//iterate through PHP array

while (list($key, $val) = each($wddx_out["names"])) {
print "$val\n<BR>";
}

print($wddx_out["name2"] . "<br>");
print($wddx_out["name3"] . "<br>");
print($wddx_out["name4"] . "<br>");

?>
```

PHP lets you modify the contents of a WDDX packet so that you can add and
delete the contents of a WDDX packet as you see fit. To show this, you first
create a PHP array containing the first two items in the packet:

```
$names = array("Andrew", "Emma");
```

You then create the other items that make up the WDDX packet:

```
$name2 = "Terry";
$name3 = "Mary";
$name4 = "Thomas";
```

You then create the WDDX packet:

```
$wddxpack = wddx_packet_start("PHP-WDDX");
```

You then add the items to the WDDX packet and close it:

```
wddx_add_vars($wddxpack, "names");

wddx_add_vars($wddxpack, "name2");
wddx_add_vars($wddxpack, "name3");
wddx_add_vars($wddxpack, "name4");

$wddxvar = wddx_packet_end($wddxpack);
```

If you look at the contents of the WDDX packet, you can see how PHP has
built it:

```
<struct>
<var name='names'>
<array length='2'>
<string>Andrew</string>
<string>Emma</string>
</array>
</var>
<var name='name2'>
<string>Terry</string>
</var>
<var name='name3'>
<string>Mary</string>
</var>
<var name='name4'>
<string>Thomas</string>
</var>
</struct>
```

It's interesting to note that PHP adds each data type (the array and other elements) separately to the WDDX packet. Also note that PHP uses named references for each data element added to the WDDX packet, such as names for the
array, name2 for "Terry", and so on.

```
$wddx_out = wddx_deserialize($wddxvar);
```

You deserialize the WDDX packet as normal. Because there are different data
types within the WDDX packet, PHP handles the deserialized data differently.
For the array, you use the list function that you used in the previous
example:

```
while (list($key, $val) = each($wddx_out["names"])) {
print "$val\n<BR>";
}
```

For the other data types, you use the reference contained in the WDDX file:

```
print($wddx_out["name2"] . "<br>");
print($wddx_out["name3"] . "<br>");
print($wddx_out["name4"] . "<br>");
```

In effect, what is returned to PHP from the WDDX packet is a hash array (or
named array). Each element in the array takes its named value from the reference in the WDDX packet.

Summary

This chapter looked at how PHP can maintain state across web applications using sessions. It also looked at how PHP can share data between web scripting languages using WDDX.

6

PHP and Databases

ADATABASE IS ONE OF THE MAINSTAYS of modern-day server-side web development. They are found everywhere, from the database that lets you buy books from Amazon to the database that lets you search the web with Yahoo!. You might find that you use a database a lot when developing web sites and web applications. As such, the development language you use should aid you in such tasks. As you will see, PHP has everything you need.

PHP's Database Querying Methods

PHP can connect to and query a database either using Open Database Connectivity (ODBC) or by directly accessing the database. The direct method uses a PHP extension that is written for the database in question (such as Oracle or MySQL). This extension can make use of the database's API to directly call the database.

However, you might find that your database has no PHP extension (although PHP does support most major database vendors). If that is the case, you can use ODBC. (Most Database Management Systems [DBMSs] have an ODBC driver.)

ODBC

ODBC is a standard way of connecting a database to an application. ODBC is often seen on the Windows platform but is also available for UNIX and Linux systems.

ODBC lets you define a connection to a data source, as shown in Figure 6.1. This can be a flat-file database such as a CSV text file or a relational database. (Databases are often managed by a DBMS. A DBMS for a relational database is called a Relational Database Management System [RDBMS]).)

Figure 6.1   Connecting PHP to a database via ODBC.

Some DBMSs let you set quite advanced settings for connecting and querying a database. Such information is best collected and stored, and ODBC lets you do this. In fact, all you need to do is call the name of the ODBC connection, and all the details that are needed for connecting to a database are passed to the database to make that connection. An ODBC connection can be used by multiple applications. So, for example, if you need to query the same database using PHP or ASP, ODBC can make this much easier. ODBC calls a connection to a database a Data Source Name (DSN).

Appendix A, "Creating an ODBC Connection," gives details on setting up a DSN. ODBC lets you set different DSN types. The two types of DSNs of interest to us are System DSNs and User DSNs.

System DSNs

A System DSN is a connection to a database that can occur when the DSN and the database are on the same computer or on different computers, as shown in Figure 6.2.

Figure 6.2   Connecting PHP to a database via ODBC using a System DSN.

User DSNs

A User DSN is the reverse of a System DSN. A User DSN can connect only to a database that resides on the same computer that the DSN is set up on (see Figure 6.3).

Figure 6.3 Connecting PHP to a database via ODBC using a User DSN.

When setting up a DSN, it's important to choose the correct DSN for your system. In other words, if your database is located on a different computer than PHP, set up a System DSN. If it isn't, use either a System DSN or a User DSN. If you set up the wrong DSN for your system, the application that uses the DSN (such as PHP) reports an error—normally the dreaded 80004005 error. If you get such an error and you can't find a problem with your application, double-check your DSN type.

For further information on ODBC, see `http://www.microsoft.com/data`.

The Direct Method

Most database vendors provide an API for connecting to and querying a database (see Figure 6.4). Using this API, applications can communicate directly with the database. PHP makes use of various database vendor APIs to achieve this aim. The MySQL API, for example, is compiled directly into PHP. Other database types such as SQL Server require their APIs be explicitly added via a PHP extension.

Figure 6.4 Connecting PHP to a database via the database API.

Using an API allows PHP to communicate directly with a database, so this method is often faster than ODBC, because you have no go-between. Your queries go directly to the database. PHP uses the direct method to query relational database systems such as SQL Server or Access, as well as flat-file databases such as text files or files in the dBASE file format.

Database Work

You work with the data in a database via a standard language called SQL (Structured Query Language). SQL lets you add, delete, and edit the tables in a database, as well as query, update, delete, and add records in a table of a database. PHP, like all languages that work with databases, uses SQL to work with the database. All PHP does is pass the SQL command to the database. If a query is being run, the database returns the result of the query to PHP. PHP can be used not only to query data from a database, but also to perform all the functions SQL can carry out.

Note

SQL has many permutations across the different DBMSs. For portability, this book uses ANSI SQL92—and I recommend that you do as well.

Querying a Database Using ODBC and PHP

Querying a database with PHP using ODBC is very straightforward, but you do need to follow the steps outlined next.

Setting Up a Database

This chapter uses a sample Microsoft Access database called php4win. (Be warned that Microsoft Access is not a suitable DBMS for use in a situation in which multiple clients access it almost simultaneously. In these circumstances, you should use a product such as Microsoft SQL Server or Oracle.) I have created a simple table called names in the database. Its fields are shown in Table 6.1.

Table 6.1   **A Table in the php4win Database**

Field Name	Field Type	Field Size
ID	AutoNumber	
Name	Text	50

Setting Up a DSN

Appendix A shows you how to set up a DSN for the php4win database. I have created the DSN as a System DSN, but if you are running the Access database and PHP on the same computer, you can use a User DSN.

Setting a Connection

If you obtained PHP as a binary distribution, ODBC is compiled straight into PHP, so you don't need to use a PHP extension for ODBC. (Due to the changing development between PHP versions, I recommend that you make sure that the binary distribution has ODBC support.) To begin using ODBC, you first connect to the database:

```php
<?php

//connect to the database
$connectionstring = odbc_connect("phpwinaccess", "", "");

?>
```

The `odbc_connect` function has three parameters: the DSN name (in this case, phpwinaccess), a username, and a password. The username and password are always required. However, if your DBMS does not need a username and password, set them to empty strings.

Although our script will connect to the database, it needs to disconnect from the database after it has finished working with it:

```php
<?php

//connect to the database
$connectionstring = odbc_connect("phpwinaccess", "", "");

//disconnect from database
odbc_close($connectionstring);

?>
```

Most databases keep connections open but impose a limit on how many are open in order to preserve database resources. When a database reaches its limit for open connections, it prevents other connections from being opened. Thankfully, PHP closes all database connections for you (with or without a close function such as `odbc_close`) unless they have been opened with a persistent function.

One such type of persistent connection is the `odbc_pconnect` function:

```php
<?php

//connect to the database
$connectionstring = odbc_pconnect("phpwinaccess", "", "");

?>
```

odbc_pconnect differs from odbc_connect in that it preserves the connection for the life of the web server process. You might think this is a bad idea, but in fact it's a good one. As soon as a connection using odbc_pconnect is opened, all PHP scripts that use the same odbc_pconnect function use that one connection (as opposed to the individual connections odbc_connect makes). Using a persistent database connection means that you are not constantly connecting to the database every time a connection is needed. Instead, one remains open for you. When using either a persistent or nonpersistent database connection, it's often best to benchmark both methods of connection and review your DBMS documentation to decide when to use either method.

Querying a Database

The next stage is to query the database to obtain the information you need:

```php
<?php

//connect to the database
$connectionstring = odbc_connect("phpwinaccess", "", "");

//SQL query
$query = "SELECT Name FROM Names";

//execute query
$result = odbc_do($connectionstring, $query);

//disconnect from database
odbc_close($connectionstring);

?>
```

This script builds on previous scripts by adding the capability to query the database. To do this, you must first set the SQL query that you need to query the database. You store it in a variable ($query). This lets you reuse the same SQL query in any later queries. (Although you don't need to do this in this example, it's always a good practice, especially if you are using advanced SQL with long syntax.) It's also useful for error checking. If you develop an error in your SQL query string, you can simply print the variable to the screen to see where you went wrong.

```php
$query = "SELECT Name FROM Names";
```

You then pass the query to the database and store its result in $result:

```php
$result = odbc_do($connectionstring, $query);
```

Query Errors

It is important when you set the SQL query to spell database and table names correctly. For example, this query:

```
$query = "SELECT Name FROM Namess";
```

returns the error shown in Figure 6.5.

Figure 6.5   PHP returning a database query error.

Query Results

If you run the preceding script, you won't see anything displayed. To see things displayed, use the following script:

```php
<?php

//connect to the database
$connectionstring = odbc_connect("phpwinaccess", "", "");

//SQL query
$query = "SELECT Name FROM Names";

//execute query
$result = odbc_do($connectionstring, $query);

//output results to standard output
odbc_result_all($result, "BORDER=1");

//disconnect from database
odbc_close($connectionstring);

?>
```

This script differs only slightly from the preceding one. It adds the `odbc_result_all` function:

```php
odbc_result_all($queryexe, "BORDER=1");
```

This function takes the result from the query you passed to the database in the `odbc_do` function and displays it in an HTML table, as shown in Figure 6.6. The second argument (`BORDER=1`) lets you pass some values that you can use to format the HTML table.

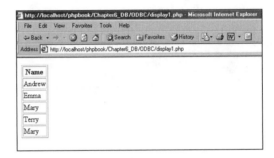

Figure 6.6   Database query results from the Access database.

Formatting Results

The problem with using the `odbc_result` function is that you have no control over how the data is presented. To do this, you must use a few other PHP ODBC functions:

```
<html>
<head></head>
<body bgcolor="#FFFFFF">
<table width="75%" border="1" cellspacing="1" cellpadding="1"
bgcolor="#FFFFFF">
  <tr bgcolor="#CCFFFF">
    <td height="22"><b>Names</b></td>

  </tr>

    <?php

    //connect to the database
    $connectionstring = odbc_connect("phpwinaccess", "", "");

    //SQL query
    $query = "SELECT Name FROM Names";

    //execute query
    $result = odbc_do($connectionstring, $query);

        //query database
        while(odbc_fetch_row($result))
```

```
         {
                 $name = odbc_result($result, 1);

                 //format results
                 print ("<tr><td>$name</td></tr>");

         }

         //disconnect from database
         odbc_close($connectionstring);

     ?>


</table>
</body>
</html>
```

Notice that you are embedding your PHP script in HTML. You need to do this in order to use HTML to improve the display of your data. First notice the use of the `odbc_fetch_row` function. This function cycles through all the rows in the database. As it cycles through each row, it will make sure that you don't run into any EOF (End Of File) or other such errors (by trying to read records when he reached the last record in the database).

```
while(odbc_fetch_row($queryexe))
```

You can then access the value of each record's columns. These are identified by number, starting at 0. Your table has the columns ID and Name, so ID would be column 0, and Name would be column 1.

```
$name = odbc_result($queryexe, 1);
```

Note that you store the value of the record in the variable `$name`. (Again, you don't have to do this, but if you need this information later in the script, it's always a good practice to store values. It also makes reading scripts a little easier.)

Now that you have the values you require, you can display them using HTML for formatting:

```
print ("<tr><td>$name</td></tr>");
```

If you run the script, you should see a result similar to the last script (refer to Figure 6.6), but with additional formatting (see Figure 6.7).

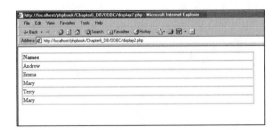

Figure 6.7   HTML-formatted database query results from the Access database.

Querying a Database Directly Using PHP

Now that we have looked at querying a database with ODBC, we can move on to looking at how you can directly query a database using PHP. PHP supports many database APIs, including mSQL, MySQL, Microsoft SQL Server, Oracle, dBASE, Postgres, Informix, Ingres, and InterBase. PHP supports so many, in fact, that covering them all would take a book in itself. Therefore, I will cover only DBMSs that are commonly found on the Windows platform.

Microsoft SQL Server

Microsoft SQL Server (hereby referred to as MS-SQL Server, pronounced "sequel server") probably needs no introduction, but if you don't know much about it, it is Microsoft's flagship database product. It is a Windows-only server that is one of the most common enterprise DBMSs in the Windows world. In fact, it has long played a role in Microsoft's enterprise strategies. As such, developers enjoy close integration between it, the Windows operating system, and other Microsoft products.

Installing MS-SQL Server and setting security settings is beyond the scope of this book, but you can learn more from the following:

- *SQL Server 7 Essential Reference* by Sharon Dooley (New Riders Publishing, 2000)
- *SQL Server System Administration* by Sean Baird and Chris Miller (New Riders Publishing, 1998)

You can find further information and a trial download at
`http://www.microsoft.com/sql/evaluation/trial/2000/default.asp`.

Setting Up MS-SQL Server with PHP

Support for MS-SQL Server within PHP resides in a PHP extension that must first be loaded by PHP in order for the SQL Server functions to work correctly. To allow this module to be loaded, you must first remove the semi-colon (;) from the following line in your PHP.ini file:

```
;extension=php_mssql.dll
```

Remember to make sure that your PHP extension path has been set. (See Chapter 2, "Installation and Optimization," for further information.) Now restart your web server. If you don't get any errors (if you do, double-check the extension path), the SQL Server functions are ready for use.

Setting Up a Database

The examples in this chapter use the Pubs database. It is installed by default when you install SQL Server.

Setting a Connection

Now that the SQL Server functions are available, you can start to use SQL Server and PHP together:

```php
<?php

//connect to database
$msqlconc = mssql_connect("emma", "sa", "");


//disconnect from database
mssql_close($msqlconc);

?>
```

First you connect to the database and store the connection in memory:

```
$msqlconc = mssql_connect("emma", "sa", "");
```

Note that the mssql_connect command requires the server name, a username, and, if required, a password. In this example, these are as follows:

- SQL Server name: emma
- Username: sa
- Password: blank

The sa user is installed by default with SQL Server. However, you should set up and use users who have the correct security settings.

In order to preserve memory and free up server resources, you disconnect from SQL Server:

```
mssql_close($msqlconc);
```

You can develop this script further using the following:

```php
<?php

//connect to database
If(!($msqlconc = mssql_connect("emma", "sa", "")))
{
    print("could not connect to MS-SQL Server database");

} else {

    print("Connected to database ");

    //disconnect from database
    mssql_close($msqlconc);

}

?>
```

When the `mssql_connect` function connects to SQL Server, it returns a link identifier if successful or FALSE on error. You can catch this in your script to detect connection values using the following:

```php
If(!($msqlconc = mssql_connect("emma", "sa", "")))
```

Then, in the success block, you can see if the expression evaluated to TRUE and the connection failed:

```php
{
    print("could not connect to MS-SQL Server database");
}
```

or if the connection was successful:

```php
else {

    print("Connected to database");

    //disconnect from database
    mssql_close($msqlconc);

}
```

As with ODBC, you can use a persistent connection:

```php
<?php

$msqlconc = mssql_pconnect("emma", "sa", "");

?>
```

This lets you create a connection that remains open for the duration of the application. This means that you don't need to keep opening and closing connections in a web application. However, you should use it carefully, because a persistent connection can't be closed with the `mssql_close` method; it closes only when the web server is stopped. Too many open connections take up server resources.

Querying a Database

Now that you have connected to a database, the next step is to query the database. As I mentioned, this chapter uses a test database called Pubs. It is pre-installed with SQL Server.

```php
<?php

//connect to database
If(!($msqlconc = mssql_connect("emma", "sa", "")))
{
    print("could not connect to MS-SQL Server database");

} else {

    mssql_select_db("pubs", $msqlconc);

    //create SQL query
    $query = "SELECT * FROM Authors";

    mssql_query($query, $msqlconc);

    //disconnect from database
    mssql_close($msqlconc);

}
```

First you select the database you want to query:

```php
mssql_select_db("pubs", $msqlconc);
```

Next you create a SQL query that queries the database and runs the SQL query against the database:

```php
$query = "SELECT * FROM Authors";

mssql_query($query, $msqlconc);
```

If you run this script, you won't see any output, because you haven't yet displayed the query results.

Displaying the SQL Server Table Structure

When you query a table within a database, you can gather information about the table itself (size, type and number of columns, and so on), as well as data within the table.

To display table information, you can use the following:

```php
<?php

//connect to database
If(!($msqlconc = mssql_connect("emma", "sa", "emma")))
{
    print("could not connect to MS-SQL Server database");

} else {

    mssql_select_db("pubs", $msqlconc);

    //create SQL query
    $query = "SELECT * FROM Authors";

    //run SQL query
    $runquery = mssql_query($query, $msqlconc);

    //gather number of fields
    $numfields = mssql_num_fields($runquery);

    print("<TABLE BORDER=""1"">\n");
    print("<TR><TD>Column Name</TD><TD>Column Type</TD></TR>");


    for ($p=0; $p < $numfields; $p++)
    {

    $fname = mssql_field_name($runquery, $p);
    $ftype = mssql_field_type($runquery, $p);


    print "<TR><TD>" . $fname . "</TD><TD>" . $ftype . "</TD></TR>";


    }


    print("</TABLE>");

    //disconnect from database
    mssql_close($msqlconc);

}

?>
```

First you create and run the SQL query that selects the table and columns you want to display:

```php
$query = "SELECT * FROM Authors";

$runquery = mssql_query($query, $msqlconc)
```

Next you see how many fields your query will return:

```
$numfields = mssql_num_fields($runquery);
```

Then you loop through each column using the number of fields to see how many you need to loop through:

```
for ($p=0; $p < $numfields; $p++)
```

Finally, you display the name and type of each column in turn:

```
$fname = mssql_field_name($runquery, $p);
$ftype = mssql_field_type($runquery, $p);
```

mssql_field_name references each column by number. This is why you must first look at how many columns you have and then loop through each one. Column references start at zero. This is why the counter is incremented.

If you run the script, you should see information about the table structure, as shown in Figure 6.8. You might wonder why you would want to do this. Table information can be handy to use in certain situations: for temporary names when displaying table data, type conversions between the database data and PHP data, and so on.

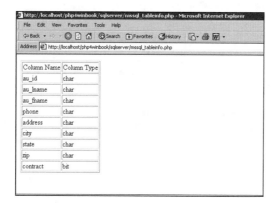

Figure 6.8 MS-SQL Server database authors table structure.

Displaying MS-SQL Server Table Data

Displaying data is not all that different from querying table information. You query the database using SQL, run the query, determine how many results the query has returned, and loop through the results to display. Instead of columns, you are dealing with rows:

```php
<?php

//connect to database
If(!($msqlconc = mssql_connect("emma", "sa", "")))
{
    print("could not connect to MS-SQL Server database");

} else {

    mssql_select_db("pubs", $msqlconc);

    //create SQL query
    $query = "SELECT * FROM Authors";

    //run SQL query
    $runquery = mssql_query($query, $msqlconc);

    //gather number of rows
    $numfields = mssql_num_fields($runquery);

    print($query . "<BR><BR>\n");

    print("<TABLE BORDER=1>\n");
    print("<TR><TD>Name<TD></TR>");

    $lname = array();
    $fname = array();

    while($db_row = mssql_fetch_array($runquery))
    {

        $lname[] = $db_row["au_lname"];
        $fname[] = $db_row["au_fname"];

    }


    $iCount = count($lname);
    for ($i=0; $iCount; $i++) {

    print("<TR<TD>" . $fname[$i] . " " . $lname[$i] . "<TD></TR>");


    }


    print("</TABLE>");

    //disconnect from database
    mssql_close($msqlconc);

}

?>
```

Here you use the `mssql_fetch_array` function. It lets you place the query results into an array:

```
while($db_row = mssql_fetch_array($runquery))
```

However, the array is a reference array. That is, the query results are formatted into an array structure. To work with the query results, you must copy the results array into a new array:

```
$lname = array();
$fname = array();
```

Each reference array is named by column name, so for every column, you create a new array for that data:

```
$lname[] = $db_row["au_lname"];
$fname[] = $db_row["au_fname"];
```

To work without new arrays, all you do is iterate through the contents:

```
$iCount = count($lname);
for ($i=0; $i<$Count; $i++) {

print("<TR<TD>" . $fname[$i] . " " . $lname[$i] . "<TD></TR>");

}
```

To be able to work with changing table sizes, you first detect the number of items within the array:

```
$iCount = count($lname);
```

This script has two arrays. It's safe to assume that both arrays are the same size, so you can use either array from your table to determine the size.

After you have the size, you iterate through the contents, referencing each element within the array by number:

```
for ($i=0; $i<$Count; $i++) {

print("<TR<TD>" . $fname[$i] . " " . $lname[$i] . "<TD></TR>");

}
```

If you run this script, you see the query results, as shown in Figure 6.9.

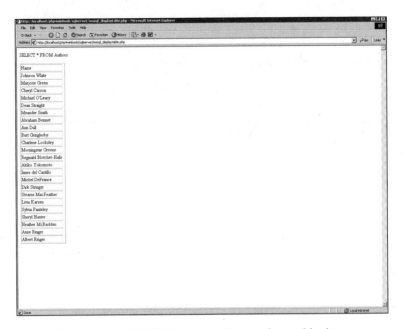

Figure 6.9   MS-SQL Server database authors table data.

Oracle

Oracle has been around a long time. I first used it on the VAX platform and have used it and seen it running on Windows, Linux, and other platforms. One of the most common enterprise RDBMSs in the world, it is used to power high-profile sites such as Yahoo! and Amazon.

Installing Oracle and setting security settings is beyond the scope of this book, but you can learn more from *Oracle8 Server Unleashed* by Joe Greene (Sams Publishing, 1998). For further information on Oracle and a trial download, go to `http://otn.oracle.com/`.

Setting Up Oracle with PHP

Support for Oracle within PHP resides in a PHP extension that must first be loaded by PHP in order for the Oracle functions to work correctly. To allow this module to be loaded, you must remove the semicolon (;) from the following line in your PHP.ini file:

```
;extension=php_oci8.dll
```

PHP supports two Oracle database versions: v7 and v8. Oracle v7 is supported through the php_oracle.dll extension, and Oracle v8 is supported through the php_oci8.dll extension. Oracle v7 functions begin with `ora` (such as `ora_logoff`), and Oracle v8 functions begin with `oci` (such as `oci_logoff`).

Most Oracle v7 functions are available in Oracle v8 (but have slightly different names, as just mentioned). As such, this book looks at Oracle v8 functions only. Oracle v9 currently is not yet supported by PHP.

The Oracle extension uses the Oracle client to pass commands to the Oracle database. Therefore, the Oracle client must be installed correctly for the PHP extension to work (this is true for both v7 and v8). Remember to make sure that your PHP extension path has also been set (see Chapter 2 for further information). Now restart your web server. If you don't get any errors (if you do, double-check the extension path), the Oracle functions are ready for use.

Setting Up a Database

Oracle sets up databases according to users. This is a security measure, so not all database tables are visible to all users. They are visible only to the database users you specify when you create your database and database tables. This chapter uses one of the default Oracle users, scott, and that user's related tables.

Setting a Connection

Now that you have the Oracle functions available, you can start to use Oracle and PHP together.

```php
<?php

//connect to database
$oracle_connection = ocilogon("scott", "tiger");

//disconnect from database
ocilogoff($oracle_connection);

?>
```

First you connect to the database and store the connection in memory:

```
$oracle_connection = ocilogon("scott", "tiger");
```

The `ocilogon` command requires a username and password. In this example, these are as follows:

- Username: scott
- Password: tiger

The scott user is installed by default with Oracle. However, I advise that you set up and use users that have the correct security settings.

In order to preserve memory and free up server resources, you disconnect from Oracle:

```
ocilogoff($oracle_connection);
```

You can develop this script further using the following:

```php
<?php

//connect to database
If(!($oracle_connection = ocilogon("scott", "tiger")))
{
    print("could not connect to Oracle database");

} else {

    print("database connected");

    //disconnect from database
    ocilogoff($oracle_connection);

}

?>
```

When the `ocilogin` function connects to Oracle, it returns a link identifier if successful or FALSE on error. You can catch this in your script to detect connection values using the following:

```php
If(!($oracle_connection = ocilogon("scott", "tiger")))
```

Then, in the success block, you can see if the expression evaluated to TRUE and the connection failed:

```php
{
    print("could not connect to Oracle database");

}
```

or if the connection was successful:

```php
else {

    print("database connected");

    ocilogoff($oracle_connection);

}
```

If you run this script, you should see that the database connected, as shown in Figure 6.10.

Figure 6.10 A successful Oracle connection.

As with SQL Server and ODBC, you can use a persistent connection:

```php
<?php

$oracle_connection = ociplogon("scott", "tiger");

?>
```

This lets you create a connection that remains open for the duration of the application. This means that you don't need to keep opening and closing connections in a web application. However, you should use this method carefully, because you can't close a persistent connection with the `ocilogoff` method. The connection closes only when the web server is stopped. As I have noted previously, too many open connections take up server resources.

Displaying Oracle Version Information

The PHP functions can handily tell you what Oracle version you are using:

```php
<?php

//connect to database
If(!($oracle_connection = ocilogon("scott", "tiger")))
{
    print("could not connect to Oracle database");

} else {

    $serverver = ociserverversion($oracle_connection);
    print("The server version is " . $serverver);

    //disconnect from database
    ocilogoff($oracle_connection);

}

?>
```

Here you use the `ociserverversion` function:

```php
$serverver = ociserverversion($oracle_connection);
```

If you run this script, you should see the Oracle server version, as shown in Figure 6.11. This function can be useful for several reasons, but it is most useful if you are running Oracle v7 and v8 and need to run the same generic script against them. Using this function can help your script choose either Oracle v7 PHP functions or Oracle v8 PHP functions.

Figure 6.11 Oracle server information.

Displaying the Oracle Database Table Structure

To display table information, you can use the following:

```php
<?php

//connect to database
If(!($oracle_connection = ocilogon("scott", "tiger")))
{
    print("could not connect to Oracle database");

} else {

    //create SQL query
    $query = "SELECT * FROM DEPT";

    //parse query ready for Oracle use
    $p_query = ociparse($oracle_connection, $query);

    ociexecute($p_query);

    if($dberror = ocierror($p_query))
    {
        print "An error occurred when attempting to run a query against the
        ➥ database, Oracle provides the following error: <BR>\n";
        print($dberror["code"] . ":" . $dberror["message"] . "<BR>\n");

    } else {

        //number of cols in database
        $numofcols = ocinumcols($p_query);

        //display the SQL query that displays the table
        print("SQL Query: " . $query . "<BR><BR>\n");
```

```
                //build HTML table
                print("<TABLE BORDER=1>\n");
                print("<TR><TD>Column Name</TD><TD>Column Type</TD>
                ➥<TD>Column Size</TD></TR>");

                //display each row in database table in HTML table
                for($cols=1; $cols <= $numofcols; $cols++)
                {
                print("<TR>");

                print("<TD>" . ocicolumnname($p_query, $cols) . "</TD>");
                print("<TD>" . ocicolumntype($p_query, $cols) . "</TD>");
                print("<TD>" . ocicolumnsize($p_query, $cols) . "</TD>");

                print("</TR>");
                }

                print("</TABLE>");


        }

        //free query from memory
        ocifreestatement($p_query);

        //disconnect from database
        ocilogoff($oracle_connection);

    }

    ?>
```

Here you create and run the SQL query that selects the table and columns
you want to display:

```
$query = "SELECT * FROM DEPT";

$p_query = ociparse($oracle_connection, $query);

ociexecute($p_query);
```

Note that the SQL query must be parsed by the `ociparse` command before it
is executed.

Next you see if the query returns any errors, catch those errors, and display
any error information:

```
if($dberror = ocierror($p_query))
    {
        print "An error occurred when attempting to run a query against the
        ➥ database, Oracle provides the following error: <BR>\n";
        print($dberror["code"] . ":" . $dberror["message"] . "<BR>\n");
```

If no errors are detected, you can move on to looking at the table structure that the query returns. The first stage is to look at the number of columns that the query has returned:

```
$numofcols = ocinumcols($p_query);
```

Next you must look at each column in turn to see its details. You do this by looping through each one using the number of columns to determine how many you must loop through:

```
for($cols=0; $cols <= $numofcols; $cols++)
{
    print("<TR>");

    print("<TD>" . ocicolumnname($p_query, $cols) . "</TD>");
    print("<TD>" . ocicolumntype($p_query, $cols) . "</TD>");
    print("<TD>" . ocicolumnsize($p_query, $cols) . "</TD>");

    print("</TR>");
}
```

As you loop through the columns, you use the `ocicolumnname` function to show the column name, `ocicolumntype` to show the column type function, and `ocicolumnsize` to show the column size. If you run the script, you should see the table information, as shown in Figure 6.12.

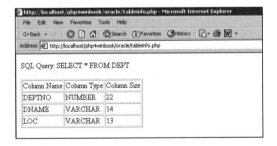

Figure 6.12   The Oracle database table DEPT structure.

Displaying Oracle Database Table Data

As alluded to earlier, displaying data is not all that different from querying table information. You query the database using SQL, run the query, determine how many results the query has returned, and loop through the results to display. Instead of columns, you are dealing with rows:

```php
<?php

//display contents of an Oracle DB table

//connect to database
If(!($oracle_connection = ocilogon("scott", "tiger")))
{
    print("could not connect to Oracle database");

} else {

    //create SQL query
    $query = "SELECT * FROM DEPT";

    //parse query ready for Oracle use
    $p_query = ociparse($oracle_connection, $query);

    ociexecute($p_query);

    if($dberror = ocierror($p_query))
    {
        print "An error occurred when attempting to run a query against the
        ➥ database, Oracle provides the following error: <BR>\n";
        print($dberror["code"] . ":" . $dberror["message"] . "<BR>\n");

    } else {

        //number of cols in database
        $numofcols = ocinumcols($p_query);

        //display the SQL query that displays the table
        print("SQL Query: " . $query . "<BR><BR>\n");

        //build HTML table
        print("<TABLE BORDER=1>\n");

        //create HTML table headers from database table headers
        print("<TR>");
        for($cols=1; $cols <= $numofcols; $cols++)
        {
        print("<TD>" . ocicolumnname($p_query, $cols) . "</TD>");
        }
        print("</TR>");

        //get each row in turn
        while(ocifetch($p_query))
        {
            print("<TR>");
            //now look over each column in the row
            for($rowcols=1; $rowcols <= $numofcols; $rowcols++)
            {
                print("<TD>" . ociresult($p_query, $rowcols) . "</TD>");
            }
```

```
                    print("</TR>");
            }

            print("</TABLE>");


    }

    //free query from memory
    ocifreestatement($p_query);

    //disconnect from database
    ocilogoff($oracle_connection);

}

?>
```

As in the previous example, you first create and run the SQL query that selects the table and columns you want to display:

```
$query = "SELECT * FROM DEPT";

$p_query = ociparse($oracle_connection, $query);

ociexecute($p_query);
```

Next you find the number of columns the query returns using the `ocinumcols` function:

```
$numofcols = ocinumcols($p_query);
```

Next you loop over the columns to display the name of each column using the `ocicolumnname` function. You use that name to name each column in the HTML table:

```
for($cols=1; $cols <= $numofcols; $cols++)
{
print("<TD>" . ocicolumnname($p_query, $cols) . "</TD>");
}
```

Now you look at the data in the table. To do this, you loop over each row the query returns:

```
while(ocifetch($p_query))
```

Next you look through each row to display the data in each column in that row using the `ociresult` function:

```
for($rowcols=1; $rowcols <= $numofcols; $rowcols++)
{
print("<TD>" . ociresult($p_query, $rowcols) . "</TD>");
}
```

If you run the script, you should see the data from the DEPT table, as shown in Figure 6.13.

Figure 6.13   The Oracle database table DEPT data.

MySQL

MySQL and PHP have long enjoyed a close relationship. One term often used in Linux circles is Linux Apache MySQL PHP (LAMP), which refers to a software toolkit.

MySQL, like PHP, is open-source. The license for MySQL is slightly different from that for PHP. MySQL is licensed under a dual license—either the GNU Public License or a proprietary license for proprietary use. MySQL is available for many OSs, including Windows and Linux. MySQL on the Windows platform is often slightly behind its Linux version in terms of versions and stability. It requires that licences must be purchased for commercial use on the Windows platform. However, if you intend to roll out your project on a Linux box, but you are developing on the Windows platform, MySQL is a great choice (and you can also run PHP and Apache on the Windows platform to further mirror your Linux solution).

Installing MySQL and setting security settings is beyond the scope of this book, but you can learn more from *MySQL* by Paul DuBois (New Riders Publishing, 1999).

You can find further information and a download of MySQL at `http://www.mysql.com/downloads/index.html`.

Setting Up MySQL with PHP

Unlike SQL Server or Oracle, MySQL support is built directly into PHP binaries for Windows. You don't need to modify the PHP.ini file. All the functions you need are immediately available.

Setting Up a Database

MySQL has no default database that we can make use of, so for the purposes of this chapter, I have set one up. First, I created a database called edb. I then created a table for that database using the following SQL script:

```
CREATE TABLE names
(
    ID INT UNSIGNED NOT NULL AUTO_INCREMENT PRIMARY KEY,
    name VARCHAR(30) NOT NULL
)
```

After the table has been created, you need to add some data to it using the following SQL script:

```
INSERT INTO names (name) VALUES ('Andrew'),('Emma'),('Terry'),
('Mary'),('Thomas')
```

Various GUI tools (including an open-source PHP version called phpMyAdmin) are available to administer PHP. However, you might find it easier to use the command line, because this is the main method of using and administering MySQL. It is well-documented. If you intend to use MySQL on both Windows and Linux, all the commands are the same. I recommend *MySQL* by Paul DuBois (New Riders Publishing, 1999) as a reference on creating databases and database tables and populating database tables using the command line.

Setting a Connection

Now that you have a database available, you can start using MySQL and PHP together:

```
<?php

$dbcon = mysql_connect("localhost", "Andrew", "");

mysql_close($dbcon);

?>
```

First you connect to the database and store the connection in memory:

```
$dbcon = mysql_connect("localhost", "Andrew", "");
```

The mysql_connect command requires a server name and address, a username, and a password. In this example, these are as follows:

- Server: localhost
- Username: Andrew
- Password: Blank

MySQL has only the root user by default, so you should set up users with the correct permissions. For this example, I have set up a new user called Andrew.

In order to preserve memory and free up server resources, you disconnect from MySQL:

```
mysql_close($dbcon);
```

You can develop this script further using the following:

```
<?php

if(!($dbcon = mysql_connect("localhost", "Andrew", "")))
{
    print("could not connect to MySQL database");

} else {

    print("database connected");

    mysql_close($dbcon);

}

?>
```

When the `mysql_connect` function connects to MySQL, it returns TRUE if it connects successfully or FALSE if the connection fails. You can catch this in your script to detect connection values using the following:

```
if(!($dbcon = mysql_connect("localhost", "Andrew", "")))
```

Then, in the `if` logic, you see if the connection failed:

```
{
    print("could not connect to MySQL database");

}
```

or if the connection was successful:

```
else {

    print("database connected");

    mysql_close($dbcon);

}
```

If you run this script, you should see that the database connected, as shown in Figure 6.14.

Figure 6.14   A successful MySQL connection.

As with Oracle, SQL Server, and ODBC, you can use a persistent connection:

```
<?php

 $dbcon = mysql_pconnect("localhost", "Andrew", "")

?>
```

This lets you create a connection that remains open for the duration of the application. This means that you don't need to keep opening and closing connections in a web application. However, you should use this method carefully, because you can't close persistent connections using the `mysql_close` method. These connections close only when the web server is stopped. Too many open connections take up server resources.

Querying a Database

MySQL gives you two ways to query a database. The first method is as follows:

```
<?php

//connect to database
If(!($dbcon = mysql_connect("localhost", "Andrew", "")))
{
    print("could not connect to MySQL database");

} else {

    if(!(mysql_select_db("edb", $dbcon)))
    {
        print("database select failed - error number: " . mysql_errno() .
        ➥ " error message: " . mysql_error() . "<BR>\n");

    } else {

        $query = "SELECT * FROM names";

        $query_result = @ mysql_query($query, $dbcon);
```

```
        //query results here

    }

    //disconnect from database
    mysql_close($dbcon);

}

?>
```

Using the `mysql_select_db` function, you first select the database you want to query, while testing that the connection was successful:

```
if(!(mysql_select_db("edb", $dbcon)))
```

If it was successful, you define the SQL query you want to run:

```
$query = "SELECT * FROM names";
```

Then, using the SQL query, you query the database using the `mysql_query` function:

```
$query_result = @ mysql_query($query, $dbcon);
```

Displaying the MySQL Database Table Structure

To display table information, you can use the following:

```
<?php

//connect to database
If(!($dbcon = mysql_connect("localhost", "Andrew", "")))
{
    print("could not connect to Oracle database");

} else {

    $query = "SELECT * FROM names";

    if(!(mysql_select_db("edb", $dbcon)))
    {
        print("database select failed - error number: " . mysql_errno() .
        ➥ " error message: " . mysql_error() . "<BR>\n");

    } else {

        $query_result = @ mysql_query($query, $dbcon);

        //display the SQL query that displays the table
        print("SQL Query: " . $query . "<BR><BR>\n");
```

```
        //build HTML table
        print("<TABLE BORDER=1>\n");
        print("<TR><TD>Column Name</TD><TD>Column Type</TD></TR>");


        for ($b = 0; $b < mysql_num_fields($query_result); $b++)
        {
            print("<TR>");
            print("<TD>" . mysql_field_name($query_result, $b) . "</TD>");
            print("<TD>" . mysql_field_type($query_result, $b) . "</TD>");
            print("</TR>");
        }

        print("</TABLE>");

    }

    mysql_close($dbcon);

}

?>
```

First you connect to and query the database:

```
$query = "SELECT * FROM names";

if(!(mysql_select_db("edb", $dbcon)))
{
    print("database select failed - error number: " . mysql_errno() .
    ➥ " error message: " . mysql_error() . "<BR>\n");

} else {
    $query_result = @ mysql_query($query, $dbcon);
```

Next, using the result from the query, you run through each column the query
returns using the mysql_num_fields function:

```
for ($b = 0; $b < mysql_num_fields($query_result); $b++)
```

As you run through each column, you display that column's name and type
using the mysql_field_name and mysql_field_type functions:

```
print("<TD>" . mysql_field_name($query_result, $b) . "</TD>");
```

```
print("<TD>" . mysql_field_type($query_result, $b) . "</TD>");
```

If you run the script, you should see that the table information is displayed, as
shown in Figure 6.15.

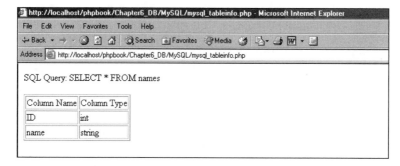

Figure 6.15   The MySQL database names table structure.

Displaying MySQL Database Table Data

Displaying data from MySQL table data is generally like displaying it from the
other databases' tables:

```php
<?php

//connect to database
If(!($dbcon = mysql_connect("localhost", "Andrew", "")))
{
    print("could not connect to Oracle database");

} else {

    $query = "SELECT * FROM names";

    if(!(mysql_select_db("edb", $dbcon)))
    {
        print("database select failed - error number: " . mysql_errno() .
        ➥ " error message: " . mysql_error() . "<BR>\n");

    } else {

        $query_result = @ mysql_query($query, $dbcon);

        //display the SQL query that displays the table
        print("SQL Query: " . $query . "<BR><BR>\n");

        //build HTML table
        print("<TABLE BORDER=1>\n");

        print("<TR>");

            //display column headers
            for ($col_count = 0; $col_count <
mysql_num_fields($query_result);
➥ $col_count++)
            {
```

```
                              print("<TD>" . mysql_field_name($query_result,
                              ➥ $col_count) . "</TD>");

                    }

           print("</TR>");

                    //display rows
                    for ($row_count = 0; $row_count <
mysql_num_rows($query_result);
➥ $row_count++) {

                    //obtain each row
                    $row = @ mysql_fetch_row($query_result);

                    print("<TR>");

                         //loop through columns within row
                         for ($col_count = 0; $col_count <
mysql_num_fields($query_result);
➥ $col_count++)
                         {

                         //display data in each column of the row
                         print("<TD>" . $row[$col_count] . "</TD>");

                         }

                    print("</TR>");



           print("</TABLE>");

      }

      mysql_close($dbcon);

}

?>
```

First you connect to and query the database:

```
$query = "SELECT * FROM names";

if(!(mysql_select_db("edb", $dbcon)))
{
    print("database select failed - error number: " . mysql_errno() .
    ➥ " error message: " . mysql_error() . "<BR>\n");

} else {
    $query_result = @ mysql_query($query, $dbcon);
```

Next you display the names of each column in the database table to make up the HTML table. You use the `mysql_numfields` and `mysql_field_name` functions, which you met in the previous example:

```
for ($col_count = 0; $col_count < mysql_numfields($query_result);
$col_count++)
{

print("<TD>" . mysql_field_name($query_result, $col_count) . "</TD>");

}
```

Next you run through each row the query returns using the `mysql_numrows` function:

```
for ($row_count = 0; $row_count < mysql_numrows($query_result); $row_count++)
{
```

You then store each row in an array as it is returned:

```
$row = @ mysql_fetch_row($query_result);
```

You then run through all the columns the query returns. Again you use the `mysql_numfields` function:

```
for ($col_count = 0; $col_count < mysql_numfields($query_result);
$col_count++)
```

As you run through each column, you use the column position to reference the row array:

```
print("<TD>" . $row[$col_count] . "</TD>");
```

This in effect lets you separate the array into individual fields referenced by the column value. If you run the script, you should see data from the names table, as shown in Figure 6.16.

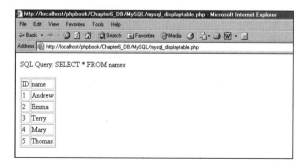

Figure 6.16 MySQL names table data.

Summary

This chapter looked at two ways PHP can query a database: using ODBC or directly. We explored both methods and developed PHP code to connect to and query a database. Using the ODBC method, we looked at how to use a Microsoft Access database and the PHP ODBC functions together. Using the direct method, we looked at the various PHP functions for working with SQL Server, Oracle, and MySQL. Chapter 10, "PHP and ADO," further explores how to use PHP and databases together. But first we will explore the relationship between PHP and COM and the emerging .NET framework in the next chapter.

Advanced PHP Programming

7

PHP, COM, and .NET

THIS CHAPTER LOOKS AT HOW YOU CAN USE PHP with COM and also how to use PHP with Microsoft .NET. We will cover what COM is, how COM developed, how to create COM components with Visual Basic (VB), and how to use them from PHP. We also will look at what Microsoft .NET is, how it developed, how to develop .NET components in Visual Basic .NET, and how to use them from PHP.

The PHP COM functions were developed by Zeev Suraski and Harald Radi.

All About COM

COM stands for component object model. We will start our look at COM with an overview of the two basic components of COM: a component and an object.

What Is a Component?

A component can be described as a piece of code that can be shared by other programs. For example, you might write a spell-checker component that could be used by a word processing package or email software.

What Is an Object?

An object can be described as code that is reusable. This sounds like a component, and indeed, a component can be made of objects. Perhaps your spell-checker has a dictionary object for checking words, a custom dictionary object for storing custom words, and an object for running through words and checking them against the dictionaries.

What Is COM?

COM is a model for creating components from objects. COM is a binary specification. In other words, it is not programming-language-bound. But all languages that support the creation of COM components must create the components to the same specification. In this way, COM components created in one programming language (such as ActiveState and Perl) can be reused in another COM-supported programming language (such as VB).

COM is still the cornerstone of Windows development. Almost everything that Microsoft does is based on COM. Windows is COM-based, Office is COM-based, Microsoft VB can create and interface with COM components—the list is endless.

Server–Side or Client–Side COM

COM components are often divided into client-side or server-side components. Although they serve different purposes, they fundamentally serve the same purpose—forming a reusable block of code in an application. A spell-checker component is an example of a client-side component, and a tax component for an e-commerce web site is an example of a server-side component. Server-side components can take advantage of newer elements for COM: Microsoft Transaction Server (MTS) and Microsoft Message Queue (MMQ). Client-side components can also be GUI components that can be used to make up a GUI for an application (such as a button).

A Brief History of COM

This section looks at how COM developed, from its early days as a way of sharing data to its current incarnation as a fully featured component system.

DDE

Dynamic Data Exchange (DDE) was developed in the late 1980s to allow Windows applications to share data (text and graphics) from the Clipboard. However, because DDE was available only to Microsoft applications, it was not a widely used or popular solution for transferring data between applications.

OLE 1

To resolve this problem, Microsoft developed OLE (Object Linking and Embedding), now called OLE 1. OLE 1 allowed you to insert a document from one application into the document of another. An example would be embedding a spreadsheet into a word processing package. Because the spreadsheet was linked, if you updated it, the update would appear in the embedded spreadsheet in the word processing document as well. OLE 1 was slow and suffered from bugs. However, Microsoft realized this and began developing OLE 2.

OLE 2

It was during the development of OLE 2 that Microsoft saw how OLE caused problems for applications. Different applications used different methods to allow the embedding of applications within themselves. OLE required many function calls and parameters that most applications achieved in different ways. Put another way, one problem lay in getting two applications to find a common way of communicating. COM was developed as a part of OLE 2 to overcome this problem.

COM/DCOM

After COM was born, it gave applications a common way of communicating. If the applications used COM, either built using COM objects or by using COM for an external interface, all COM applications would have a common way of communicating. COM applications could be COM objects themselves or could be made of COM objects.

Distributed COM (DCOM) was developed later to allow COM objects to communicate over a network (rather than the same computer). It's often described as "COM with a long wire."

COM+

Microsoft began a concentrated effort to allow developers to use COM as a way to build applications from components. With the arrival of COM support in ASP and DCOM, Microsoft saw how developers were building applications from COM components that were housed on several different computers.

To build on this, Microsoft added Microsoft Transaction Server (MTS) and Microsoft Message Queue (MSMQ) to the Windows NT 4 service pack.

MTS added transaction services that COM objects could call on, and MSMQ allowed messages between COM objects to be stored in a queue. If a message could not get through, it could be stored and forwarded later.

With the arrival of Windows 2000, however, Microsoft developed a version of COM to integrate MTS and MSMQ within COM so that natively it had DCOM, transaction, and messaging services available. Microsoft called this version COM+.

What Makes Up a COM Object?

In its simplest form, a COM object consists of one or more classes, as shown in Figure 7.1. Each class consists of a collection of methods, and within these methods is the code that makes up your object. Methods can be *private,* meaning that they can be used only by other methods within the same class. Methods can also be *public,* meaning that they can be used by all methods and are exposed to the outside world (and thus are the only kinds of functions you can use when calling a COM object).

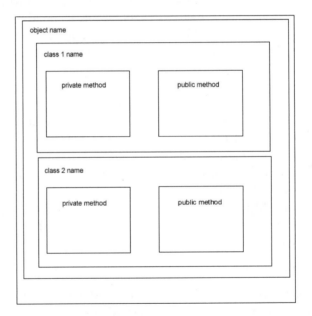

Figure 7.1   A COM object in its simplest form.

COM has a lot more to it than what I have described. However, because an in-depth discussion of COM's internals is beyond the scope of this book, I recommend the books listed in the next section for further information.

How Are COM Objects Created?

COM objects can be created in any programming language that supports the COM binary specification. All Microsoft programming tools (such as Visual Basic and Visual C++) support COM, as do ActiveState programming tools (Perl, Python, TCL) and Borland programming tools (such as Delphi), to name just a few.

If you are interested in learning more about COM's internals and COM development, I suggest the following books:

- Appleman, Dan. *Dan Appleman's Developing COM/ActiveX Components with Visual Basic 6*. Sams Publishing, 1998.
- Brill, Gregory. *Applying COM+*. New Riders Publishing, 2000.

Creating a Server-Side COM Component in VB 6.0

Creating a COM object in VB is very straightforward. First, open VB and select ActiveX DLL, as shown in Figure 7.2.

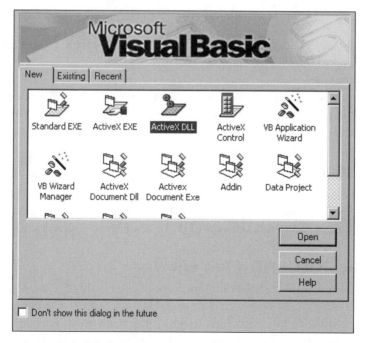

Figure 7.2   Selecting an ActiveX DLL project type in Visual Basic.

Call the project php4winbook and name the class Examples, as shown in Figure 7.3.

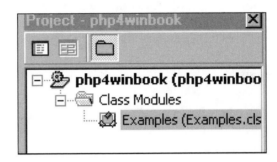

Figure 7.3   The object and class name of your COM object.

Next, add the following code to the examples:

```
Option Explicit
Public Function HelloFunc(ByRef uname As Variant) As Variant
     HelloFunc = "hello " & uname
End Function
```

Note that you have created a single function called HelloFunc; this will become important to remember later in this chapter.

Finally, compile the component. This gives you php4winbook.dll. Because you have built your COM component from within VB, it is registered for use on the system you built the COM component on. If you want to use the COM component on another system, you must register it using the following command:

```
RegSvr32 php4winbook.dll
```

Also note that if you create COM components in VB that use the ByRef statement, they might not work in PHP 4.0.4. This appears to be because of an issue with the ByRef statement and PHP. This has been resolved in PHP 4.0.6.

How Are COM Objects Referenced?

Programming languages have different ways of referencing COM objects, but they all call the COM component's name. The call to the COM component's name is passed to Windows, which looks up the name in its Registry. After the name is found, Windows looks up the COM component's location (stored in its Registry entry) and loads it into memory. The memory location of the COM object is then passed back to the calling application. When the calling application has finished with the COM object, it should pass this information back to Windows so that Windows can unload the COM object from memory (to preserve system resources). Most languages support an automatic feature that does this for them. Nevertheless, it is a good practice to include this in your code when using COM components.

When working with the Microsoft IIS web server, it is possible to create your own memory space for your web site (Microsoft calls them web applications) so that all COM components you use are created by Windows within that memory space. It's important to note, however, that IIS holds that COM component in memory space until the web application or web server is stopped. This increases the speed with which IIS can pass COM objects back to calling applications, but it does mean that you must unload them from the web application if you want to change or recompile your COM object (or Windows will hold them as locked).

Interfacing with a COM Component in Classic ASP

As an example, we can look at how classic ASP (called ASP in the rest of this chapter) handles COM components. ASP supports the interfacing of COM, not the creation of COM objects. However, its main scripting languages, VBScript and JScript, can both be exposed as COM objects.

Let's start with some ASP code:

```
<%

set test = Server.CreateObject("php4winbook.Examples")

hellmes = test.HelloFunc ("Andrew")

set test = nothing

Response.write hellmes

%>
```

In this code, ASP loads into memory the php4winbook COM component you created a moment ago.

Let's look at each line of the code:

```
set test = Server.CreateObject("php4winbook.Examples")
```

Note that you have interfaced with the Examples class. COM can interface with only one class of a COM component in any one recall. Different applications can call on different classes of the same component, but in one call it's one class only.

```
hellmes = test.HelloFunc ("Andrew")
```

This line says to pass some information to the `HelloFunc` function of the Examples class and store its return result in hellmes.

That result is then printed to the screen, as shown in Figure 7.4.

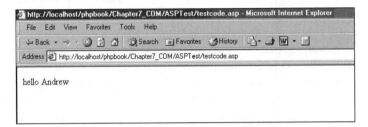

Figure 7.4   The output of your COM object from ASP.

Note that you also unload the COM component from memory:

```
set test = nothing
```

How Does PHP Handle COM?

Like ASP, PHP supports the interfacing of COM, but not the creation of COM objects. In other words, it can interface with any COM object, but you cannot yet create COM objects with PHP code.

PHP's COM Functions

PHP has featured COM support since PHP 3.03. These same functions are still available in PHP 4. You can interface with your php4winbook COM component in the following way:

```php
<?php

//load COM component into memory
$comobj = com_load("php4winbook.Examples");

//set the property of the function to a value
com_set($comobj, "HelloFunc", "Andrew");

//obtain the result of the function
$hellmes = com_get($comobj, "HelloFunc");

print($hellmes);

?>
```

Let's look at some of these code lines:

```php
$comobj = com_load("php4winbook.Examples");
```

This line loads the COM component into memory. Note that, as in the ASP example, you can do this on only a single class level.

You then set the value of the `HelloFunc` function to the value `Andrew`:

```
com_set($comobj, "HelloFunc", "Andrew");
```

You then obtain the return result of the `HelloFunc` function:

```
$hellmes = com_get($comobj, "HelloFunc");
```

Although you are guaranteed backward compatibility between versions of PHP, the syntax can become messy. PHP 4 has a shorthand version for using COM components:

```
<?php

$comobj = new COM("php4winbook.Examples");
$hellmes = $comobj->HelloFunc("Andrew");

print($hellmes);

?>
```

Let's look at a couple of these code lines:

```
$comobj = new COM("php4winbook.Examples");
```

This loads the COM component into memory. What happens here is that when you call the COM component using PHP's COM class, you create a link between the COM component and PHP. Note that when you call the PHP component, you can do so at only a single class level and access public functions in that class. So when you call a function of the COM component, PHP translates that call into data that the COM component can understand (such as changing data types). Note the different syntax for loading the COM component into memory between ASP and PHP.

```
$hellmes = $test->HelloFunc("Andrew");
```

Next you pass some information to the `HelloFunc` function and store its return result in `$hellmes`. This is a better method of setting and getting the value of functions, because you can do so in one line of code and don't need to use PHP functions. PHP makes the function call within the COM component for you. Note the PHP forward notation.

Finally, the result is printed to the screen, as shown in Figure 7.5.

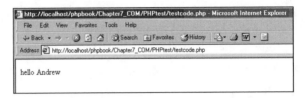

Figure 7.5   The output of your COM object from PHP.

If you think there is very little difference between the way the ASP and PHP code works, you are right. Both languages must load the COM component into memory, where they then call its functions. This also demonstrates one of the beauties of using COM. You wrote the COM component in VB and accessed it in both ASP and PHP. And you could rewrite the COM component in C++—it makes no difference to your ASP or PHP code.

PHP and .NET

Now that we have examined COM, we will finish with a look at Microsoft .NET.

What Is Microsoft .NET?

It is important to remember that .NET is *not* COM, and vice versa. .NET is a brand-new strategy from Microsoft. As mentioned at the start of this chapter, COM is the cornerstone of the current Microsoft platform. .NET, however, is the cornerstone of future Microsoft development. .NET applications run not only on Microsoft platforms but on any device (your PC, your WebTV, your handheld, and so on).

.NET is a combination of things. Largely, it's a framework that encompasses a Common Language Runtime (CLR, discussed in a moment) and common class set (also covered in a moment). It also gives application developers new ways of working with the platform they are targeting and creating the applications they want to deploy. As we will see, .NET is a far more powerful way of working than COM and is decidedly COM's successor.

What Makes Up Microsoft .NET?

Microsoft .NET is a broad concept that Microsoft splits into four terms:

- .NET framework
- .NET development tools
- .NET OSs and servers
- .NET services

.NET Framework

This is how .NET applications are created; they use the CLR and a common class set. Microsoft provides the .NET framework SDK to allow you to do this.

The .NET framework also gives you several new languages that make use of the CLR and common class set: Visual Basic .NET, a new version of Visual Basic; C# (pronounced "C sharp"), a language with the control and power of C and C++ but with the rapid application development capability of a language like Visual Basic; and J# (pronounced "J sharp"), which is a version of Java for the .NET framework.

.NET Development Tools

Microsoft offers Visual Studio .NET for easy .NET development. You don't need Visual Studio .NET to create .NET applications, but it has been developed to aid in this process.

.NET OSs and Servers

Microsoft has rebranded most of its product line to use the .NET name. However, Microsoft OSs and servers don't yet use the .NET framework. (However, plans are underway to include the CLR in future versions of Microsoft Server 2000 and to allow the creation of stored procedures in C# for SQL Server.) Microsoft also plans to release the next version of Windows 2000 as Windows .NET. This OS won't be based on the .NET framework, but it will contain parts of the .NET framework.

.NET Services

Web services (discussed in Chapter 9, "PHP and Web Services") are a big part of Microsoft .NET. They are very easy to build and deploy using Microsoft .NET. To aid in this sort of development, Microsoft is building a set of web services called Microsoft MyServices to allow your web service applications to connect to Microsoft services such as Microsoft Passport and HotMail.

What Makes Up the .NET Framework?

The .NET framework is split into two parts: the CLR and the common class set.

CLR

The Common Language Runtime (CLR) is the runtime of the .NET framework. In a .NET language (such as Visual Basic .NET or C#), the compiler compiles the code to something called MSIL (Microsoft Intermediate

Language). MSIL can then be run on any CLR. The CLR itself can be targeted at any platform (Windows, Linux, Solaris, UNIX, and so on), so instead of your having to rewrite your .NET application to suit the platform, all the platform needs is a suitable CLR. In theory, this means that your applications can target any application that has a suitable CLR.

> **Note**
> The CLR is to be ported to the FreeBSD UNIX platform by Microsoft and to Linux by several third parties.

This approach might be familiar to Java developers. In the case of Java, the common runtime is called the Java Runtime Environment (JRE).

Common Class Set

The .NET framework provides a common class set that a .NET-compatible language can use. The common class set provides you with classes for many things, from handling data such as strings and variables to working with the Win32 API. The class set handles much of the functionality that was often difficult, such as working with databases with ADO (now called ADO.NET).

.NET Applications

.NET applications can be several different things, from conventional Windows GUI applications to console applications, web services, Windows services, and .NET components (which is the .NET equivalent of COM components).

All .NET applications can make use of something called an assembly. Microsoft .NET assemblies allow a .NET application to package itself into a single compact unit. For example, an assembly can contain an application's .exe file, any related component (DLL) files, and graphics files. The assembly spells the end of "DLL hell," in which different versions of the same DLL could be installed to a computer, causing compatibility problems. Now an application needs to look no further than its assembly.

Assemblies can be of two types: private and shared. In a private assembly, the assembly's contents are available only to the application within that assembly (any DLL files in that assembly can be used by that assembly's application). A shared assembly can be accessed by files (applications, DLLs, and so on) in other assemblies. A shared assembly is stored in the GAC (Global Assembly Cache), which you can view under C:\WINNT\Assembly\ if you have the .NET framework installed. You can use the shfusion.dll (a Windows shell extension that comes with the .NET framework) to obtain more information about the GAC.

Obtaining the .NET Framework

The .NET framework currently is in version 1.0. It is available for Windows XP, Windows 2000, and Windows NT 4.0 platforms only. You can download the .NET framework from `http://www.gotdotnet.com`. You can also order it on a CD for free (there is a small shipping charge).

.NET and PHP

PHP currently does not support .NET natively. You can access .NET libraries, but PHP has no support for the CLR. Daniel Beulshaushen of `php4win.com` has developed a version of PHP and a related PHP extension that can access .NET libraries. However, this is currently in beta and cannot be used with standard PHP extensions. However, you can access .NET libraries and other features by wrapping them into .NET components and exposing such components to PHP using a feature of .NET called COM Interop.

COM Interop lets you create a COM wrapper around your .NET components. The .NET component remains a .NET component, but it uses the CLR and is built using the .NET framework. However, it is built in such a way that Windows thinks it's a COM component and makes it available to all calling COM clients.

In this way, you can make a .NET component available to PHP via the same COM features of PHP discussed earlier. To use a .NET component with PHP successfully, you must make sure that you place your .NET component in the GAC. Unlike COM, .NET does not use the Registry to find components; it uses the GAC. In order for your PHP script to find your component, you must place it in the GAC.

Creating the .NET Component

The first step is to create the .NET component. You could use Visual Studio .NET for this, but all you need is the .NET framework installed. As such, you will use a simple text editor (Notepad is fine) and the command line.

Creating the examples.vb File

Create the file examples.vb using the following code:

```
Namespace php4winbook

    Public Class examples

        Public Function showname(ByVal name As String)
```

```
        Return "hello " & name

    End Function

End Class

End Namespace
```

This is Visual Basic .NET code, but you can use any .NET language you choose (such as C#). Save the file as examples.vb.

Creating a Key File

Every component in the GAC must be versioned and signed. To do this, you will use a cryptographic key. You create the key from the command line by typing the following:

```
sn -k key.snk
```

This creates a cryptographic public key (a private key to encrypt and a public key to decrypt) called key.snk. To create this key, the CLR uses the contents of the assembly using a private key it creates itself. Anyone can use the public key to decrypt the assembly. It helps ensure that the assembly has not been tampered with. (If the assembly's contents have changed, the public key would be different.)

Creating a Reference File

You must now add a reference to the component and use that reference to sign the assembly. Create the file AssemblyInfo.vb and add the following:

```
Imports System.Runtime.CompilerServices

<assembly: AssemblyVersion("1.0.*")>
<assembly: AssemblyKeyFile("key.snk")>
```

Note that you need to use the `Imports` statement and that

```
<assembly: AssemblyKeyFile("key.snk")>
```

must point to the directory containing the key.snk file (in case it's in the same directory as the VB.NET files).

Compiling a Reference File

You must now compile the reference file with the following:

```
vbc /t:module /out:AssemblyInfo.dll AssemblyInfo.vb
```

Compiling examples.vb with a Reference File

Now that you have the compiled reference file, you can use it when you compile the examples.vb file. This indicates to the CLR that you have a reference file and that it can be used to sign the assembly.

The following line creates the assembly file examples.dll:

```
vbc /t:library /addmodule:AssemblyInfo.dll examples.vb
```

A Shortcut for Creating a Signed Assembly File

You can add the reference file directly to the VB.NET code:

```
Imports System.Reflection
Imports System.Runtime.CompilerServices

<assembly: AssemblyVersion("1.0.*")>
<assembly: AssemblyKeyFile("key.snk")>

Namespace php4winbook

    Public Class examples

        Public Function showname(ByVal name As String)

            Return "hello " & name

        End Function

    End Class

End Namespace
```

You can compile with this:

```
vbc /t:library examples.vb
```

However, if you have many components in your assembly, you might want to keep the reference file and the code for various assembly contents separate (thus making changes to the reference file code easier to make), as you did in the first example.

Adding examples.dll to the GAC

You must now add the signed assembly file to the GAC using the following:

```
drive letterProgram Files\Microsoft.NET\FrameworkSDK\Bin\gcutil /i
examples.dll
```

If you open the GAC in Windows Explorer (*drive letter*\WINNT\Assembly\), you should see the entry for your component (see Figure 7.6).

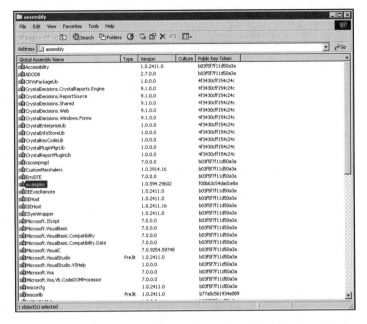

Figure 7.6 The Global Assembly Cache displayed in Windows Explorer.

Adding the Assembly to the Registry

In order to complete the process of fooling Windows, you must create a type library (TLB) file for your assembly. COM requires TLB files so that it can gather the information it needs about the component to access its public functions correctly (that is, what data type the function is and what data type it needs to send and receive from those functions).

```
Regasm examples.dll /tlb:examples.tlb
```

Remember that Windows looks for COM components in the Windows Registry, but .NET components reside in the GAC. Regasm fools Windows by adding information to the Registry about your component, but instead of loading the COM component from the file system, it loads from the GAC.

Creating the PHP File

Create the file testcode.php with the following code:

```php
<?php

$test = new COM("php4winbook.examples");
$hellmes = $test->showname("Andrew");
```

```
print($hellmes);

?>
```

Notice that you have used the same syntax as the COM example you built earlier in this chapter. As far as PHP is concerned, you are using a COM component.

Running the PHP File

If you now run the testcode.php file, you should see the result printed to the screen, as shown in Figure 7.7.

Figure 7.7   The output of your .NET component in PHP.

Summary

In this chapter, we looked at what COM is and how it developed. We looked at how to create a COM component in VB and use that COM component in ASP and PHP. We then moved on to look at Microsoft .NET and how you can use .NET's COM Interop feature to write a .NET component in Visual Basic .NET and use that object from within PHP. Hopefully, you can use the knowledge you have acquired here to use COM within your PHP applications. In later chapters, you will see how useful COM can be for a host of applications.

8

PHP and XML

U NLESS YOU HAVE BEEN IN A DEEP freeze for the last three years, you have heard of XML (Extensible Markup Language). This chapter looks at what XML is, how it began, and how you can use it with PHP. I will provide just a general overview. However, XML is such a big subject that it warrants books in its own right. If you want to learn more about XML, I recommend *Inside XML* by Steve Holzner (New Riders Publishing, 2000).

A Brief History of XML

To help you understand what XML is, let's first look at how it came about. The following sections trace a brief history of how XML developed.

GML

Generalized Markup Language (GML) was created by Charles Goldfarb, Ed Mosher, and Ray Lorie at IBM in 1969. GML (it was also known within IBM as Text Description Language [TDL]) was one of the first markup languages. Its purpose was to allow a document's form (its structure) and its content to be separated.

SGML

By 1978, the ISO (International Organization for Standardization) wanted to create a standards-based markup language based on GML. In 1986, this standard was agreed on, and it was called Standard Generalized Markup Language (SGML).

HTML

In 1989, Tim Berners-Lee, a CERN scientist, borrowed from SGML for his latest project—a hypertext idea. He combined the tag-based approach of SGML with typesetters' style sheets and hyperlinking to create a new markup language called Hypertext Markup Language (HTML).

XML

HTML grew in popularity and served its purpose well, but it was decided that its tag set was too limited. Switching back to SGML was not a good idea, because it was too complex for the web. In 1994, Tim Berners-Lee set up a new standards body at MIT called the World Wide Web Consortium (W3C). In 1996, a new working group at the W3C was formed to create a simple version of SGML (called within the group "SGML for the web") that, like HTML, could be used on the web. They called it Extensible Markup Language (XML). In 1998, the XML specification was agreed on, and XML officially became a W3C standard.

What Is XML?

XML is a language for creating metadata. Metadata is data that describes itself. To explain this further, let's look at a sample XML document:

```
<?xml version="1.0" encoding="UTF-8"?>
<PEOPLE>
    <PERSON>
        <NAME>Andrew</NAME>
    </PERSON>
</PEOPLE>
```

Don't worry if you have never encountered XML. I will explain how XML is made up later in this chapter. In this example, the data is a name: Andrew. Using XML, you can turn Andrew into metadata by describing it as a NAME:

```
<NAME>Andrew</NAME>
```

Each NAME belongs to a PERSON, which in turn belongs to PEOPLE. You can have multiple items of data that are all names, and you can describe them as such using the same method:

```
<?xml version="1.0" encoding="UTF-8"?>
<PEOPLE>
    <PERSON>
        <NAME>Andrew</NAME>
    </PERSON>
    <PERSON>
        <NAME>Emma</NAME>
    </PERSON>
    <PERSON>
        <NAME>Terry</NAME>
    </PERSON>
    <PERSON>
        <NAME>Mary</NAME>
    </PERSON>
    <PERSON>
        <NAME>Thomas</NAME>
    </PERSON>
</PEOPLE>
```

The elements that make up XML documents are called *nodes*. The sample XML document has the following nodes:

```
<NAME></NAME>

<PERSON></PERSON>

<PEOPLE></PEOPLE>
```

The most interesting thing to note about this example is that I made it up. XML is not really a language as such but a method that lets you create your own markup languages to then create metadata. You might have seen markup languages before; HTML is perhaps the most common markup language. (A version of HTML developed in XML is called XHTML.)

Reading XML

The software that reads and displays an XML document is called an XML *parser*. PHP contains the Expat XML parser. However, using PHP's COM interface, you can also use the Microsoft XML (MSXML) parser (which is used throughout the Microsoft product line). The parser's job is to allow you to work with XML documents—creating them, deleting them, or adding to them as well as displaying them.

The job of displaying an XML document varies, depending on the XML parser. In a web browser such as Internet Explorer, you can use the MSXML parser to display the document directly in the browser, as shown in Figure 8.1. You can use Expat to display the XML document, but you must use a language such as PHP to finish displaying the document (that is, output the XML to a displayable format, such as HTML). You will often use an XML parser in this sense. Displayed in its raw form (as can be done in Internet Explorer, as shown in Figure 8.1), it is confusing to read and would not fit into most web applications. What you often need to do is use the parser to read the XML document and display it in an easy-to-read manner. Luckily, both Expat and MSXML let you do this. (It's luckier still that MSXML is dual-purpose in this sense—it can parse and display.) Later in this chapter you will see how to display an XML document. First, let's look more carefully at what makes up an XML document.

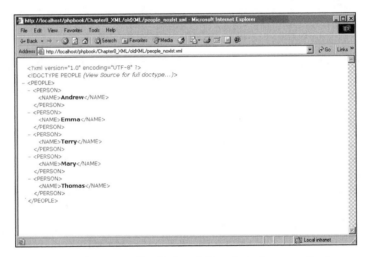

Figure 8.1   The XML file displayed directly in Internet Explorer.

What Makes Up XML?

XML is made up of several different things. In its most basic form, it can just be an XML document. However, it can also include a DTD document and an XSL document.

Document Type Definition (DTD) Document

When you create your own language using XML, you need to make sure that all the XML documents you create using your XML language follow the rules of your language; thus, you create a Document Type Definition (DTD) document.

To create an XML document, you don't need a DTD document, but if you want to enforce that all your XML documents follow the same language schema, you need a DTD document. So what does a DTD document look like? Let's look at a sample DTD for our sample XML document:

```
<?xml version="1.0" encoding="UTF-8"?>
<!ELEMENT NAME (#PCDATA)>
<!ELEMENT PEOPLE (PERSON+)>
<!ELEMENT PERSON (NAME)>
```

The language for creating DTD documents is set by the XML standard. Thus, you use the same language to create all DTD documents. The third line of the example defines the PEOPLE node as containing multiple instances of the PER-SON node. In line four, the PERSON node is defined as containing the NAME node. The NAME node is defined in the first line as containing data (such as Andrew). This sounds like the XML example. In fact, with this DTD document, your XML documents *must* have this structure, or they will be invalid (and validating XML parsers will report them as such). Save your DTD to a file called people.dtd, ready for use in your XML file.

Now that you have a DTD document, how do you make use of it in your XML file? You embed it as follows:

```
<?xml version="1.0" encoding="UTF-8"?>
<!DOCTYPE PEOPLE SYSTEM
"http://localhost/phpbook/Chapter8_XML/XML/people.dtd">
<PEOPLE>
    <PERSON>
        <NAME>Andrew</NAME>
    </PERSON>
    <PERSON>
        <NAME>Emma</NAME>
    </PERSON>
    <PERSON>
        <NAME>Terry</NAME>
    </PERSON>
    <PERSON>
        <NAME>Mary</NAME>
    </PERSON>
    <PERSON>
        <NAME>Thomas</NAME>
    </PERSON>
</PEOPLE>
```

Specifically, you use the DOCTYPE, a special XML node for embedding the DTD document:

```
<!DOCTYPE PEOPLE SYSTEM
"http://localhost/phpbook/Chapter8_XML/XML/people.dtd">
```

Here I have used an HTTP URL, but you can also use a file path.

Extensible Style Sheet Language (XSL) Document

As you saw in Figure 8.1, XML displayed in its raw form is not easy to read. Thankfully, the W3C developed a standard to allow us to display XML files in a much easier-to-read manner. They called it Extensible Style Sheet Language (XSL).

If you think XSL sounds like the HTML Cascading Style Sheet (CSS) language, you are correct. XSL and CSS serve a similar purpose—to apply styles and formatting. CSS and XSL also serve different purposes, but they complement each other. For example, XSL can transform documents, but CSS can only style them. XSL can produce HTML/CSS from XML, but CSS can't.

The XSL language, like the DTD language, is fixed. The XSL language is an XML language, and it's a standard, so all XSL documents you create must follow that standard. What does an XSL document look like? Let's look at a sample XSL document for our sample XML document:

```
<?xml version="1.0" encoding="UTF-8"?>
<xsl:stylesheet version="1.0"
xmlns:xsl="http://www.w3.org/1999/XSL/Transform">
    <xsl:template match="/">
        <html>
            <head/>
            <body>
                <xsl:apply-templates/>
            </body>
        </html>
    </xsl:template>
    <xsl:template match="NAME">
        <span style="display:list-item; font-family:Arial">
            <span style="display:list-item; font-family:Arial">
                <xsl:apply-templates/>
            </span>
        </span>
    </xsl:template>
</xsl:stylesheet>
```

First, you must include the required XSL header:

```
<xsl:stylesheet version="1.0"
xmlns:xsl="http://www.w3.org/1999/XSL/Transform">
```

This is so that the parser knows which version of XSL you are using. In the XSL document, you will format your XML document into an HTML document. To ensure that your XML document is displayed correctly within HTML, you place your XML content within the <BODY></BODY> HTML tags:

```
<xsl:template match="/">
    <html>
        <head/>
        <body>
            <xsl:apply-templates/>
        </body>
    </html>
</xsl:template>
```

The only node within your XML document that holds character data is the NAME node. To ensure that this is what is displayed within the HTML, you target that node:

```
<xsl:template match="NAME">
```

You then specify all formatting to apply to the NAME node:

```
<span style="display:list-item; font-family:Arial">
<xsl:apply-templates/>
</span>
```

In this case, you list the items and display in the Arial font. You save your XSL file to a file called people.xstl. You can then embed it as follows:

```
<?xml version="1.0" encoding="UTF-8"?>
<!DOCTYPE PEOPLE SYSTEM
"http://localhost/phpbook/Chapter8_XML/XML/people.dtd">
<?xml-stylesheet type="text/xsl"
href="http://localhost/phpbook/Chapter8_XML/XML/people.xslt"?>
<PEOPLE>
    <PERSON>
        <NAME>Andrew</NAME>
    </PERSON>
    <PERSON>
        <NAME>Emma</NAME>
    </PERSON>
    <PERSON>
        <NAME>Terry</NAME>
    </PERSON>
    <PERSON>
        <NAME>Mary</NAME>
    </PERSON>
    <PERSON>
        <NAME>Thomas</NAME>
    </PERSON>
</PEOPLE>
```

Specifically, you use the `xml-stylesheet` tag, a special XML node for embedding the XSL document:

```
<?xml-stylesheet type="text/xsl"
href="http://localhost/phpbook/Chapter8_XML/XML/people.xslt"?>
```

If you now display the XML document, you will see it in a formatted form, as shown in Figure 8.2.

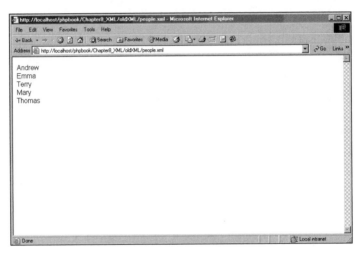

Figure 8.2 The XML file formatted with XSL.

How Is XML Structured?

When you define XML languages and create XML documents, you must follow a few rules. DTD documents help you keep your XML documents consistent, but a few more rules must be followed.

Always Remember the Header

In all the examples, you might have noticed the special XML header:

```
<?xml version="1.0" encoding="UTF-8"?>
```

This is always required. It tells the parser what version of XML and what encoding you are using so that the parser can display the XML document correctly. If you don't include the header, the parser returns an error. XML encoding is required in XML documents. XML supports two types—UTF-8 and UTF-16. When you set XML encoding, you tell the XML parser what encoding type to use to encode the XML document into a format the computer processor will understand. (A computer processor understands only numbers, so you use encoding to state how all the characters in the XML relate to their numeric counterparts.) Encoding differs depending on what encoding type you set. In other words, the letter-to-number encoding differs depending on whether you use UTF-8 or UTF-16.

Always Close Nodes

XML languages always need a close tag. Unlike, say, HTML, which can have single tags as well as open and close tags, XML tags always require an open tag and a close tag. For example, our XML language has the NAME tag, which we open with <NAME> and close with </NAME>.

> **Note**
>
> If XML doesn't have tags within tags, do you always need a close tag? In theory, yes, but you can use a shorthand syntax. For example, in HTML, the <IMG> tag has no tags within it. However, the XHTML version of the tag still needs a close tag. Thus, you can use <IMG/>, a shorthand form of a close tag. Also note that XML is case-sensitive, so the correct syntax would be <img/>. Furthermore, some browsers require a space before the ending slash, or they won't recognize the tag, so it's always good form to write it as <img />.

Never Cross Nodes

XML tags must never cross one another. For example, the following would be invalid:

```
<?xml version="1.0" encoding="UTF-8"?>
<PEOPLE>
     <PERSON>
          <NAME>Andrew</PERSON></NAME>
</PEOPLE>
```

Here, the PEOPLE node is closed before the NAME node is closed. In theory, you can get away with this without the parser's returning an error, but you will get unexpected results when you try to work with the XML document. You can enforce the rule about not crossing nodes within the DTD document—another reason why it is important to have one.

Using PHP with XML

Now that you have an idea of what XML is and how it is made up, you can start using it with PHP. The place to start is with Expat.

PHP and Expat

As I explained earlier, PHP utilizes the Expat library to make use of its native XML support. Expat is an open-source XML parser that is used in several applications; the PHP XML extension is just one. You can find out more about Expat at `http://www.jclark.com/xml/`.

XML support is built into PHP, so you can use it without modifying your php.ini file. To start, load and display your XML file:

```php
<?php

//path to XML file
$file_path = "C:\\Book\\Code\\Chapter8_XML\\XML\\";

//XML file
$xml_file = $file_path . "people.xml";

//display the contents of the XML file
function display($xmlp, $data) {

    Print($data);

}

//create the XML parser
$xmlp = xml_parser_create();

//set what function to call when you call the xml_parse method
xml_set_character_data_handler($xmlp, 'display');

//open the XML file as read-only
$file = fopen($xml_file, 'r') or die('cannot open xml file');

//loop through XML file contents
while($data = fread($file, filesize($xml_file))) {

    //call xml_parse method to read XML file
    xml_parse($xmlp, $data, feof($file)) or die ('xml error');

}

//free XML parser from memory
xml_parser_free($xmlp);

?>
```

First, you define the location and filename of the XML file you want to read:

```
//path to XML file
$file_path = "C:\\Book\\Code\\Chapter8_XML\XML\\";

//XML file
$xml_file = $file_path . "people.xml";
```

Next, you define a function that you use to display the contents of the XML document when character data is encountered:

```
//display the contents of the XML file
function display($xmlp, $data) {

    Print($data);

}
```

Then you create an XML parser instance and return a handle to it:

```
$xmlp = xml_parser_create();
```

Then you specify how to handle data from the XML document using the xml_set_character_data_handler function:

```
xml_set_character_data_handler($xmlp, 'display');
```

Here you supply the name of the function to be called by the processor (such as display) when character data is encountered in the parsing of the XML document.

Next you open the XML file and cycle through its contents:

```
//open the XML file as read-only
$file = fopen($xml_file, 'r') or die('cannot open xml file');

//loop through XML file contents
while($data = fread($file, filesize($xml_file))) {
```

Next you call the xml_parse function of the XML extension to parse through the XML document:

```
xml_parse($xmlp, $data, feof($file)) or die ('xml error');
```

Here the xml_parse function passes the contents of the XML file to the xml_set_character_data_handler function. If the xml_set_character_data_handler function encounters character data, it looks to see what function it has available for displaying data (which you set up when you set the xml_set_character_data_handler function earlier in the code). The display function then displays that character data, as shown in Figure 8.3.

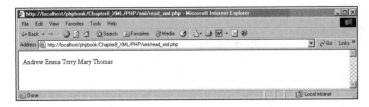

Figure 8.3   The XML file displayed using the PHP XML extension.

If your XML file contains a lot of data, the `xml_parse` function lets you read the file in chunks. To do this, all you need to do is modify the `fread` function as follows:

```
while($data = fread($file, 4000)) {

    //call xml_parse method to read XML file
    xml_parse($xmlp, $data, feof($file)) or die ('xml error');

}
```

Here the XML document is read in 4000-byte chunks rather than the whole document (as you did previously using the `filesize` function to pass the entire XML document to the `fread` function).

PHP and MSXML

PHP also lets you work with another XML parser: the Microsoft XML (MSXML) parser. Using the MSXML parser differs slightly from using the Expat parser in that the MSXML parser exists as a COM object as opposed to a native library like Expat. When using PHP with MSXML, you will encounter some issues, as shown here:

```
<%

'create MSXML parser
set source = Server.CreateObject("Microsoft.XMLDOM")

source.async = False

'load XML document into parser
source.load("http://localhost/phpbook/Chapter8_XML/XML/people.xml")

'node to find
set tagtofind = source.getElementsByTagName("NAME")

'how many tags we have
taglength = tagtofind.length
```

```
'iterate through nodes
For i = 0 To taglength - 1

'display data within tags
Response.write(tagtofind(i).Text & "<BR>")

Next

'free MSXML parser from memory
set source = nothing
%>
```

Here, using ASP, you use the MSXML parser to load the XML document and look up the NAME node. This creates an array holding a COM reference to each NAME node. You then iterate through the array, displaying the value of each NAME node in the array. Using PHP, this looks like the following:

```php
<?php

//create an MSXML parser as a COM object
$source = new COM("Microsoft.XMLDOM");

$source->async = false;

//load an XML document into the parser
$source->load("http://localhost/Book/Code/Chapter8_XML/XML/people.xml");

//tag to find
$nodecoll = $source->getElementsByTagName("NAME");

//how many tags we have
$numnodes = $nodecoll->length;

//iterate through tags
for ($i = 0; $i < $numnodes; $i++) {
    $item =& $nodecoll->item($i);
    print "Found: {$item->xml}\n";
}

?>
```

First, you load the MSXML parser COM object:

```php
$source = new COM("Microsoft.XMLDOM");
```

Next you load the XML document into the MSXML parser:

```php
$source->load("http://localhost/phpbook/Chapter8_XML/XML/people.xml");
```

Next you look up the tag you want to find:

```php
$tagtofind = $source->getElementsByTagName("NAME");
```

Next you see how many tags you have:

```
$numnodes = $nodecoll->length;
```

You then iterate through each of the tags:

```
for ($i = 0; $i < $numnodes; $i++) {
```

Next you display data within each of the tags. PHP does not support anonymous object dereferencing when using COM, so the syntax is as follows:

```
$item =& $nodecoll->item($i);
print "Found: {$item->xml}\n";
```

Although it's easy enough to use the MSXML parser directly in your code, wrapping the code directly into a COM object gives you additional speed and modularization.

```
<?php /* -*- mode: c++; minor-mode: font -*- */

// Create an MSXML parser as a COM object.
$source = new COM("Microsoft.XMLDOM");

$source->async = false;

// Load an XML document into the parser.
$source->load("http://localhost/Book/Code/Chapter8_XML/XML/people.xml");

// Search for any NAME tags.
$nodecoll = $source->getElementsByTagName("NAME");

// Number of matching nodes in the document.
$numnodes = $nodecoll->length;

echo "Number of matching tags: $numnodes.\n";

// Iterate over the collection of found nodes.
for ($i = 0; $i < $numnodes; $i++) {
    $item =& $nodecoll->item($i);
    echo "Found: {$item->xml}\n";
}

?>
```

Creating the MSXML Wrapper COM Object

Your COM object lets you do several things. It lets you pass the XML file you want to query, along with the node you want to look up, and returns an array holding all the data with that node. If you start Visual Basic and create a new ActiveX DLL project, you can add the following code:

```
Public Function DisplayXML(ByRef xmlfile As Variant, ByRef TagName As
Variant)

'array to hold tags
Dim Tags(10)

'load MSXML COM object
Dim source As DOMDocument
Set source = New DOMDocument

source.async = False

'load XML file
source.Load (xmlfile)

'look up node
Set TagsToLookup = source.getElementsByTagName(TagName)

'look up number of nodes
TagsAmount = TagsToLookup.length

'iterate through nodes
For i = 0 To TagsAmount - 1

    'copy tag contents to array
    Tags(i) = TagsToLookup(i).Text

Next

'return array
DisplayXML = Tags

'unload MSXML
Set source = Nothing

End Function
```

I set my project name to `Chapter8` and class name to `XML`, but you can use anything you want. Before you compile the DLL, remember to add a reference to
the MSXML COM object in your Visual Basic project references, as shown in
Figure 8.4.

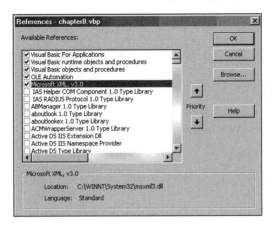

Figure 8.4   Adding the MSXML COM object to your Visual Basic project references.

The code for the COM object works much like it did before. First, you define the array that will hold the data of the tag you are looking up:

```
Dim Tags(10)
```

Visual Basic requires you to set the array size. My array size is quite small. Remember to set it large enough to accommodate all the nodes in your XML document.

Next you load the MSXML parser COM object:

```
Dim source As DOMDocument
Set source = New DOMDocument
```

Next you load the XML document into the MSXML parser. Note that you reference the parameter (that is, the path to the XML document) that you pass to your COM object:

```
source.Load (xmlfile)
```

Next you look up the node you want to find in the XML document. Note that you reference the parameter (that is, the node to find) that you pass to your COM object:

```
Set TagsToLookup = source.getElementsByTagName(TagName)
```

Next you see how many nodes occur within the XML document:

```
TagsAmount = TagsToLookup.length
```

Next you iterate through each of these nodes:

```
For i = 0 To TagsAmount - 1
```

As you iterate through the nodes, you populate your array with the data in the nodes:

```
Tags(i) = TagsToLookup(i).Text
```

Finally, after your array is populated, you use it as a return type for your COM object:

```
DisplayXML = Tags
```

Using the MSXML Feeder COM Object in PHP

After you have built and compiled the COM object, you can use it in PHP as follows:

```php
<?php


$source = new COM("chapter8.xml");
$xmlnode = $source->DisplayXML("http://localhost/phpbook/Chapter8
➥_XML/XML/people.xml", "NAME");

for ($i = 0; $i <= count($xmlnode); $i++)
{
    if($xmlnode[$i]) {
    print($xmlnode[$i] . "<BR>");
    }

}


?>
```

First, you load your COM object:

```php
$source = new COM("chapter8.xml");
```

Next, to obtain an array of results, you call the `DisplayXML` function, remembering to pass the location of your XML file and the node to find:

```php
$xmlnode = $source->DisplayXML("http://localhost/phpbook/Chapter8
➥_XML/XML/people.xml", "NAME");
```

Next you iterate through the array. Note that I have used the PHP `count` function to test how many elements are in the array:

```php
for ($i = 0; $i <= count($xmlnode); $i++)
```

The array might be larger than the number of nodes in your XML document, so some elements in the array might be empty. You avoid displaying these elements as follows:

```php
if($xmlnode[$i] <> "") {
```

To finally display data within your array, you use the following:

```
print($xmlnode[$i] . "<BR>");
```

If you run this script, you should see data from your NAMES nodes displayed, as shown in Figure 8.5.

Figure 8.5   The data from the NAMES node displayed using PHP and your MSXML feeder COM object.

Formatting XML with PHP and XSL

We looked at how to format XML using XSL earlier in this chapter. In that case, you embedded the XSL document directly into the XML document. Sometimes, however, that approach might not be best. Imagine if you needed to format the XSL document as either HTML or WAP, depending on the browser being used. You could create two versions of the same XML file and embed them. However, this approach is not ideal. Making changes to the documents or keeping them current can present a lot of problems. So how do you use XML and two different XSL documents? Thankfully, both Expat and MSXML let you embed an XSL document into an XML document. Here you can use PHP to detect the browser type, select the matching XSL document, and use either Expat or MSXML to embed the XSL document.

Using the PHP XSL Extension for XSL Formatting

PHP uses Expat and another open-source library called Sablotron. Sablotron is an XSL parser library and is used in combination with Expat to make up PHP's XSL extension. Support is planned for other libraries, such as the Xalan and libxslt libraries.

To enable XSLT support in PHP, you must uncomment the following line in your PHP.ini file:

```
extension=php_xslt.dll
```

You can use the PHP XSLT extension in two ways. You can load the XML and XSL documents directly into the extension, or you can load the documents into memory first. You can use the second method if the XML and XSL documents come from a non-file-based source, such as a database.

The Direct Method

The following code loads the XML and XSL files directly into the XSLT extension:

```php
<?php

//path
$file_path = "C:\\Book\\Code\Chapter8_XML\\XML\\";

//XML file
$xml_file = "file://" . $file_path . "people.xml";

//XSL file
$xsl_file = "file://" . $file_path . "people.xslt";

//allocate a new XSLT instance
$xh = xslt_create();

//process the document
$result = xslt_process($xh, $xml_file, $xsl_file);

//display the document
print $result;

//unload XSLT
xslt_free($xh);

?>
```

First you set up the paths to the XML and XSL files:

```php
$file_path = "C:\\Book\\Code\Chapter8_XML\\XML\\";

$xml_file = "file://" . $file_path . "people.xml";

$xsl_file = "file://" . $file_path . "people.xslt";
```

Note that I have used a local file path; Sablotron has no support for loading files over HTTP. Also note that each file begins with `"file://"`. This is required so that Sablotron knows that you are referencing a file. You will receive an error if you omit it.

The next stage is to create an instance of the XSLT extension:

```php
$xh = xslt_create();
```

Next you call the xslt_process function of the XSLT extension, passing the instance of the XSLT extension as well as the locations of your XML and XSL files:

```
$result = xslt_process($xh, $xml_file, $xsl_file);
```

You store the result of the xslt_process function in a variable ($result), which you can now display:

```
print $result;
```

To complete your code, you erase your instance of the XSLT extension from memory:

```
xslt_free($xh);
```

The Load into Memory Method

The second method you can use is to load the XML and XSL files into memory and then style the XML file with the XSL file. Using PHP, you do this as follows:

```
<?php

//path
$file_path = "http://localhost/phpbook/Chapter8_XML/XML/";

//XML file
$xml_file = $file_path . "people.xml";

//XSL file
$xsl_file = $file_path . "people.xslt";

//open XML file
$xmlfile = fopen ($xml_file, "r");
while (!feof ($xmlfile)) {
    $xml_file_contents .= fgets($xmlfile, 4096);
}
fclose ($xmlfile);

//open XSLT contents
$xslfile = fopen ($xsl_file, "r");
while (!feof ($xslfile)) {
    $xsl_file_contents .= fgets($xslfile, 4096);
}
fclose ($xslfile);

$arguments = array(
    '/_xml' => $xml_file_contents,
    '/_xsl' => $xsl_file_contents
);
```

```
//allocate a new XSLT processor
$xh = xslt_create();

//process the document
$result = xslt_process($xh, 'arg:/_xml', 'arg:/_xsl', NULL, $arguments);

print $result;

xslt_free($xh);

?>
```

First, you set up the paths to the XML and XSL files:

```
$file_path = "http://localhost/phpbook/Chapter8_XML/XML/";

$xml_file = $file_path . "people.xml";

$xsl_file = $file_path . "people.xslt";
```

The next stage is to read both the XML and XSL files into memory using PHP's file functions. Here you use the `fopen` function to load the XML and XSL files and loop through each file, reading it into a variable using the `fgets` function. As mentioned earlier, Sablotron does not support reading files over HTTP. However, when you use file functions, this has no bearing if the file is coming from a local file system or via HTTP.

```
$xmlfile = fopen ($xml_file, "r");
while (!feof ($xmlfile)) {
    $xml_file_contents .= fgets($xmlfile, 4096);
}
fclose ($xmlfile);

$xslfile = fopen ($xsl_file, "r");
while (!feof ($xslfile)) {
    $xsl_file_contents .= fgets($xslfile, 4096);
}
fclose ($xslfile);
```

Next you set up a parameters array. This links both the XML and XSL files to a set of parameters that you will reference in Sablotron:

```
$arguments = array(
    '/_xml' => $xml_file_contents,
    '/_xsl' => $xsl_file_contents
);
```

Here you link `'/_xml'` to the XML file and `'/_xsl'` to the XSL file. Now that you have everything ready, you can load the Sablotron functions. First, you create a new instance of Sablotron:

```
$xh = xslt_create();
```

Next you call the `xslt_process` function. Here you pass a handle to the Sablotron parser, as well as the references to the parameters array:

```
$result = xslt_process($xh, 'arg:/_xml', 'arg:/_xsl', NULL, $arguments);
```

Here, the `xslt_process` function matches `'arg:/_xml'` and `'arg:/_xsl'` against values in the parameters array (`$arguments`). If it finds a match, it replaces each with the value from the array.

You store the result from the `xslt_process` function to a variable (`$result`). To complete the example, you display that result and then unload Sablotron from memory:

```
print $result;

xslt_free($xh);
```

Using PHP and MSXML for XSL Formatting

The MSXML parser includes XSL formatting functions. You don't need to call on any other parsers for XSL formatting. Using the XSL functions is very simple:

```php
<?php

//Load the XML
$xml = new COM("Microsoft.XMLDOM");
$xml->async = false;
$xml->load("http://localhost/phpbook/Chapter8_XML/XML/people.xml");

//Load the XSL
$xsl = new COM("Microsoft.XMLDOM");
$xsl->async = false;
$xsl->load("http://localhost/phpbook/Chapter8_XML/XML/people.xslt");

$output = $xml->transformNode($xsl);

print $output;

?>
```

You first create a new instance of the MSXML COM object and load the XML file using that object:

```
$xml = new COM("Microsoft.XMLDOM");
$xml->async = false;
$xml->load("http://localhost/phpbook/Chapter8_XML/XML/people.xml");
```

You then create another instance of the MSXML COM object and load the XSL file using that object:

```
$xsl = new COM("Microsoft.XMLDOM");
$xsl->async = false;
$xsl->load("http://localhost/phpbook/Chapter8_XML/XML/people.xslt");
```

Next you call the `transformNode` method of the XML file object. This method
expects a COM instance of the XSL file, so you pass the second MSXML
COM object you created:

```
$output = $xml->transformNode($xsl);
```

Finally, you display the output of the `transformNode` object:

```
print $output;
```

Summary

This chapter looked at the history of XML and what XML is. We looked at
what makes up an XML document and how you can create well-formed
XML documents. We also looked at how you can use PHP's XML extension
and how you can use PHP with MSXML and COM. Finally, we looked at
formatting XML documents with XSLT and how you can use PHP and
XSLT with the PHP XSLT extension, MSXML, and COM.

9

PHP and Web Services

WEB SERVICES ARE ONE OF THE MOST talked-about technologies of the day.
They are set to change how data is exchanged on the Internet as the Internet
itself evolves to deliver content not only to web browsers on PCs but also to
PDAs and other devices. Further still, the evolution of "Internet-ready" software and hardware will see web services being used in applications such as
MP3 players, personal stereos, and game consoles. PHP is a great language for
developing web services, and this chapter shows you just what a web service is
and how it is made up. Then we will look at how you can use PHP to develop
web services.

What Makes Up a Web Service?

A web service is made up of four parts, as shown in Figure 9.1. The first part is
the component that wants to act as a web service. It can be any part of an
application: the executable, a COM component, a JavaBean, and so on. The
web service component exposes public methods and functions that other
applications can query. Your component could be one that you have created
for this purpose, but normally you can expose any component that has public
methods as a web service.

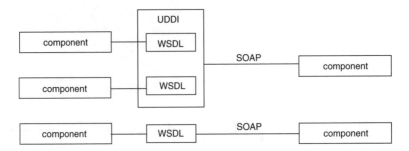

Figure 9.1   The makeup of web services.

You must allow your components to be accessed by other applications as a web service. To do this, you must allow other applications to see what public functions and methods your components have. You don't allow applications to do this directly. To accomplish this, you create a file based on an XML-based metalanguage called Web Services Description Language (WSDL).

Next you must allow applications to query the WSDL file and exchange data with the web service.

For this purpose, you use another XML-based metalanguage called Simple Object Access Protocol (SOAP).

Using SOAP, you look up the web service component's public methods and functions using the WSDL file and then query those methods and functions. However, you don't always know where to find a web service's WSDL file. In that case, you can look at an XML-based database (also called a *registry*) of WSDL addresses. This database is called a Uniform Description, Discovery, and Integration (UDDI) registry.

The easiest way to remember the component parts of a web service is to think in terms of these three concepts:

- Discovery: UDDI lets you discover web services.
- Query: WSDL lets you query web services.
- Transport: SOAP lets you transmit those queries back and forth from the web service.

Don't worry if some of these terms are new to you. They are covered in further detail later in this chapter. Now that we have identified all the component parts of a web service, let's look at each in detail.

SOAP (Simple Object Access Protocol)

In Chapter 5, "PHP and Sessions," SOAP was mentioned briefly when we looked at how WDDX developed. SOAP, like WDDX, is an XML-based language. Unlike WDDX, however, and like another XML-based language,

XML-RPC, it is used for RPC (Remote Procedure Call) via XML. XML-RPC started life as an idea of Dave Winer of UserLand software. He discussed his ideas with Microsoft, and from his ideas, SOAP was born. (XML-RPC continues to develop as a protocol separate from SOAP.)

Other companies (such as IBM) joined Microsoft in developing SOAP. Soon after that, implementations of SOAP for languages such as Java (via IBM) and Visual C++ and Visual Basic (via Microsoft) were released.

Using SOAP

So how is SOAP used? SOAP is an XML-based language, so in effect, all SOAP implementations do is create XML files or strings that facilitate passing data and calling methods between (normally remote) applications. SOAP does not have to be strictly about web services; in other words, it does not require WSDL or UDDI to work and can be used in a standard RPC manner. SOAP is often described as passing objects between applications; this can be both misleading and confusing. All SOAP does is allow a public function or method to be queried via an XML interface. It does not pass physical objects in the same way that Java serialization does, for example.

When an application queries a public function or another application's methods, it passes some data to that function or method and might get results in return. A public function or method does not always do this, but it is good practice that such functions or methods at least return some handshake data (a simple code that allows the calling application to see that the public function or method has received the data it sent).

When dealing with remote applications, you might face data type problems. That is, different languages have different ways of representing data. You might have some success on this front. For example, Java and PHP have very similar data types, but when dealing with calling applications that might be made up of languages such Perl, Python, and C++, you will face a nightmare.

If you imagine that your remote application is developed in Java and your calling clients are made up of PHP and Visual Basic, you might face few problems with the PHP application calling the remote Java application. But you will face a lot of problems when you do the same with a Visual Basic application.

Luckily, SOAP deals with this by presenting a standard way of representing data. Imagine that your remote Java application function accepts a string. Using SOAP, you translate the calling application data into the SOAP equivalent and pass that to the remote Java application. The Java application then translates the SOAP string data into the Java equivalent.

This can work in reverse too so that if your Java application returns a result, it does so as SOAP data for your client applications to translate back into native data types. So, in effect, SOAP does not really let you pass objects between applications. Instead, it provides the means to interface between different objects in different languages.

I was once asked if SOAP, based on part of its definition (simple object), is for simple objects only. Its meaning is not to be confused with objects in the sense we use them in OOP languages such as C++. It does not need to know what an object does, how it exists, or how it works. In fact, the very use of the word *object* can be misleading. SOAP does not require objects to exist in a true OOP sense. They can be nothing more than public functions and methods and are not subject to OOP concepts such as encapsulation.

SOAP Transparency

Because SOAP is XML-based, it is nothing more than ASCII data that is being transmitted (and therefore is as simple as standard text). This is one of key benefits of SOAP. It uses simple character encoding (ASCII) as a file format. It can be transmitted on any protocol that supports the transmission of ASCII data. As it happens, most TCP/IP protocols do. This allows SOAP to be used across HTTP (the most common protocol to be used with SOAP), FTP, SMTP, and so on. This brings an added benefit in that such protocols don't require special ports and security measures such as firewalls. They run through commonly used ports. (This advantage is also enjoyed by other XML-based RPC methods, such as XML-RPC.)

This property is also apparent when you compare SOAP to other RPC methods. In PHP, you can also make use of DCOM (which is used with COM), CORBA (which uses the IIOP protocol), and Java (which natively supports the RMI protocol). Protocols that facilitate RPC are called *wire protocols* because they are low-level and require special ports. SOAP, however, has no such requirements.

SOAP's Makeup

What exactly is SOAP made of? A SOAP message is called a SOAP *envelope.* The following code exemplifies a SOAP envelope:

```
<?xml version="1.0" encoding="UTF-8" standalone="no" ?>
<SOAP-ENV:Envelope SOAP-ENV:encodingStyle=
➥"http://schemas.xmlsoap.org/soap/encoding/"
➥ xmlns:SOAP-ENV="http://schemas.xmlsoap.org/soap/envelope/">

</SOAP-ENV:Envelope>
```

An envelope contains a body, which can be either a SOAP body call or a SOAP body response.

SOAP Body Call

When a call is made to a public function or method, this is done with a SOAP body call. Such a body call looks something like this:

```
<SOAP-ENV:Body>
<SOAPSDK1:HelloFunc xmlns:SOAPSDK1="http://tempuri.org/message/">
<uname xmlns:SOAPSDK2="http://www.w3.org/2001/XMLSchema-instance"
➥ xmlns:SOAPSDK3="http://www.w3.org/2001/XMLSchema"
➥ SOAPSDK2:type="SOAPSDK3:string">Andrew</uname>
</SOAPSDK1:HelloFunc>
</SOAP-ENV:Body>
```

Here the `HelloFunc` method is passed a string of data called `"Andrew"`. Note that SOAP has added a mapping of what data we are passing to the public service or method:

```
type="SOAPSDK3:string"
```

A completed SOAP envelope calling a public service or method looks like the following:

```
<?xml version="1.0" encoding="UTF-8" standalone="no" ?>
<SOAP-ENV:Envelope SOAP-ENV:encodingStyle=
➥ "http://schemas.xmlsoap.org/soap/encoding/"
➥ xmlns:SOAP-ENV="http://schemas.xmlsoap.org/soap/envelope/">
<SOAP-ENV:Body>
<SOAPSDK1:HelloFunc xmlns:SOAPSDK1="http://tempuri.org/message/">
<uname xmlns:SOAPSDK2="http://www.w3.org/2001/XMLSchema-instance"
➥ xmlns:SOAPSDK3="http://www.w3.org/2001/XMLSchema"
➥ SOAPSDK2:type="SOAPSDK3:string">Andrew</uname>
</SOAPSDK1:HelloFunc>
</SOAP-ENV:Body>
</SOAP-ENV:Envelope>
```

SOAP Body Response

In response to a call to a public function or method, SOAP can respond to that call using the SOAP body response:

```
<SOAP-ENV:Body>
<SOAPSDK1:HelloFuncResponse xmlns:SOAPSDK1="http://tempuri.org/message/">
<Result xmlns:SOAPSDK2="http://www.w3.org/2001/XMLSchema-instance"
➥ xmlns:SOAPSDK3="http://www.w3.org/2001/XMLSchema"
➥ SOAPSDK2:type="SOAPSDK3:string">hello Andrew</Result>
<uname xmlns:SOAPSDK4="http://www.w3.org/2001/XMLSchema-instance"
➥ xmlns:SOAPSDK5="http://www.w3.org/2001/XMLSchema"
➥ SOAPSDK4:type="SOAPSDK5:string">Andrew</uname>
</SOAPSDK1:HelloFuncResponse>#
</SOAP-ENV:Body>
```

The SOAP body result contains any data that the public function or method returns:

```
<Result xmlns:SOAPSDK2="http://www.w3.org/2001/XMLSchema-instance"
➥ xmlns:SOAPSDK3="http://www.w3.org/2001/XMLSchema"
➥ SOAPSDK2:type="SOAPSDK3:string">hello Andrew</Result>
```

along with the original method call:

```
<uname xmlns:SOAPSDK4="http://www.w3.org/2001/XMLSchema-instance"
➥ xmlns:SOAPSDK5="http://www.w3.org/2001/XMLSchema"
➥ SOAPSDK4:type="SOAPSDK5:string">Andrew</uname>
```

Web Services Description Language (WSDL)

In the web services sense, although SOAP helps you exchange data between the public functions or methods of a web service, it can't help you explain which public functions or methods are available and what they do. Without this information, you can't use SOAP to exchange data, because you have no idea what is available to help you facilitate the exchange.

For this purpose, we have Web Services Description Language (WSDL). Like SOAP, WSDL is an XML-based file format for describing what public functions and methods are available in a web service. Other applications use the WSDL file to find this information and then use SOAP against those described public functions or methods.

WSDL File Makeup

```
<?xml version='1.0' encoding='UTF-8' ?>
 <!-- Generated 09/24/01 by Microsoft SOAP Toolkit WSDL File Generator,
➥ Version 1.02.813.0 -->
<definitions  name ='PHP4WINSOAP'
➥    targetNamespace = 'http://tempuri.org/wsdl/'
      xmlns:wsdlns='http://tempuri.org/wsdl/'
      xmlns:typens='http://tempuri.org/type'
      xmlns:soap='http://schemas.xmlsoap.org/wsdl/soap/'
      xmlns:xsd='http://www.w3.org/2001/XMLSchema'
      xmlns:stk='http://schemas.microsoft.com/soap-toolkit/wsdl-extension'
      xmlns='http://schemas.xmlsoap.org/wsdl/'>
  <types>
    <schema targetNamespace='http://tempuri.org/type'
      xmlns='http://www.w3.org/2001/XMLSchema'
      xmlns:SOAP-ENC='http://schemas.xmlsoap.org/soap/encoding/'
      xmlns:wsdl='http://schemas.xmlsoap.org/wsdl/'
      elementFormDefault='qualified'>
    </schema>
  </types>
  <message name='Examples.HelloFunc'>
```

```
      <part name='uname' type='xsd:anyType'/>
    </message>
    <message name='Examples.HelloFuncResponse'>
      <part name='Result' type='xsd:anyType'/>
      <part name='uname' type='xsd:anyType'/>
    </message>
    <portType name='ExamplesSoapPort'>
      <operation name='HelloFunc' parameterOrder='uname'>
        <input message='wsdlns:Examples.HelloFunc' />
        <output message='wsdlns:Examples.HelloFuncResponse' />
      </operation>
    </portType>
    <binding name='ExamplesSoapBinding' type='wsdlns:ExamplesSoapPort' >
      <stk:binding preferredEncoding='UTF-8'/>
      <soap:binding style='rpc' transport=
    ➥'http://schemas.xmlsoap.org/soap/http' />
      <operation name='HelloFunc' >
        <soap:operation soapAction=
    ➥'http://tempuri.org/action/Examples.HelloFunc' />
        <input>
          <soap:body use='encoded' namespace='http://tempuri.org/message/'
              encodingStyle='http://schemas.xmlsoap.org/soap/encoding/' />
        </input>
        <output>
          <soap:body use='encoded' namespace='http://tempuri.org/message/'
              encodingStyle='http://schemas.xmlsoap.org/soap/encoding/' />
        </output>
      </operation>
    </binding>
    <service name='PHP4WINSOAP' >
      <port name='ExamplesSoapPort' binding='wsdlns:ExamplesSoapBinding' >
        <soap:address location='http://localhost/phpbook/Chapter9
      ➥_SOAP/SOAP/Server/PHP4WINSOAP.ASP' />
      </port>
    </service>
  </definitions>
```

As you can see, the WSDL file format is quite a complicated one. The three
most important pieces are the port type, binding, and service name.

Port Type

The port type defines which public functions or methods are available. It uses
the full name, which in this case is the HelloFunc method of the Examples
class:

```
<portType name='ExamplesSoapPort'>
  <operation name='HelloFunc' parameterOrder='uname'>
    <input message='wsdlns:Examples.HelloFunc' />
    <output message='wsdlns:Examples.HelloFuncResponse' />
  </operation>
</portType>
```

Binding

Binding describes how calls are made to each public method or function of a
web service. In other words, it describes what encoding a client application
should use when querying that public method or function.

```
<binding name='ExamplesSoapBinding' type='wsdlns:ExamplesSoapPort' >
    <stk:binding preferredEncoding='UTF-8'/>
    <soap:binding style='rpc'
  ➥ transport='http://schemas.xmlsoap.org/soap/http' />
    <operation name='HelloFunc' >
      <soap:operation soapAction=
    ➥'http://tempuri.org/action/Examples.HelloFunc' />
      <input>
        <soap:body use='encoded' namespace='http://tempuri.org/message/'
            encodingStyle='http://schemas.xmlsoap.org/soap/encoding/' />
      </input>
      <output>
        <soap:body use='encoded' namespace='http://tempuri.org/message/'
            encodingStyle='http://schemas.xmlsoap.org/soap/encoding/' />
      </output>
    </operation>
  </binding>
```

This line describes what encoding will use of the binding:

```
<stk:binding preferredEncoding='UTF-8'/>
```

This must match the encoding for your XML file (the encoding specified in
the XML header). Next you specify what the binding is (RPC) and its transport (HTTP):

```
<soap:binding style='rpc' transport='http://schemas.xmlsoap.org/soap/http' />
```

Next you specify what function you will call as `Hello Func`:

```
<operation name='HelloFunc' >
<soap:operation soapAction='http://tempuri.org/action/Examples.HelloFunc' />
```

The WSDL file describes the encoding you use to query the web service and
obtain a result:

```
<input>
<soap:body use='encoded' namespace='http://tempuri.org/message/'
➥ encodingStyle='http://schemas.xmlsoap.org/soap/encoding/' />
</input>
<output>
<soap:body use='encoded' namespace='http://tempuri.org/message/'
➥ encodingStyle='http://schemas.xmlsoap.org/soap/encoding/' />
</output>
```

Although it's important to understand the structure of a WSDL file, you won't
often need to write a WSDL file yourself. Most web service toolkits have tools
for creating WSDL files for you.

Service Name

The service name defines where the WSDL gateway will be. A WSDL gateway is used to query the web service's component. A WSDL file passes the gateway information back to the client application. Such queries from the client application go to the gateway and on to the web service component and back.

```
<service name='PHP4WINSOAP' >
  <port name='ExamplesSoapPort' binding='wsdlns:ExamplesSoapBinding' >
    <soap:address location='http://localhost/phpbook/Chapter9
    ➥_SOAP/SOAP/Server/PHP4WINSOAP.ASP' />
  </port>
</service>
```

A gateway is language-independent. For instance, our example uses ASP, but the gateway can be developed in any language you like, as long as it supports XML. All it does is work in unison with the WSDL file to allow client applications to pass SOAP queries back and forth between the web service and the client application.

Uniform Description, Discovery, and Integration (UDDI)

Although you can now look up and query a web service's public methods and functions, finding a web service presents a problem. It can't be found using normal means such as a web search engine. If your company wants to make use of web services, it needs to make them generally available to all calling applications, not simply provide URLs on web pages for people to connect to.

Web services need a source of information all their own that an application can search and use to find WSDL files to query. UDDI was created for this purpose (see `http://www.uddi.org`). UDDI is another emerging standard for web services. It allows a company to register its company details, web page, and so on with a business group (for example, a car dealership could register with an automotive association). A person can then search the UDDI for companies within a business group or type via an application or directly via a web browser. More interestingly, UDDI allows companies to publish details of what web services are available (using brief descriptions and keywords) as well as the URLs of the WSDL files. An application can use this information to discover which web services a company has available.

Several public UDDI registries have been set up to allow companies to test and publish details of real-world web services. The Microsoft UDDI registry (`http://uddi.microsoft.com`), shown in Figure 9.2, serves such a purpose.

Figure 9.2 Microsoft's UDDI web site.

Microsoft also provides a test UDDI registry at `http://test.uddi.microsoft.com` (see Figure 9.3). Other UDDI registries are available from IBM at `http://www.ibm.com/developerworks/webservices/`.

Figure 9.3 Microsoft's UDDI web site for testing.

The Future of Web Services

In May 2000, SOAP was submitted to the W3C for standardization. (That group included Microsoft, UserLand, DeveloperMentor, and IBM. The submission can be found at `http://www.w3.org/Submission/2000/05/`.) In time, SOAP will become part of a brand-new protocol that the W3C is calling XML Protocol. (It's called XP for short, but don't confuse it with the Microsoft operating system of the same name.) XP will serve exactly the same purpose as SOAP but will be the first standardized XML-based RPC protocol. The drafting of XP is under way, with the W3C XP working group releasing a draft of the SOAP 1.2 specification. Further details on XP can be found at `http://www.w3.org/2000/xp/`.

Using PHP to Create Web Services

Now that we have looked at what a web service is and what comprises it, let's now look at how you can create a web service in PHP.

Creating the Web Service

To create your web service, you will use the Microsoft SOAP SDK (`http://msdn.microsoft.com/webservices/`). It gives you all you need to create web services and web service clients (connecting to and querying web services). The client portion of the SDK is included in the Windows XP operating system. The SDK is continually updated by Microsoft as the various protocols (such as SOAP and WSDL) change. The SDK used in this chapter is the Microsoft SOAP SDK 2.0 SP2 (see Figure 9.4).

Figure 9.4   The Microsoft SOAP SDK installer dialog box.

Other SOAP SDKs are also available, such as the IBM web service SDK, which includes web service libraries and a WSDL file generator (http:// www-106.ibm.com/developerworks/webservices/). Both IBM and Microsoft provide SDKs for UDDI that are separate from their SOAP/WSDL SDKs.

Creating a Web Service Component

The base of your web service (the one that provides the public functions or methods that you want to query against) is the simple COM component you developed in Chapter 7, "PHP, COM, and .NET." You developed this in Visual Basic using the following code:

```
Option Explicit
Public Function HelloFunc(ByRef uname As Variant) As Variant
      HelloFunc = "hello " & uname
End Function
```

All this COM component does is take a string as its argument (such as "every-one") and return a string (such as "hello everyone"). You can either compile a new version of this COM component for use with your web service or simply reuse the same COM component exactly as you left it in Chapter 7.

Creating a WSDL File

As soon as you have your COM component, you need to make a WSDL file to turn it into a web service. Although you can write this by hand, as you have seen, this is quite complicated. Luckily, the Microsoft SOAP SDK provides you with a handy WSDL generation tool called wsdlgen.exe. (You can access it by selecting Start, SOAP SDK.) When you start the WSDL generation tool, you see a welcome screen, as shown in Figure 9.5.

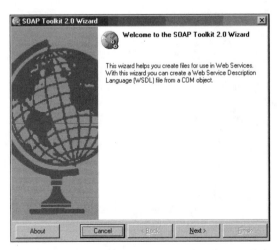

Figure 9.5   The Microsoft WSDL Wizard welcome dialog box.

If you click Next, you can select which COM component you want to create the WSDL file for (its physical file location), as shown in Figure 9.6. Also select a name for your WSDL. You can use any name, but it is best to choose something short and easy to use.

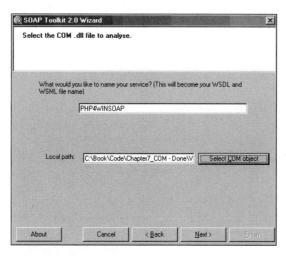

Figure 9.6   The Microsoft WSDL Wizard COM object selection dialog box.

When you click Next, the tool checks what public functions and methods your COM component has available and allows you to select which ones you want to expose in the WSDL file, as shown in Figure 9.7. You might not want to expose them all, but you can do so if you want to.

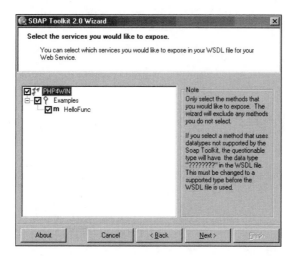

Figure 9.7   The Microsoft WSDL Wizard function selection dialog box.

When you click Next, you reach the SOAP listener information dialog box, shown in Figure 9.8. This is quite an important section, because this is where you map the WSDL file to your COM component. This tool lets you create either an ASP listener or an ISAPI listener (also called a gateway). The listener can be stored in either the same place as your COM component or elsewhere. Make sure, however, that the directory you choose is accessible by the web server.

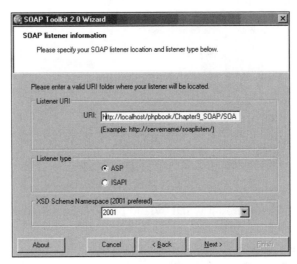

Figure 9.8 The Microsoft WSDL Wizard listener setup dialog box.

After you click Next, you select where you want to store the tool you will create (see Figure 9.9). The WSDL file can be separate from the COM component if you want.

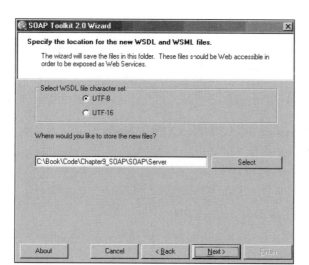

Figure 9.9 The Microsoft WSDL Wizard file storage dialog box.

Click Next. The WSDL file is created (see Figure 9.10).

Figure 9.10 The Microsoft WSDL Wizard completion dialog box.

Client Application

To make use of the services your web service provides, you must access the WSDL file. Your client application does just this. You can use two methods in PHP to create the client application. You can use the COM objects that the Microsoft SOAP SDK provides, or you can use a native PHP implementation.

Using the Microsoft SOAP SDK COM Objects

When using the COM objects in the SDK, you can approach creating the client application using two methods. You can use the COM objects directly from PHP, or you can wrap them into a single COM object.

Using COM Objects Directly from PHP

The SOAP SDK provides you with a set of COM objects for querying a web service, as follows:

```php
<?php

//load COM SOAP client object
$soapob = new COM("MSSOAP.SoapClient");

//connect to web service
$soapob->mssoapinit("http://localhost/phpbook/Chapter9
➥_SOAP/SOAP/Server/PHP4WINSOAP.WSDL");

//obtain result from web service method
$soapmessage = $soapob->HelloFunc("Andrew");

//print result
print($soapmessage);

?>
```

First, you load the SOAP client COM object into memory:

```php
$soapob = new COM("MSSOAP.SoapClient");
```

Next you connect to your web service. (Remember to use the full URL of where you stored the WSDL file you created earlier in this chapter.)

```php
$soapob->mssoapinit("http://localhost/phpbook/Chapter9
➥_SOAP/SOAP/Server/PHP4WINSOAP.WSDL");
```

Next you call the HelloFunc method of your web service, passing the string "Andrew" and storing its return result:

```php
$soapmessage = $soapob->HelloFunc("Andrew");
```

Finally, you display the result:

```php
print($soapmessage);
```

If you run the PHP script, you should see the result from the `HelloFunc` method of your web service, as shown in Figure 9.11.

Figure 9.11   Your web service displaying data.

If you change the call to the web service method, the output changes. For example, if you change the following line in your script:

```
$soapmessage = $soapob->HelloFunc("Elle and Jack");
```

the output changes, as shown in Figure 9.12.

Figure 9.12   Your web service displaying different data.

Your Web Service Wrapped into a Single COM Object

You might want to reuse the same SOAP client application code across different scripts. In such a case, you can wrap the client application into a COM object.

If you start Visual Basic and create an ActiveX DLL called php4winsoap with a class called `Output`, you can add the following code:

```
Public Function getdata()

Set sc = New SoapClient

On Error Resume Next

sc.mssoapinit "http://localhost/phpbook/Chapter9
➥_SOAP/SOAP/Server/PHP4WINSOAP.WSDL"

If Err <> 0 Then
```

```
    getdata = "initialization failed " + Err.Description

End If

getdata = sc.HelloFunc("Andrew")


End Function
```

If you try to compile this code, you will get an error. You must also reference the SOAP COM objects in your visual basic project, as shown in Figure 9.13.

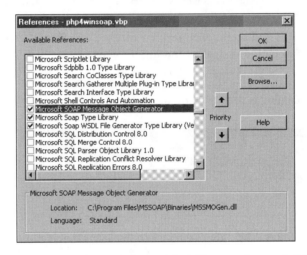

Figure 9.13   The Microsoft SOAP SDK COM library reference in Visual Basic.

As soon as the COM object is compiled, you can use it from within PHP:

```php
<?php

//load SOAP client COM object
$soapob = new COM("php4winsoap.output");

//call getdata method to obtain result of SOAP exchange
$soapmessage = $soapob->getdata();

//output result
print($soapmessage);

?>
```

If you run this script, the web service output is displayed, as in the previous example (see Figure 9.14).

Figure 9.14   Running your web service using a wrapped COM object.

Native PHP Implementation

PHP also lets you not use COM objects at all and connect and query WSDL files directly from PHP. This is made possible by the Simple Web Services API (SWSAPI). It is an open-source API whose creation has been led by the ActiveState Corporation in order to establish the same standard syntax for connecting and querying WSDL files in several different languages. SWSAPI currently is in beta and is available for Perl, Python, and PHP. It is expected to be made available for Ruby.

Using a native implementation means that you use your PHP libraries. In this case, the SWSAPI is a PHP library that builds on a native PHP implementation for SOAP called SOAP4X. To make use of the SWSAPI, you must unzip the PHP files into a directory you can access. You then make use of the SWSAPI via the following code:

```php
<?php

require_once('webservice.php');

$soapob = WebService::ServiceProxy('http://localhost/phpbook/Chapter9
➡_SOAP/SOAP/Server/PHP4WINSOAP.WSDL');

$soapmessage = $soapob->HelloFunc("Andrew");

print($soapmessage);

?>
```

Here you load up the SWSAPI functions from the SWSAPI PHP library:

```php
require_once('webservice.php');
```

What remains is very much like what you have seen using the Microsoft SOAP SDK COM objects. First, you call the WSDL file and store it in a variable:

```php
$soapob = WebService::ServiceProxy('http://localhost/phpbook/Chapter9
➡_SOAP/SOAP/Server/PHP4WINSOAP.WSDL');
```

You then call a function of the web service and store the result in a variable:

```
$soapmessage = $soapob->HelloFunc("Andrew");
```

Finally, you display the result:

```
print($soapmessage);
```

If you run the script, you can see the result of calling your web service using the SWSAPI, as shown in Figure 9.15.

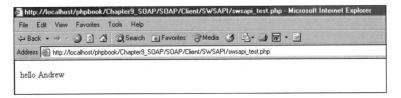

Figure 9.15   Running your web service using the SWSAPI.

Further information, downloads, and the SWSAPI specification can be found at `http://aspn.activestate.com/ASPN/WebServices/SWSAPI/`.

Useful Tools

One of the most useful tools that the toolkit provides is the Trace utility (MsSoapT.exe). You access it by selecting Start, SOAP SDK. Trace lets you view SOAP message exchanges between client applications and the web service at either the web service or the client application side.

If you monitor the web service side, you must modify the service name portion of the WSDL file as follows:

```
<soap:address location='http://localhost:8080/phpbook/Chapter9
➥_SOAP/SOAP/Server/PHP4WINSOAP.ASP' />
```

Here you add a port number (8080) to the web service gateway's URL. If you start the Trace utility and select formatted trace, you are asked for the local port to listen on, as shown in Figure 9.16. In this case, because you are using port 8080, specify port 8080.

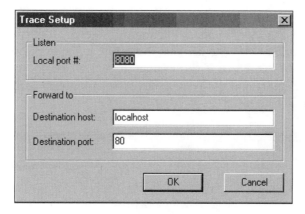

Figure 9.16 The Trace Setup dialog box.

If you click OK to start the trace, you see the Trace window, shown in Figure 9.17.

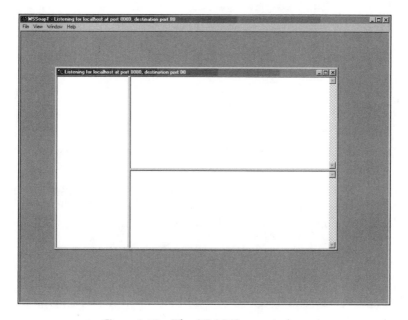

Figure 9.17 The SOAP Trace window.

If you run the web service client PHP script again, the Trace window stores the result of the SOAP message exchange. This exchange is stored under the IP that the web service was delivered from (in this case, the local host address of 127.0.0.1). The top pane of the Trace window contains the SOAP message that calls the web service's public function or method. The bottom pane contains the resulting SOAP message that the public function or method returns (see Figure 9.18). Note that if you change the WSDL file to support listening with the Trace utility and the Trace utility is not running, your web service reports an error.

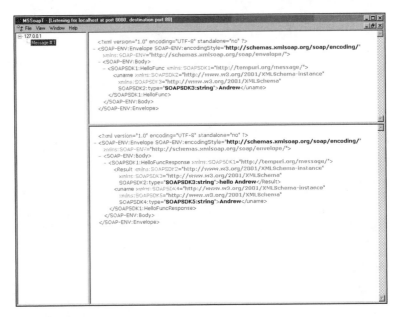

Figure 9.18 The SOAP Trace window displaying SOAP messages.

The Trace utility is very useful in helping you see what SOAP messages are exchanged between the web service and client applications. It therefore helps you debug any problems in your web services.

Summary

This chapter looked at what web services are, what comprises them (UDDI, WSDL, and SOAP), and how you can use PHP to create, look up, and query web services.

10

PHP and ADO

THIS CHAPTER LOOKS AT HOW YOU CAN use PHP with Microsoft Active Data Objects (ADO). We will then look at how you can use PHP with a PHP database function library called ADODB.

The History of ADO

Let's begin this chapter by looking at how ADO has evolved.

ODBC

We met ODBC in Chapter 6, "PHP and Databases." To review, ODBC (Open Database Connectivity) presents a standard way of allowing an application to connect to and work with a database. ODBC presents a middle layer for database connectivity. Your application uses ODBC commands to connect to and query the database, and ODBC then translates these commands to commands specific to your database vendor. To connect to and query a database either directly or using ODBC, your application needs some means of accessing the necessary APIs. Microsoft created its first group of APIs with DAO.

DAO

Data Access Objects (DAO) was a collection of OLE objects that wrapped around the APIs for using the Microsoft Jet engine. The Jet engine is the engine that Microsoft Access uses. Because the DAO objects mirrored objects within a Microsoft Access database (such as tables and queries), DAO provided the quickest and simplest means of accessing Access databases.

However, DAO suffered when used with other databases via ODBC. The Jet engine had to translate the DAO objects into ODBC and from ODBC into queries your database could understand. If it was a database other than Microsoft Access, often a lot of functionality was lost, because many objects could not be translated to ODBC, and the performance was not good.

DAO also suffered when it came to remote data sources such as SQL Server. To operate in a correct client/server fashion, data retrieved from the database is phrased first on the server, and then the client receives only the data it requested. However, DAO pulled all the data to the client so that the Jet engine could parse the data.

RDO

Remote Data Objects (RDO) came next. They overcame the problem of accessing remote data sources. RDO was a new set of COM objects that reflected ODBC APIs rather than Jet APIs. Because ODBC was used, no translation beyond ODBC translation was needed, so RDO operated a lot faster than DAO.

ODBCDirect

ODBCDirect came next. It was introduced into the DAO COM objects. ODBCDirect in fact used RDO to connect and query a database rather than using ODBC APIs directly; however, it gave DAO objects a way of accessing a database without the need to go through the Jet engine.

OLE DB

Microsoft was aware of several RDO shortcomings. Although it provided a set of COM objects for accessing databases via ODBC, it was limited when accessing Jet or ISAM data sources.

The solution Microsoft provided was OLE DB. OLE DB not only wrapped around the ODBC APIs, but it also provided its own API so that database vendors could write OLE DB drivers for their databases. OLE DB also provided you with the means to connect to and query these databases.

ADO

Unfortunately, OLE DB was very tricky to work with. To simplify this, Microsoft introduced Active Data Objects (ADO). ADO is a set of COM objects that wrap around OLE DB to simplify writing code to connect to and query a database using OLE DB.

ADO.NET

Chapter 7, "PHP, COM, and .NET," looked at how Microsoft .NET is evolving. ADO.NET is a part of the .NET framework and, like the .NET framework, does not use COM as its basis. Here Microsoft has redeveloped data access once more, this time to take advantage of common classes, to be easier to work with, and to be more available to .NET programming languages. ADO.NET still provides a wrapper for OLE DB should you need to work with it. However, it is much richer in functionality (for example, you can work with XML data) and for the first time provides database vendors with a way of writing drivers that can be accessed directly by ADO.NET. This is doing away with OLE DB.

What Is ADO to You as a PHP Programmer?

ADO as a common set of objects for connecting to and working with a database is fairly unique. Remember that ADO can work with any database that supports OLE DB and the code is always the same, so you have a common set of objects for working with a range of databases.

PHP does not really have anything like this; the closest it has is the ADODB library (covered later in this chapter). However, ADO, as you shall discover, is fully useable from PHP.

Installing ADO

ADO is installed by default in products such as Microsoft SQL Server and Microsoft Office. You can also download ADO from http://www.microsoft.com/data/.

A word of warning with ADO: It is not backward-compatible, so if you install the most recent version of ADO and then you install an application that installs a later version of ADO, you could end up with a very messy computer. This is classic "DLL hell" (see Chapter 7), in which you end up with different versions of the same COM objects. Sorting out this mess is often very difficult (and I speak from experience). As a general rule, avoid very recent versions of ADO as much as you can.

Using PHP with ADO

Now that you have an idea of what ADO is, how do you use it with PHP? Chapter 7 looked at how PHP can use COM. Because ADO is a set of COM objects, all you need in order to access ADO is PHP's COM support.

Accessing ADO.NET is trickier, because PHP has no direct support for .NET. However, as discussed in Chapter 7, it is possible to emulate a COM object in .NET. As such, it's certainly possible to write a COM wrapper object for certain ADO.NET functions and thus make them useable by PHP.

For the purposes of this chapter, I'll show you how to use ADO first in ASP and then in PHP. The ASP code is included for reference. If you don't have an ASP background, don't worry. The PHP code is fully explained.

Database Example

For the purposes of this chapter, I have created a simple database called php-book in SQL Server 2000 with a simple table called Names. ADO can work with any database that supports OLE DB, such as Microsoft Access and Oracle. The Names table contains the fields shown in Table 10.1.

Table 10.1   **Names Table Fields**

Name	Type	Length
Id	Int	4
fname	Nvarchar	15
lname	Nvarchar	15

I then created a sample record within the database table, as shown in Figure 10.1.

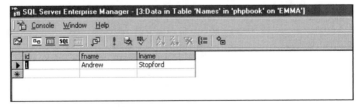

Figure 10.1   A sample record with the Names table of the phpbook sample database.

To finish setting up the database, I created a DSN (see Appendix A, "Creating an ODBC Connection") to the database called phpbook.

Using the ADO Connection and Recordset Objects

The ADO Connection and Recordset objects must be used together, as shown in Figure 10.2.

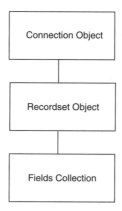

Figure 10.2 The ADO Connection and Recordset objects, as well as the Recordset Fields collection in the ADO object model.

The ADO Connection object is the first object that can be used in ADO. Its purpose is quite simply to allow you to connect to the database. Using the Connection object, you can connect via ODBC or directly.

The ADO Recordset object is what you use to work with data within a database table. Using the Recordset object, you can display fields within a table, as well as add, edit, and delete fields. Recordset objects hold a mirror copy of a database table that is directly linked to a table on a database. As you work through the fields in the Recordset object, you are also working through the fields in the database table that are linked to that Recordset object. However, ADO provides you with disconnected recordsets. You still use the Recordset object, but rather than staying connected to the database as you work through a table, you hold that table within the Recordset object, work with the table, and then update the table on the database when you are done.

Finally, you have the Fields collection of the Recordset object. It references each field within the database table.

Querying a Database Table Using ADO

Now that you have an idea of what the ADO objects are, let's put them to use by querying a database.

Querying Using ASP

Using ADO with a web scripting language is pretty straightforward. ADO is commonly used with ASP, so Listing 10.1 looks at how you can use it with ASP.

Listing 10.1 **ADO with ASP**

```
<%


'create ADO Connection object
set objcon = Server.CreateObject("ADODB.Connection")

dbcon = "DSN=phpbook;UID=sa;PWD=;"

'open database connection using the ADO Connection object
objcon.Open dbcon

     sqlquery = "SELECT * FROM Names"

     'run sql query against database using the ADO connection; returns an
     'ADO recordset
     set objrs = objcon.Execute(sqlquery)

          'cycle through database rows using the ADO recordset
          while not objrs.EOF


               'display database fields
               Response.write(objrs("fname") & " " & objrs("lname") & "<BR>")

               'move to next record in the ADO recordset
               objrs.MoveNext

          Wend


     objrs.close
     set objrs = nothing

objcon.close
set objcon = nothing


     %>
```

Querying Using PHP

Now that you have used ADO with ASP, Listing 10.2 looks at how you can use ADO with PHP.

Listing 10.2 **ADO with PHP**

```php
<?php

//create ADO Connection object
$objcon = new COM("ADODB.Connection");

$dbcon = "DSN=phpbook;UID=sa;PWD=;";

//open database connection using the ADO Connection object
$objcon->Open($dbcon);

    $sqlquery = "SELECT * FROM Names";

    //run sql query against database using the ADO connection; returns an
    //ADO recordset
    $objrs = $objcon->Execute($sqlquery);

    //note we have to look up the field directly
    $fname = $objrs->Fields(1);
    $lname = $objrs->Fields(2);

    //cycle through database rows using the ADO recordset
    while(!$objrs->EOF) {

            //display database fields
            //note we have to show the value directly
            print($fname->value . " " . $lname->value . "<BR>");

            //move to next record in the ADO recordset
            $objrs->MoveNext();

    }

    $objrs->close;

$objcon->close;

?>
```

First you create the ADO connection object using PHP's COM function:

```php
$objcon = new COM("ADODB.Connection");
```

Next you establish a connection that uses the DSN you set up previously:

```
$dbcon = "DSN=phpbook;UID=sa;PWD=;";

$objcon->Open($dbcon);
```

Then you set a connection string:

```
$dbcon = "DSN=phpbook;UID=sa;PWD=;";
```

The connection string always follows a fixed format of DSN name (such as phpbook), database username, and database password. If your database does not require a username or password, you should just leave these fields blank (such as `DSN=phpbook;UID=;PWD=;`).

Next you open a connection to the database using your connection string:

```
$objcon->Open($dbcon);
```

Then you define a SQL query that you will run against your database and use in the Execute function of the ADO Command object. This returns an ADO Recordset object, in which the SQL query's results are placed:

```
$sqlquery = "SELECT * FROM Names";

$objrs = $objcon->Execute($sqlquery);
```

To complete the query, you cycle through each record with the Recordset object and display each field within the record:

```
while(!$objrs->EOF) {

print($fname->value . " " . $lname->value . "<BR>");

$objrs->MoveNext();

}
```

Note that PHP does not support anonymous object dereferencing. In other words, you cannot reference an object by an object; you must first load the object and then reference it. Therefore, to display the value of the database field, you use this:

```
$fname = $objrs->Fields(1);
$fname->value
```

You first load the database field object into a variable:

```
$fname = $objrs->Fields(1);
```

You then reference the object:

```
$fname->value
```

In ASP, this equates to the following:

```
objrs.Fields("fname").Value
```

In PHP, you must reference the fields and then display their values. PHP cannot use named references in fields; it must reference them by their values. If you run the script, you can see the result of the ADO query, as shown in Figure 10.3.

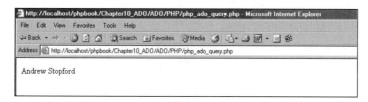

Figure 10.3   The result of running the ADO query in PHP.

Using Cursors and Locking

Cursors let you control how your Recordset object and the database table communicate with one another. You control how you use cursors using the CursorType (see Table 10.2) and CursorLocation (see Table 10.3) properties of the Recordset object.

Table 10.2   **CursorTypes**

Constant	Value	Description
adForwardOnly	0	Known as a forward-only cursor, this type of cursor lets you move through a database table one row at a time. If you intend to query the database table only once, this type of cursor offers the best type of performance.
adOpenKeySet	1	Known as a keyset cursor, this type of cursor is a fixed cursor, in which the data within the Recordset object stays current with the database table but does not show deletions or additions to the database table.
adOpenDynamic	2	Known as a dynamic cursor, this type of cursor always stays concurrent with the data in the database table. Dynamic cursors are not always supported by the database vendor's OLE DB implementation.

continues

Table 10.2 **Continued**

Constant	Value	Description
adOpenStatic	3	Known as a static cursor, this type of cursor is a fixed cursor that holds a copy of the database table. It does not stay current with the database table.

Table 10.3 **CursorLocations**

Constant	Value	Description
adUseNone	1	No cursor location
adUseServer	2	Server-side location
adUseClient	3	Client-side location

When you use disconnected recordsets, you set a client-side location, because the Recordset object holds an offline copy of the database table and thus must be held on the client side.

Locking lets you control how a database is accessed when you change it by updating, deleting, or adding. ADO supports the use of locking using the LockType property of the Recordset object. The LockType properties are listed in Table 10.4.

Table 10.4 **LockTypes**

Constant	Value	Description
adLockReadOnly	1	The database table is read-only and cannot be altered.
adLockPessimistic	2	The database table is locked by the database as soon as editing of the database starts and is unlocked when editing is finished.
adLockOptimistic	3	The database table is locked by the database during ADO Update actions and is unlocked when editing is finished.
adLockBatchOptimistic	4	The database table is locked by the database during ADO UpdateBatch actions and is unlocked when editing is finished.

Setting these properties requires a change in syntax. When you queried the database using ADO earlier in this chapter, you returned the Recordset object from the Execute method of the Connection object. This is known as an *implicit* recordset. To make use of cursors and locking, you must create an *explicit* recordset using the following in PHP:

```
$objrs = new COM("ADODB.Recordset");
```

In ASP, you use the following:

```
set objrs = Server.CreateObject("ADODB.Recordset")
```

> **Note**
>
> You can use explicit and implicit recordsets for querying when working with pages of database records, for example.

Because the Recordset object must be tied to the Connection object, you tie them together using the Open property of the Recordset object. Let's explore this further.

Adding to a Database Table Using ADO

We begin our exploration of the explicit Recordset object, cursors, and locking by looking at adding to a database using ADO.

Adding to a Database Using ASP

Like the previous example, let's first look at using ADO to insert data in a database using ASP (see Listing 10.3).

Listing 10.3 **Inserting Data Using ASP**

```
<%

'create ADO Connection object
set objcon = Server.CreateObject("ADODB.Connection")

'open database connection using the ADO Connection object
dbcon = "DSN=phpbook;UID=sa;PWD=emma;"

objcon.Open dbcon

    'update code

    'create ADO Connection object
    set objrs = Server.CreateObject("ADODB.Recordset")

    'set cursor and locktype
    objrs.CursorLocation = 2
    objrs.CursorType = 0
    objrs.LockType = 3
```

continues

Listing 10.3   **Continued**

```
'set what range of records the recordset will hold by querying
'the database
sqlquery = "SELECT * FROM Names"

'run query using the Connection object
objrs.Open sqlquery, objcon

'call the AddNew method of the Recordset object to prepare the
'recordset to add new data
objrs.AddNew

'new data to add
objrs("fname") = "Emma"
objrs("lname") = "Stopford"

'call Update method of Recordset object to update database table with
'new data
objrs.Update

'refresh data
objrs.Requery

objrs.Close

set objrs = nothing

'query code

sqlquery = "SELECT * FROM Names"

set objrs = objcon.Execute(sqlquery)

    while not objrs.EOF

        Response.write("Record added <BR><BR>")

        Response.write(objrs("fname") & " " & objrs("lname") & "<BR>")

    objrs.MoveNext

    Wend


    objrs.close
    set objrs = nothing

objcon.close
set objcon = nothing


%>
```

Adding to a Database Using PHP

Now that you know how to use ADO to insert data with ASP, Listing 10.4 shows you how to use ADO to insert data with PHP.

Listing 10.4 **Inserting Data Using PHP**

```php
<?php

//create ADO Connection object
$objcon = new COM("ADODB.Connection");

//open database connection using the ADO Connection object
$dbcon = "DSN=phpbook;UID=sa;PWD=emma;";

$objcon->Open($dbcon);

    //update code

    //create ADO Recordset object
    $objrs = new COM("ADODB.Recordset");

    //set cursor and locktype
    $objrs->CursorLocation = 2;
    $objrs->CursorType = 0;
    $objrs->LockType = 3;

    //set what range of records the recordset will hold by querying
    //the database
    $sqlquery = "SELECT * FROM Names";

    //run query using the Connection object
    $objrs->Open($sqlquery, $objcon);

    //call the AddNew method of the Recordset object to prepare the
    //recordset to add new data
    $objrs->AddNew();

    //new data to add
    $test1 = $objrs->Fields(1);
    $test2 = $objrs->Fields(2);

    $test1->value = "Emma";
    $test2->value = "Stopford";

    //call Update method of Recordset object to update database table with
    //new data
    $objrs->Update();

    //refresh data
    $objrs->Requery();
```

continues

Listing 10.4   **Continued**

```
    $objrs->Close();

    //query code

    print("Record added <BR><BR>");

    $sqlquery = "SELECT * FROM Names";

    $objrs = $objcon->Execute($sqlquery);

        while(!$objrs->EOF) {

            $test1 = $objrs->Fields(1);
            $test2 = $objrs->Fields(2);

            print($test1->value . " " . $test2->value . "<BR>");

            $objrs->MoveNext();

        }

    $objrs->close();

$objcon->close();

?>
```

In this listing, you first create a Connection object. Remember that recordsets when implicit or explicit are dependent on an associated Connection object.

```
$objcon = new COM("ADODB.Connection");
```

Next you open a connection to the database using your Connection object:

```
$dbcon = "DSN=phpbook;UID=sa;PWD=emma;";

$objcon->Open($dbcon);
```

Then you explicitly create a Recordset object:

```
$objrs = new COM("ADODB.Recordset");
```

Now that you have a Recordset object, you can set its cursor and locktype information:

```
$objrs->CursorLocation = 2;
$objrs->CursorType = 0;
$objrs->LockType = 3;
```

Using Tables 10.2 and 10.4, this translates to the following:

`CursorLocation` = Use server-side cursor

`CursorType` = Forward-only cursor

`Locktype` = Optimisic locking

Next, you tie the Connection object to the Recordset object and use a SQL query to specify which data within the database (such as which fields) the Recordset object can use. Your Recordset object now has a useable range of data, but remember that you must work within that range. In other words, you can update a record if the field is not specified in the SQL query.

```
$sqlquery = "SELECT * FROM Names";

$objrs->Open($sqlquery, $objcon);
```

To begin the add process, you must call the `AddNew` method of the Recordset object. This prepares the Recordset for the add process:

```
$objrs->AddNew();
```

Next you specify which database fields you are adding data to. As you saw in the query example, PHP does not support default collections, so you must specify the fields in full.

```
$test1 = $objrs->Fields(1);
$test2 = $objrs->Fields(2);
$test1->value = "Emma";
$test2->value = "Stopford";
$objrs->Update();
```

To complete the add process, you call the Update and Requery methods of the Recordset object. The Update method updates the data in the database with that in the Recordset object, and the Requery method then refreshes the data in the Recordset from the new contents of the database table.

```
$objrs->Requery();

$objrs->Close();
```

You can now make use of the Recordset object to query the database table. If you run the script shown in Listing 10.4, you should see that the data has been added to the database and is displayed, as shown in Figure 10.4.

Figure 10.4   Data added to the database using ADO and PHP.

Editing a Database Table

You can also use explicit Recordset objects to edit the data within a database. We will explore this using ASP and then follow up with PHP. Because you will change existing data in the database, I will assume that you have the database set up with the necessary data.

Editing Database Data Using ASP

As with the previous example, let's first look at using ADO to update data to a database using ASP (see Listing 10.5).

Listing 10.5   **Updating with ASP**

```
<%

'create ADO Connection object
set objcon = Server.CreateObject("ADODB.Connection")

'open database connection using the ADO Connection object
dbcon = "DSN=phpbook;UID=sa;PWD=emma;"

objcon.Open dbcon

    'update code

    'create ADO Connection object
    set objrs = Server.CreateObject("ADODB.Recordset")

    'set cursor and locktype
    objrs.CursorLocation = 2
    objrs.CursorType = 0
    objrs.LockType = 3

    'set what range of records the recordset will hold by querying
    'the database
    sqlquery = "SELECT * FROM Names WHERE fname = 'Andrew'"
```

```
        'run query using the Connection object
        objrs.Open sqlquery, objcon

        'new data to add
        objrs("fname") = "Elle"
        objrs("lname") = "Stopford"

        'call Update method of Recordset object to update database table with
        'new data
        objrs.Update

        'refresh data
        objrs.Requery

        objrs.Close

        set objrs = nothing

        'query code

        sqlquery = "SELECT * FROM Names"

        set objrs = objcon.Execute(sqlquery)

            while not objrs.EOF

                Response.write("Record edited <BR><BR>")

                Response.write(objrs("fname") & " " & objrs("lname") & "<BR>")

            objrs.MoveNext

            Wend


        objrs.close
        set objrs = nothing
objcon.close
set objcon = nothing


%>
```

Editing Database Data Using PHP

Now that you have seen how to use ADO to update data with ASP, Listing 10.6 shows you how to use ADO to update data with PHP.

Listing 10.6 **Updating with PHP**

```php
<?php

//create ADO Connection object
$objcon = new COM("ADODB.Connection");

//open database connection using the ADO Connection object
$dbcon = "DSN=phpbook;UID=sa;PWD=emma;";

$objcon->Open($dbcon);

    //update code

    //create ADO Recordset object
    $objrs = new COM("ADODB.Recordset");

    //set cursor and locktype
    $objrs->CursorLocation = 2;
    $objrs->CursorType = 0;
    $objrs->LockType = 3;

    //set what range of records the recordset will hold by querying
    //the database
    $sqlquery = "SELECT * FROM Names WHERE fname = 'Andrew'";

    //run query using the Connection object
    $objrs->Open($sqlquery, $objcon);

    //new data to add
    $test1 = $objrs->Fields(1);
    $test2 = $objrs->Fields(2);

    $test1->value  = "Elle";
    $test2->value = "Stopford";

    //call Update method of Recordset object to update database table with
    //new data
    $objrs->Update();

    //refresh data
    $objrs->Requery();

    $objrs->Close();

    //query code

    print("Record edited <BR><BR>");

    $sqlquery = "SELECT * FROM Names";
```

```
$objrs = $objcon->Execute($sqlquery);

    while(!$objrs->EOF) {

        $test1 = $objrs->Fields(1);
        $test2 = $objrs->Fields(2);

        print($test1->value . " " . $test2->value . "<BR>");

        $objrs->MoveNext();

    }

$objrs->close();

$objcon->close();

?>
```

If you think this code looks very similar to the add process code, you're correct. The only difference, in fact, is that you don't call the AddNew method of the Recordset object. If you run the script, you can see that the data in the database has been updated, as shown in Figure 10.5.

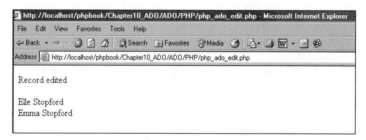

Figure 10.5   The results of editing data in the database using ADO and PHP.

Deleting from a Database Table

You can also delete records from a database table using ADO. Again we'll start with ASP and then move on to PHP.

Deleting Using ADO and ASP

Deleting with ASP is demonstrated in Listing 10.7.

Listing 10.7   **Deleting with ASP**

```
<%

'create ADO Connection object
set objcon = Server.CreateObject("ADODB.Connection")

'open database connection using the ADO Connection object
dbcon = "DSN=phpbook;UID=sa;PWD=emma;"

objcon.Open dbcon

    'create ADO Recordset object
    set objrs = Server.CreateObject("ADODB.Recordset")

    'set cursor and locktype
    objrs.CursorLocation = 2
    objrs.CursorType = 0
    objrs.LockType = 3

    'set range of data
    sqlquery = "SELECT * FROM Names WHERE lname = 'Stopford'"

    'run query using the Connection object
    objrs.Open sqlquery, objcon

    'loop through recordset
    while not objrs.EOF

        'delete records
        objrs.Delete
        objrs.MoveNext

    Wend

    objrs.Close

    set objrs = nothing

objcon.close
set objcon = nothing

Response.write("Record deleted")

%>
```

Deleting Using ADO and PHP

Deleting data using ADO with PHP is exemplified in Listing 10.8.

Listing 10.8 **Deleting Data from a Database**

```php
<?php

//create ADO Connection object
$objcon = new COM("ADODB.Connection");

//open database connection using the ADO Connection object
$dbcon = "DSN=phpbook;UID=sa;PWD=emma;";

$objcon->Open($dbcon);

    //create ADO Recordset object

    $objrs = new COM("ADODB.Recordset");

    //set cursor and locktype
    $objrs->CursorLocation = 2;
    $objrs->CursorType = 0;
    $objrs->LockType = 3;

    //set range of data
    $sqlquery = "SELECT * FROM Names where lname = 'Stopford'";

    //run query using the Connection object
    $objrs->Open($sqlquery, $objcon);

    //loop through recordset
    while(!$objrs->EOF) {

            //delete records
            $objrs->Delete();
            $objrs->MoveNext();

    }

    $objrs->Close();

$objcon->close();

print("Record deleted");

?>
```

Note that, as with the add and edit process examples, you create a Connection object to connect to the database and then create an explicit Recordset object that you tie to the Connection object. As before, you set the range of data within your recordset using a SQL query. To complete the delete process, you must first loop through each record in the table:

```php
while(!$objrs->EOF) {
```

You can then delete each record as you cycle through using the Delete method of your Recordset object:

```
$objrs->Delete();
```

Querying a Database Table Using Stored Procedures

Stored procedures are very commonly found in DBMSs such as Microsoft SQL Server and Oracle. Not only do they allow you to store and reuse SQL code in a central place, but they also make use of the DBMS's own language (a kind of extended SQL) for working with databases (for example, Microsoft SQL Servers use TSQL). Here we will look at using PHP with a simple query-based stored procedure.

Creating a Stored Procedure in Microsoft SQL Server

I created a simple procedure called `sp_LookUpNames` to query the Names table, as shown in Figure 10.6. This stored procedure uses the parameter `@lname` to look up the lname column in your table.

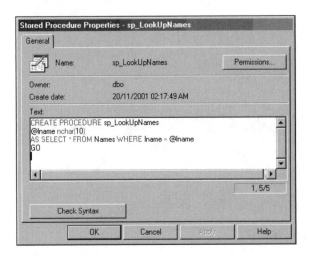

Figure 10.6   A simple stored procedure to query the database.

If you are interested in learning more about stored procedures, I recommend *Writing Stored Procedures for Microsoft SQL Server* by Matthew Shepker (Sams Publishing, 2000).

SQL Method

You can make use of your stored procedure using standard SQL, ADO, and PHP as shown in Listing 10.9.

Listing 10.9   **Making Use of Stored Procedures**

```php
<?php

$objcon = new COM("ADODB.Connection");

$dbcon = "DSN=phpbook;UID=sa;PWD=emma;";

$objcon->Open($dbcon);

    //use the SQL EXEC statement to make use of a stored procedure
    $sqlquery = "EXEC sp_LookUpNames Stopford";

    //all other code standard for query

    $objrs = $objcon->Execute($sqlquery);

    $fname = $objrs->Fields(1);
    $lname = $objrs->Fields(2);

    while(!$objrs->EOF) {

            print($fname->value . " " . $lname->value . "<BR>");
            $objrs->MoveNext();

    }

    $objrs->close;

$objcon->close;

?>
```

This code is similar to the query code used at the beginning of this chapter.
You can use implicit or explicit Recordset objects. You must reference database
fields in full. The major difference is that rather than type the SQL code
directly into the script, you call on the SQL code within your stored procedure using the SQL EXEC command:

```
$sqlquery = "EXEC sp_LookUpNames Stopford";
```

The EXEC command has the following syntax:

```
EXEC "stored procedure name" ["parameters"]
```

Using parameters with the EXEC command is optional. However, should you
need parameters, you can include as many as the stored procedure needs.

ADO Command Method

ADO gives you another method of using stored procedures in the form of the
ADO Command object (see Figure 10.7). The Command object is *not* solely

for use with stored procedures; it's for issuing commands against a database. As such, it can be used to query a database using standard SQL or stored procedures. This example, however, uses the Command object to query using stored procedures.

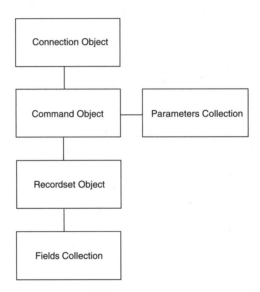

Figure 10.7 The ADO Command object and its parameter collection in the ADO object model.

When you use the Command object, things differ slightly from what you have used before. Specifically, the Command object is used directly with the Connection object. From the Connection object, you explicitly take the Recordset object. Before, you took the Recordset object explicitly from the Connection object. As the preceding EXEC SQL example shows, you can still use this method and stored procedures together. Using the Command object, however, gives you greater control over the stored procedure.

To summarize, using the Command object, you use the Command and Connection objects together to connect to and query the database. The Command object uses the Connection object for its database connection (via its ActiveConnection property). The Command object has a parameters collection that you link to the Command object. When you call the Execute method of the Command object, a Recordset object is implicitly returned, and you can navigate the database table as normal. Let's now look at the code for using the Command object.

Using the ADO Command Object and ASP

Listing 10.10 illustrates the use of the ADO Command object with ASP.

Listing 10.10 **ADO Command Object with ASP**

```
<%

set objcon = Server.CreateObject("ADODB.Connection")

dbcon = "DSN=phpbook;Database=phpbook;UID=sa;PWD=emma;"

objcon.Open dbcon

     'create ADO Command object
     set objcoman = Server.CreateObject("ADODB.Command")

     objcoman.CommandText = "sp_LookUpNames"
     objcoman.CommandType = 4

     'set connection to Connection object
     set objcoman.ActiveConnection = objcon

          'create parameter
          set objSpParam = objcoman.CreateParameter ("@lname", 130, 1, 10,
          ➥ "Stopford")

          'add parameter to Connection object
          objcoman.Parameters.Append objSpParam

          'run Execute method to get Recordset object
          set objrs = objcoman.Execute()

               while not objrs.EOF

                    Response.write(objrs("fname") & " " & objrs("lname") &
                    ➥ "<BR>")

                    objrs.MoveNext

               Wend

          objrs.close

          set objrs = nothing

          set objSpParam = nothing

     set objcoman = nothing
objcon.close
set objcon = nothing

%>
```

Using the ADO Command Object and PHP

Next let's look at how you can use ADO directly with PHP to use the stored procedure (see Listing 10.11).

Listing 10.11   **ADO Command Object with PHP**

```php
<?php

$objcon = new COM("ADODB.Connection");

$dbcon = "DSN=phpbook;Database=phpbook;UID=sa;PWD=emma;";

$objcon->Open($dbcon);

    //create ADO Command Object
    $objcoman = new COM("ADODB.Command");

    $objcoman->CommandText = "sp_LookUpNames";
    $objcoman->CommandType = 4;

    //set connection to Connection object
    $objcoman->ActiveConnection = $objcon;

        //create parameter
        $objSpParam = $objcoman->CreateParameter ("@lname", 130, 1, 10,
        ➥ "Stopford");

        //add parameter to Connection object
        $objcoman->Parameters->Append = $objSpParam;

        //run Execute method to get Recordset object
        $objrs = $objcoman->Execute();

        $fname = $objrs->Fields(1);
        $lname = $objrs->Fields(2);

            while(!$objrs->EOF) {

            //note we have to show the value directly
            print($fname->value . " " . $lname->value . "<BR>");
            $objrs->MoveNext();

            }

        $objrs->close();

$objcon->close();

?>
```

First you create the Connection object and open the database using a DSN connection:

```
$objcon = new COM("ADODB.Connection");

$dbcon = "DSN=phpbook;Database=phpbook;UID=sa;PWD=emma;";

$objcon->Open($dbcon);
```

Next you create the Command object:

```
$objcoman = new COM("ADODB.Command");
```

Next you set some properties of the Command object—namely, the CommandText and CommandType properties:

```
$objcoman->CommandText = "sp_LookUpNames";
$objcoman->CommandType = 4;
```

The CommandText property is the query you will run against the database (in this case, the stored procedure sp_LookUpNames). The CommandType property is the type of command you will run against the database (see Table 10.5).

Table 10.5 **CommandTypes**

Constant	Value	Description
adCmdText	1	Executes a SQL statement against a database table.
adCmdTable	2	Opens a database table.
adCmdTableDirect	512	Directly opens a database table. Some databases don't support this, so it's best to use the adCmdTable type instead.
adCmdStoredProcedure	4	Uses a stored procedure.
adCmdFile	256	Opens a recordset using data saved with the Recordset object's SAVE method. This type lets you use disconnected recordsets.
adCmdUnknown	8	The command type is unknown.

The CommandText and CommandType properties are directly linked. For example, if you wanted to open your database using standard SQL, you would use the following:

```
$objcoman->CommandText = "SELECT * FROM Names";
$objcoman->CommandType = 1;
```

You can shorten this to

```
$objcoman->CommandText = "Names";
$objcoman->CommandType = 2;
```

Next you set the ActiveConnection property of the Command object to that of the Connection object:

```
$objcoman->ActiveConnection = $objcon;
```

Next you create a parameter using the CreateParameter method of the Command object. Parameters are for use with stored procedures, so the CommandText and CommandType properties must be set accordingly.

```
$objSpParam = $objcoman->CreateParameter ("@lname", 130, 1, 10, "Stopford");
```

The CreateParameter property breaks down as follows:

```
CreateParameter(Parameter Name, Parameter Type, Parameter Direction,
➥ Parameter Size, Parameter Value)
```

The Parameter Name is the name of the stored procedure parameter. In the case of our stored procedure, it's @lname. The Parameter Type is the type of data that parameter will hold. This property is indicated by an ADO DataTypeEnum value (see Table 10.6).

Table 10.6   **ADO DataTypeEnum Values**

Constant	Value
adChar	129
adCurrency	6
adDate	7
adDouble	5
adNumeric	131
adWChar	130

Note

Table 10.6 is incomplete. It lists only the common types you're likely to use. A full list is available in the ADO documentation.

The Parameter Direction indicates how the type of the parameter is assigned: directly in your code or automatically by the database. The Parameter Size indicates the size of the value you are passing in the parameter. Make sure that this value is large enough to reflect the size of the value you are passing, or you will receive an error message. The Parameter Value is the value you will pass into the stored procedure to complete the SQL query within the stored procedure.

As soon as you have a completed parameter, you tie it to the Command object:

```
$objcoman->Parameters->Append = $objSpParam;
```

Finally, you call the Execute method of the Command object to implicitly receive the Recordset object:

```
$objrs = $objcoman->Execute();
```

ADODB and PHP

Now that we have looked at ADO and PHP, we will look at a database library for PHP called ADODB. ADODB was developed in PHP by John Lim. As he states in his *ADODB Manual* v1.12, "PHP's database access functions are not standardised. This creates a need for a database class library to hide the differences between the different databases (encapsulate the differences) so we can easily switch databases." Thus, ADODB provides an ADO-like syntax for connecting to the various PHP-supported databases.

When you use ADODB, remember that ADODB is not ADO. ADODB is a PHP library that wraps around PHP-supported databases, whereas ADO is a set of COM objects that wrap around OLE DB. Thus, it is for use with any database that supports OLE DB.

Installing ADODB

You can download ADODB from `http://php.weblogs.com/ADODB`. You can download a zip file for Windows or a tgz file for UNIX systems. All you need to do then is uncompress the file's contents into a directory that your code can access.

Using ADODB

To use the ADODB library, you use the library's functions and objects to query your database in same way as the ADO examples earlier in this chapter. Listing 10.12 shows you how to do this.

Listing 10.12 **Querying the Database**

```php
<?php

include('Files\adodb.inc.php');

$db = &ADONewConnection('ado');
```

continues

Listing 10.12 **Continued**

```
$myDSN="SERVER=emma;DATABASE=phpbook;";

$db->Connect($myDSN, "sa", "emma", 'SQLOLEDB');

    $objrs = &$db->Execute('select * from Names');

    while(!$objrs->EOF) {

        print $objrs->fields[1] . " " . $objrs->fields[2] . "<BR>";
        $objrs->MoveNext();
    }

$db->close();

?>
```

At first glance, you can see that this code is indeed similar to the ADO code
we developed earlier in this chapter. However, because the ADODB library
wraps around the standard PHP-supported database types, you are subject to
the same rules concerning database support on various platforms (for example,
ADO works only on Windows platforms, but ADODB works on all the supported PHP platforms) and the same rules concerning database library requirements (such as the Oracle client for connecting to Oracle databases). Let's look
at how the query code works.

You use ADODB simply by making use of the ADODB.inc.php file. This
file provides you with the necessary functions and objects of the ADODB
library. You therefore include this file in your PHP code every time you use
ADODB.

```
include('Files\adodb.inc.php');
```

Here the ADODB library is installed in a directory called Files, which is directly
below the directory the code is in. After you include the ADODB.inc.php file,
you need to define what kind of database type you will query:

```
$db = &ADONewConnection('ado');
```

Here you create an ADO database type. Thus, your database connection and
query are run through ADO. Next, you need to create the connection to the
database:

```
$myDSN="SERVER=emma;DATABASE=phpbook;";

$db->Connect($myDSN, "sa", "emma", 'SQLOLEDB');
```

Here you set up a new DSN connection within the Connection method. Next you run a SQL statement against the database using your connection:

```
$objrs = &$db->Execute('select * from Names');
```

Just like with ADO, calling the Execute method returns a Recordset object, and that lets you run through the records in the database table:

```
while(!$objrs->EOF) {

    print $objrs->fields[1] . " " . $objrs->fields[2] . "<BR>";
    $objrs->MoveNext();
}
```

As soon as the query is complete, you close the connection:

```
$db->close();
```

If you run the script, you can see that the database data is displayed, as shown in Figure 10.8.

Figure 10.8 Querying the database using the ADODB library and PHP.

Using the ADODB Library or ADO

The ADODB library not only provides you with ADO-like syntax for querying, updating, adding to, and deleting from PHP-supported databases, but it also implements a session back end for PHP 4 sessions, includes database debugging facilities, and handles database transactions.

However, the ADODB Library does not provide all the functionality of using ADO directly in code. For example, it has no wrapper code for creating recordsets unless they are created with a Connection object, and it has no support for ADO Parameter objects.

Summary

This chapter looked at what ADO is and how it has evolved. We then looked at using ADO in both ASP and PHP. We went on to look at how you can use ADO and stored procedures. We finished with a look at the ADODB function library and how it provides ADO-like syntax for use against PHP's supported databases.

11

PHP and Active Directory

THIS CHAPTER LOOKS AT WHAT AN X.500 directory is, what Active Directory is, and how you can use PHP to work with Active Directory.

What Is an X.500 Directory?

X.500 is an ITU-U standard that directory services can make use of. An X.500 directory service has a top-down tree-like structure called a *domain tree*. At the top of the tree is the root, and below that are forests and trees.

> **Note**
> The X.500 directory service standard is a set of directory service standards covering electronic directory services such as white pages, Knowbot, and Whois.

Figure 11.1 shows a sample tree. The root of the tree is Web Widgets Inc. It contains two forests—Web Widgets UK and Web Widgets US. In the Web Widgets UK forest are the trees Whitby and Stockport.

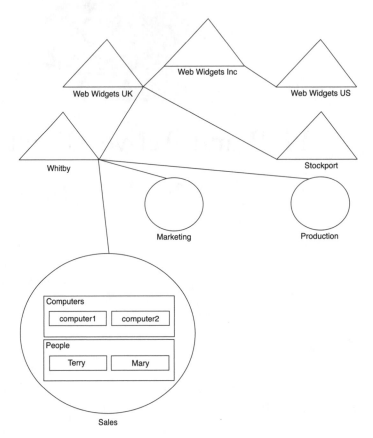

Figure 11.1   A sample X.500 directory structure.

An X.500 directory is then broken up into *organizational units* (OUs). As you can see in Figure 11.1, the Whitby tree contains three OUs—Sales, Marketing, and Production. An OU acts as a container. Within it are resources such as details on people (users), computers, printers, and so on. The kind of information an X.500 directory holds varies according to the software implementing the directory. For users, for example, you can store items such as name, last name, password, email address, postal address, telephone number, and department. X.500 directories are implemented in various types of software. Here is a partial list of various operating systems and applications:

- Windows 2000 Active Directory
- NetWare
- Netscape Directory Server
- IBM Lotus Notes

What Is LDAP?

Lightweight Directory Access Protocol (LDAP) is often confused with X.500 directories (X.500 directories are often called LDAP directories). LDAP is a way of administering (adding, editing, deleting) and querying resources within an X.500 directory (such as forests, trees, OUs, computers, printers, and people). All X.500 directories support LDAP. It's the most common way of working with items within an X.500 directory.

What Is Active Directory?

When an OS such as Windows 2000 uses X.500, it bases its domain model on the X.500 structure. Not only is the directory a resource directory (of users, computers, printers, and so on) and an information store of the resources (names, email addresses, and so on), but it is also the basis of the domain model. (Other OSs, such as NetWare, also use X.500 as the basis of their domain model.)

Microsoft calls its directory service Active Directory. In Active Directory, everything is based on DNS (Domain Name System). For example, in Figure 11.2 the root of Active Directory has two forests—webwidgetsinc.co.uk for the UK division of Web Widgets Inc. and webwidgetsinc.com for the U.S. division. The root never has a domain name, but forests under the root always do. Each tree under a forest is thus a subdomain. In Figure 11.2, under the webwidgetsinc.co.uk domain (and thus the Web Widgets Inc. UK forest), each tree is named whitby.webwidgetsinc.co.uk for the Whitby division and stockport.webwidgetsinc.co.uk for the Stockport division.

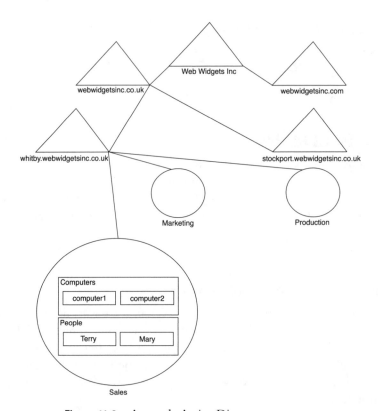

Figure 11.2 A sample Active Directory structure.

Active Directory domains do not need to know about one another to exist; they can be self-contained or can "trust" other domains if you want to access resources in that domain. Also, resources are allocated to users depending on user groups, and each user group has permissions. In this way you can control what a user can access in your domain.

For example, if Terry works in the Whitby Division, his domain is whitby.webwidgetsinc.co.uk. If Terry belongs to the Administrator group, when he logs into a computer in the whitby.webwidgetsinc.co.uk domain, he has Administrator permissions. However, he doesn't have those permissions in other domains such as stockport.webwidgetsinc.co.uk unless that domain is a trusted domain.

In Active Directory, resources can be allocated to domains (forests) and sub-domains (trees). However, the same rules for trusted domains still apply.

Active Directory differs from X.500 directories in the manner in which users are grouped. In most X.500 directories, users are grouped into OUs.

Although it is still possible to do that with Active Directory, users are still listed in the domain model under the subdomain to which they belong. This is because all users log into the subdomain to which they belong, so all users are listed by Active Directory under that subdomain and not under OUs within that subdomain. We will explore this further later in the chapter.

Active Directory Resource Properties

Every Active Directory resource has properties. As an X.500-compliant directory service, Active Directory uses X.500 directory syntax to indicate a resource's properties. If you have used an X.500 directory in the past, you might be familiar with some of these properties. For example, for a user resource, these can be items such as common name, first name, and last name.

Working with Active Directory

Active Directory gives you two means of administering and querying the Windows directory service: ADSI and LDAP. (These are scripting interfaces; the easiest method is to use the GUI tools that Windows 2000 provides.)

ADSI

Active Directory Services Interface (ADSI) is what Active Directory exposes to the outside world to let you administer and query Active Directory. ADSI is a set of APIs that software can use to make use of content with Active Directory. (The Windows 2000 GUI tools for working with Active Directory all use ADSI.)

LDAP Over ADSI

If ADSI is used as the interface to Active Directory, what about using LDAP as well? Active Directory does indeed support LDAP, both as an ADSI provider (that is, running LDAP over ADSI) and natively. However, using native LDAP support is not suitable for administrative tasks (such as adding and deleting resources), because Active Directory does not support this.

LDAP has its own syntax when dealing with X.500 resource properties. Because Active Directory is an X.500-compliant directory, you use the same LDAP syntax for accessing Active Directory resource properties as any other X.500-compliant directory (for example, cn = common name, sn = last name, and so on).

Using PHP with Active Directory

Now that you have an idea of what Active Directory is, let's look at how you can make use of content within it.

The following examples use a simple structure for Active Directory (see Figure 11.3). It contains one domain called a–coda.com (the root of Active Directory is not shown in Figure 11.3, but assume that one is present) and under it an OU called myplace.

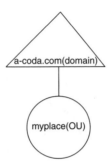

Figure 11.3   A sample Active Directory structure.

In the following examples you will build a simple web application to list members in, add members to, and delete members from both the a–coda.com domain and the myplace OU.

Using the PHP LDAP Extension

PHP has an LDAP extension that you can use to query X.500 directories.

Before you can make use of the LDAP extension, you must uncomment the following line in your PHP.ini file:

```
extension=php_ldap.dll
```

You can use the LDAP extension as shown in Listing 11.1.

Listing 11.1   **Using PHP's LDAP Extension to Query Active Directory**

```
<html>
<body>

<p><font size="4">Active Directory Members</font></p>
<table width="100%" border="1" cellspacing="0" cellpadding="0">

<?php
```

```php
//connect to LDAP server
if(!($ldap = ldap_connect("localhost"))) {
die ("ldap server can not be reached");
} else {

$oudc = "ou=myplace,dc=a-coda,dc=com";
$dn2 = "cn=terry, " . $oudc;
$password = "terry";

    //look up OU
    if (!($res = @ldap_bind($ldap, $dn2, $password))) {
    print(ldap_error($ldap) . "<BR>");
    die ("Could not bind to $dn");
    } else {

        //set search critia for OU
        $filter="cn=*";

                //search OU
                $sr=ldap_search($ldap,$oudc,$filter);
                if (!$sr) {
                        die("search failed\n");
                } else {

                    //get fields from search
                    $info = ldap_get_entries($ldap, $sr);

                    for ($i=0; $i<$info["count"]; $i++) {

                            //display fields
                        print("<TR");
                            print("<TD width=15%>" .
$info[$i]["cn"][0] .
➡ " " . $info[$i]["sn"][0] . "</TD>");
                            print("<TD width=85%>" .
$info[$i]["mail"][0] .
➡ "</TD>");

                            print("</TR>");


                    }

                }

            }
//disconnect from LDAP server
ldap_unbind($ldap);
}


?>

</table>
```

continues

Listing 11.1   **Continued**

```
</body>
</html>
```

Using the `ldap_connect` function, you first connect to the Windows 2000 server that is hosting your Active Directory. (In this case, it is localhost, but you can also use a computer's name or IP address if it is known in that Windows 2000 domain.)

```
if(!($ldap = ldap_connect("localhost"))) {
```

Next you look up the LDAP server's OU using the `ldap_bind` function:

```
$oudc = "ou=myplace,dc=a-coda,dc=com";
$dn2 = "cn=terry, " . $oudc;
$password = "terry";

if (!($res = @ldap_bind($ldap, $dn2, $password))) {
```

The `ldap_bind` method requires that you know the OU's name and which domain it is in. In most cases, the `ldap_bind` function also requires a username and password. However, this is optional. The `ldap_bind` function will still work if no username and password are required and you want to connect anonymously. Active Directory keeps users visible on a global level, but LDAP lets you query only the contents of an OU, not globally (whereas as ADSI does). For security reasons, Active Directory only lets you query an OU using a user contained within that OU. Your OU, myplace, has the user Terry, so you use his username and password.

Next, using the `ldap_search` function, you search the OU for the details you want to extract from the OU:

```
$filter="cn=*";
$sr=ldap_search($ldap,$oudc,$filter);
```

Here you look up the common name (cn) of all the users in the myplace OU.

Next, using the `ldap_get_entries` function, you obtain the results of the search:

```
$info = ldap_get_entries($ldap, $sr);
```

Next you iterate through the results and display them:

```
for ($i=0; $i<$info["count"]; $i++) {
print("<TR>");
print("<TD width=15%>" . $info[$i]["cn"][0] . " " . $info[$i]["sn"][0] .
"</TD>");
print("<TD width=85%>" . $info[$i]["mail"][0] . "</TD>");
```

```
print("</TR>");
}
```

The results are returned as an array. You iterate through the array using a for loop:

```
for ($i=0; $i<$info["count"]; $i++) {
```

As you iterate through the array, you display each value in the array in turn:

```
print("<TD width=15%" . $info[$i]["cn"][0] . " " . $info[$i]["sn"][0] .
"</TD>");
print("<TD width=85%>" . $info[$i]["mail"][0] . "</TD>");
```

To display each value in the array, you use the iterating value from the for loop (in this case, $i) and the Active Directory resource property you want to display. (Because you are using LDAP, you must use LDAP syntax to access Active Directory resources. In this case, this means cn, or common name, and mail, or the email address.) The results returned by ldap_get_entries are all Active Directory properties (even those that don't hold any data).

As soon as your loop is complete, use the ldap_unbind function to disconnect from the Active Directory to free up system resources:

```
ldap_unbind($ldap);
```

If you run the script, you can see the contents of the myplace OU, as shown in Figure 11.4. As I mentioned, all the Active Directory properties are returned by the ldap_get_entries method, even those that don't hold data. You can see this in Figure 11.4, where the terry vasey user has an email address but the Mary Vasey user does not.

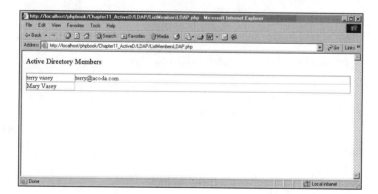

Figure 11.4   The results of the Active Directory myplace
OU returned using the PHP LDAP extension.

Using PHP, COM, and ADSI

To make use of ADSI in PHP, you must make use of COM. Here you will see how to use COM, ADSI, and PHP to query and administer Active Directory.

ADSI's API is wrapped in a COM object (called the Active DS Type Library); however, PHP's COM methods do not support many of the data types the ADSI COM object returns. To overcome this, you will create an ADSI wrapper COM object in Visual Basic to expose some of the functionality of the ADSI COM object and to provide return types that you can use in PHP.

The ADSI Wrapper COM Object

Open Visual Basic and create a new ActiveX DLL. I have named my ActiveX DLL chapter11 and my ClassModule AD, but you can use any names you want as long as you reflect them in your PHP code. You also need to add a reference to the Active DS type library, as shown in Figure 11.5.

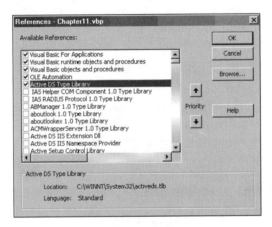

Figure 11.5   Adding a reference to the Active DS type library.

Using the ADSI Wrapper COM Object

The next stage is to add functions such as list, add, and delete to your ADSI COM wrapper object.

Using ADSI to List Global Users Within Active Directory

Remember that Active Directory sees users on a global scale and that using ADSI means access to this global scale. Therefore, this method lists all users, whether they are within an OU or not. Here you first add the function that does this to your COM object and then create the PHP code that makes use of this function.

You start by adding the function to your COM object. You add the following to your class's general declarations:

```
Public MemberCount As Variant
```

This is a global variable (it can be used across all your functions) that you use to keep track of how many users are in Active Directory. Next you add the function shown in Listing 11.2.

Listing 11.2 **A Function to List Members Via ADSI**

```
Public Function ListMembers(ByRef adserver As String)

    'array of users in AD
    Dim MemberArray(100)

    'AD type for AD user
    Dim User As IADsUser

    'AD type for AD container
    Dim Container As IADsContainer

    'variable of how many users in AD
    Dim Count

    'connect to AD
    Set Container = GetObject("WinNT://" & adserver)

        'select only users
        Container.Filter = Array("User")

        'iterate through users
        For Each User In Container
        'count users
        Count = Count + 1
        'add user's name to array
        MemberArray(Count) = User.Name

        Next

        'add count to global user count
        MemberCount = Count

        'return array
        ListMembers = MemberArray

    Set Container = Nothing

End Function
```

The function takes the name of a Windows 2000 server as its reference and returns all the global users within the Active Directory of that server as an array. To start, you declare some variables. Here you declare the size of the array you will use to store usernames and return from the function:

```
Dim MemberArray(100)
```

Next you declare an Active Directory reference, `IADsUser`. This variable type is a COM object associated with an Active Directory user:

```
Dim User As IADsUser
```

Next you declare an Active Directory reference, `IADsContainer`. This variable type is a COM object associated with an Active Directory reference:

```
Dim Container As IADsContainer
```

To complete your variable declaration, you declare the variable that counts how many users are in Active Directory:

```
Dim Count
```

Next you connect to Active Directory using the reference to the server you passed to the function:

```
Set Container = GetObject("WinNT://" & adserver)
```

Remember that Active Directory can contain many resources, including users, computers, and printers. Because you are only interested in users, you filter Active Directory to return only users:

```
Container.Filter = Array("User")
```

Next you iterate through each user in Active Directory:

```
For Each User In Container
```

As you iterate, you count each user. Using the count value as a reference, you add each name to the users array:

```
Count = Count + 1

MemberArray(Count) = User.Name
```

As soon as the array is populated, you add the value of your users count to the global users count and return the array to your function:

```
MemberCount = Count


ListMembers = MemberArray
```

To make use of the array your function returns, you must get at the value of your users count (because you used this value as the reference in your array). To do this, you use another function:

```
Public Function GetMemberCount()

    GetMemberCount = MemberCount

End Function
```

This simple function returns the global count value.

Using the ADSI COM wrapper object in PHP is very straightforward. You can use the two functions shown in Listing 11.3.

Listing 11.3 **PHP Code That Uses the ListMembers Function to List Members Within Active Directory**

```php
<?php

//load the ADSI COM wrapper object
$adsicom = new COM("chapter11.AD");

//users in Active Directory
$members = $adsicom->ListMembers("emma");

//count of users in Active Directory
$membercount = $adsicom->GetMemberCount();

//iterate through users in Active Directory
for ($i = 1; $i <= $membercount; $i++)
{
    print("<TR>");
    print("<TD width=15%>$members[$i]</TD>");
    print("<TD width=85%><A
HREF=ListMembers.php?delmem=yes&mem=$members[$i]>
➥Delete Member</A></TD>");
    print("</TR>");
}

?>
```

First you add a reference to your ADSI COM wrapper object:

```
$adsicom = new COM("chapter11.AD");
```

Next you call on your ListMembers function, adding a reference to the target Windows 2000 server (and thus Active Directory). You receive the array of users in Active Directory of that Windows 2000 server:

```
$members = $adsicom->ListMembers("emma");
```

Next you call on the `GetMemberCount` function to see how many users are in the array:

```
$membercount = $adsicom->GetMemberCount();
```

Then you iterate through your array using the value from the `GetMemberCount` function to discover when you have reached the final value in the array:

```
for ($i = 1; $i <= $membercount; $i++)
```

Finally, as you iterate through the array, you display each value within the array:

```
print("<TD width=15%>$members[$i]</TD>");
```

If you run this script, you see all the users within Active Directory, as shown in Figure 11.6. Using ADSI means that users are seen globally, so your users (Terry and Mary) from the myplace OU are displayed here.

Figure 11.6   Global users of Active Directory returned using the ADSI COM wrapper object and PHP.

Using ADSI to Delete Global Users Within Active Directory

You can also delete members from Active Directory. Listing 11.4 adds the function that does this to your COM object and then creates the PHP code that uses this function.

Listing 11.4   **A Function to Delete Members from Active Directory Using ADSI**

```
Public Function RemoveMemberADSI(ByRef adserver As String, ByRef usertogo
➥ As String)
    'AD type for AD container
    Dim Container As IADsContainer

    'connect to AD
    Set Container = GetObject("WinNT://" & adserver)

        'delete user
        Container.Delete "User", usertogo

        RemoveMemberADSI = True

    Set Container = Nothing

End Function
```

As a reference, this function takes the name of the Windows 2000 server (and thus Active Directory) and the name of the user to delete. Within the function, you first declare your variables—in this case, Active Directory COM type IADsContainer:

```
Dim Container As IADsContainer
```

Next you connect to Active Directory using the reference to the server you passed to the function:

```
Set Container = GetObject("WinNT://" & adserver)
```

Finally you delete the user, using the name you passed to the function:

```
Container.Delete "User", usertogo
```

In order for this function to work, the name you pass to the function and the name listed in Active Directory must match. A possible upgrade to this function that you could make is to search for the user, confirm that the user exists, and then delete the user (returning an error message if the user cannot be found).

To use this function, you add a link to allow users to be deleted:

```
print("<TD width=85%><A HREF=ListMembers.php?delmem=yes&mem=$members[$i]>
➥Delete Member</A></TD>");
```

Here you link back to your PHP script, passing a flag (to indicate you want to delete) and the name of the user to delete. In your PHP, you see if the delete flag has been raised. You call the delete function of the ADSI COM wrapper if it has:

```
$adsicom = new COM("chapter11.AD");
if ($_REQUEST['delmem'] == "yes") {

        $adsicom->RemoveMemberADSI("emma", $mem);

}
```

In your script, you first load your ADSI COM wrapper object:

```
$adsicom = new COM("chapter11.AD");
```

Next you check to see if the delete flag has been raised:

```
if ($_REQUEST['delmem'] == "yes") {
```

If it has, you call the RemoveMemberADSI function to delete the user. You must also pass the user's name to the function:

```
$adsicom->RemoveMemberADSI("emma", $mem);
```

If you look back at the running script (refer to Figure 11.6), you can see that as usernames are displayed, so is the option to delete the user. If you click the delete link, the user is deleted from Active Directory. (Note that Windows 2000 protects some users from deletion.) A possible upgrade to the script would be to catch such messages. (As the script currently stands, it displays an ugly error message.)

Using ADSI to Add Global Users to Active Directory

The final ADSI function to add to your ADSI COM wrapper is the capability to add users to Active Directory. Here you use a simple HTML form to post user details to the PHP script. Next you add the function that adds the user in your COM object and then creates the PHP code that joins the HTML to form the COM object.

The HTML form you will use is a simple form that adds the user's username, password, and full name. It is shown in Listing 11.5.

Listing 11.5 **An HTML Form to Add Users to Active Directory**

```
<html>
<head>
<title>Untitled Document</title>
<meta http-equiv="Content-Type" content="text/html; charset=iso-8859-1">
</head>
```

```
<body bgcolor="#FFFFFF" text="#000000">
<p><font size="4">Add an Active Directory Member </font></p>
<form method="post" action="ListMembers.php?postdata=yes">
  <table width="100%" border="0" cellspacing="0" cellpadding="0">
    <tr>
      <td width="10%">User Name</td>
      <td width="90%">
        <input type="text" name="uname">
      </td>
    </tr>
    <tr>
      <td width="10%">Password</td>
      <td width="90%">
        <input type="password" name="pword">
      </td>
    </tr>
    <tr>
      <td width="10%">Full Name</td>
      <td width="90%">
        <input type="text" name="fname">
      </td>
    </tr>
  </table>
  <p>
    <input type="submit" name="Submit" value="Submit">
    <input type="reset" value="Reset">
  </p>
</form>
</body>
</html>
```

You post the form values back to your PHP script, as well as a flag to indicate
that you are adding users:

```
<form method="post" action="ListMembers.php?postdata=yes">
```

Now that your HTML form has been created, you can create a function in
your COM object to add the users to Active Directory. See Listing 11.6.

Listing 11.6 A Function to Add Users to Active Directory Using ADSI

```
Public Function AddMemberADSI(ByRef adserver As String, ByRef uname As
➥ String, ByRef pword As String, ByRef fname As String)

    'AD type for AD user
    Dim User As IADsUser

    'AD type for AD container
    Dim Container As IADsContainer
```

continues

Listing 11.6 **Continued**

```
'connect to AD
Set Container = GetObject("WinNT://" & adserver)

'create user
Set User = Container.Create("User", uname)

    'set password
    User.SetPassword (pword)

    'set full name
    User.FullName = fname

    'save user to AD
    User.SetInfo

    AddMemberADSI = True

Set User = Nothing
Set Container = Nothing

End Function
```

As a reference, this function takes the name of the Windows 2000 server (and thus Active Directory), the username, the user's password, and the user's full name. To start, you declare some variables. Here you declare an Active Directory reference, IADsUser. This variable type is a COM object associated with an Active Directory user.

```
Dim User As IADsUser
```

Next you declare an Active Directory reference, IADsContainer. This type is a COM object associated with an Active Directory reference:

```
Dim Container As IADsContainer
```

Next you connect to Active Directory using the reference to the server you passed to the function:

```
Set Container = GetObject("WinNT://" & adserver)
```

Next you create your user using the reference to the username you passed to the function:

```
Set User = Container.Create("User", uname)
```

The Container.Create method can create various Active Directory objects, including computers and users. Thus, you must explicitly declare that you are creating a user when using this method.

Next you set the user's password and full name using the references you passed to the function:

```
User.SetPassword (pword)

User.FullName = fname
```

Finally, you save the user to the Active Directory:

```
User.SetInfo
```

To tie together your HTML form and the `AddMemberADSI` function of your ADSI COM wrapper object, you modify your PHP script as follows:

```
if($_REQUEST['postdata'] == "yes") {

    $adsicom = new COM("chapter11.AD");
    $adsicom->AddMemberADSI("emma", $uname, $pword, $fname);

}
```

You first see if the HTML form was posted to the PHP script by catching the flag from your HTML form:

```
if($_REQUEST['postdata'] == "yes") {
```

If the HTML form was posted to your script, you first load your ADSI COM wrapper object:

```
$adsicom = new COM("chapter11.AD");
```

Finally, you call your `AddMemberADSI` function, passing the username, password, and full name values from your HTML form:

```
$adsicom->AddMemberADSI("emma", $uname, $pword, $fname);
```

If you load the HTML form and add a new user, you see that a new user has been added.

Using PHP, COM, and LDAP Over ADSI

As I mentioned, you can also use LDAP with ADSI. To do this, you use the ADSI COM wrapper object once more, but you add new functions to list and add and delete users via LDAP over ADSI.

Using LDAP Over ADSI to List Users Within an Active Directory OU

Remember that with LDAP, you see only users with a specified OU, so you must specify the OU in the script. Note that I have hard-coded the OU login username and password into the script. Normally you need some kind of login and password form. (Also remember that you should use secure logins utilizing SSL.)

Visual Basic Code

To the general declarations of your class, you add the following:

```
Public LDAPMemberCount As Variant
```

This is a global variable (usable across all your functions) that you use to keep track of how many users are in the OU. Next you add the function shown in Listing 11.7.

Listing 11.7 **A Function to List Members of an OU Within Active Directory Using LDAP Over ADSI**

```
Public Function ListMembersLDAP(ByRef host As String, ByRef parent As String,
➥ ByRef ounit As String, ByRef LDAPLogInName As String,
➥ ByRef LDAPLogInPassword As String)

    'variable of how many users in OU
    Dim LDAPMemberArray(100)

    'AD type for AD container
    Dim Container2 As IADsContainer

    'AD type for LDAP
    Dim dso As IADsOpenDSObject

    Dim parent_length, parent_one, parent_two, ldap_connect, child

    'number of characters in parent variable e.g. a-coda.com = 10
    parent_length = Len(parent)

    'split front portion of parent variable e.g. a-coda
    parent_one = Left(parent, parent_length - 4)

    'split back portion of parent variable e.g. com
    parent_two = Right(parent, 3)

    'make up LDAP connection string using variables passed to function and
    'parent one and parent two
    ldap_connect = "LDAP://" & host & "/ou=" & ounit & ",dc=" & parent_one &
➥ ",dc=" & parent_two

    'create ADSI LDAP object
    Set dso = GetObject("LDAP:")

    'connect to AD using LDAP
    Set Container2 = dso.OpenDSObject(ldap_connect, LDAPLogInName,
➥ LDAPLogInPassword, 0)

        'filter only users
        Container2.Filter = "User"
```

```
        'iterate through users
        For Each child In Container2

            'count users
            LDAPMemberCount = LDAPMemberCount + 1

            'add users to array
            LDAPMemberArray(LDAPMemberCount) = Mid(child.Name, 4,
Len(child.Name))
        Next

    'return array
    ListMembersLDAP = LDAPMemberArray

End Function
```

The function takes the name of a Windows 2000 server (and thus Active Directory), the domain name, the OU, and the OU login username and password as its reference. It then returns all the users within the specified OU of that server as an array. To start, you declare some variables. Here you declare the size of the array you will use to store usernames and return from the function:

```
Dim LDAPMemberArray(100)
```

Next you declare an Active Directory reference, IADsContainer. This variable type is a COM object associated with an Active Directory reference:

```
Dim Container2 As IADsContainer
```

Next you declare an Active Directory reference, IADsOpenDSObject. This variable type is a COM object associated with an LDAP object:

```
Dim dso As IADsOpenDSObject
```

Next you split the domain name into two component parts (for example, a-coda.com becomes a-coda and com):

```
parent_length = Len(parent)

parent_one = Left(parent, parent_length - 4)
parent_two = Right(parent, 3)
```

Next you create the LDAP connection string:

```
ldap_connect = "LDAP://" & host & "/ou=" & ounit & ",dc=" & parent_one &
",dc="
➡ & parent_two
```

Next you create an LDAP object and, using that object and the connection string, connect to Active Directory:

```
Set dso = GetObject("LDAP:")

Set Container2 = dso.OpenDSObject(ldap_connect, LDAPLogInName,
LDAPLogInPassword
```

Remember that Active Directory can contain many resources, from users to computers and printers. Because you are only interested in users, you filter Active Directory to return users only:

```
Container2.Filter = "User"
```

Next you iterate through each user in Active Directory:

```
For Each child In Container2
```

As you iterate, you count each user. Using the global count value as a reference, you add each name to your users array:

```
LDAPMemberCount = LDAPMemberCount + 1

LDAPMemberArray(LDAPMemberCount) = Mid(child.Name, 4, Len(child.Name))
```

After your array is populated, you return the array to your function:

```
ListMembersLDAP = LDAPMemberArray
```

To make use of the array your function returns, you must get at the value of the users count (because you used this value as the reference in your array). To do this, you use another function:

```
Public Function GetLDAPMemberCount()

    GetLDAPMemberCount = LDAPMemberCount

End Function
```

This simple function returns the global count value.

PHP Code

Using the ADSI COM wrapper object in PHP is very straightforward. You can use the two functions shown in Listing 11.8.

Listing 11.8 **PHP Code That Uses the _ListMembersLDAP_ Function to List Members of an OU Within Active Directory**

```
<?
//no OU found
if ($_REQUEST['ou'] == "") {
print "Error: No organizational unit";
} else {
```

```
    //load ADSI COM wrapper object
    $adsicom = new COM("chapter11.AD");

    //get users in OU
    $members = $adsicom->ListMembersLDAP("emma", "acoda.com", $ou, "terry",
    ➥ "terry");

    //get count of users in OU
    $membercount = $adsicom->GetLDAPMemberCount();

    //iterate through users
    for ($i = 1; $i <= $membercount; $i++)
    {
        print("<TR>");
        print("<TD width=15%>$members[$i]</TD>");
        print("<TD width=85%>
➥<A HREF=ListMembers_LDAP.php?ou=$ou&delmem=yes&mem=$members[$i]>
➥Delete Member</A></TD>");
        print("</TR>");
    }

}
?>
```

First you check to see if an OU has been specified in the URL to your PHP
script:

```
if ($_REQUEST['ou'] == "") {
```

To ensure that your ADSI COM wrapper object does not raise any errors
if no OU is specified, you instead display an error message, as shown in
Figure 11.7.

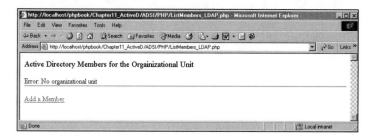

Figure 11.7   Error message diplayed if no OU is specified.

Accessing an OU with the ADSI COM Wrapper Object with No OU Specified

If you do specify an OU, your script continues. Here you first load the ADSI COM wrapper object:

```
$adsicom = new COM("chapter11.AD");
```

Next you call the `ListMembersLDAP` function, passing the Windows 2000 (and hence Active Directory) server name, the domain name, the OU (remember that you pass it in your script's URL), and the username and password for a user within the specified OU. From this function, you get back the array of users in the specified OU.

```
$members = $adsicom->ListMembersLDAP("emma", "acoda.com", $ou, "terry",
"terry");
```

Next you call the `GetMemberCount` function so that you know how many users are in the array:

```
$membercount = $adsicom->GetLDAPMemberCount();
```

Next you iterate through the array using the value from the `GetMemberCount` function to discover when you have reached the final value in the array:

```
for ($i = 1; $i <= $membercount; $i++)
```

Finally, as you iterate through the array, you display each value in the array:

```
print("<TD width=15%>$members[$i]</TD>");
```

If you run this script using the myplace OU you used earlier in the chapter, you will see all the users in that OU, as shown in Figure 11.8.

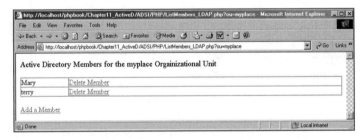

Figure 11.8 Accessing an OU with the ADSI COM wrapper object.

Using LDAP Over ADSI to Delete Users Within an Active Directory OU

You can delete members from an Active Directory OU as described in the following sections.

Visual Basic Code

The Visual Basic code is shown in Listing 11.9.

Listing 11.9 **A Function to Delete Users Within an Active Directory OU Using LDAP Over ADSI**

```
Public Function RemoveMemberLDAP(ByRef host As String, ByRef parent As
➥ String, ByRef ounit As String, ByRef LDAPLogInName As String,
➥ ByRef LDAPLogInPassword As String, ByRef usertogo As String)

    'AD type for AD container
    Dim Container2 As IADsContainer

    'AD type for LDAP
    Dim dso As IADsOpenDSObject
    Dim parent_length, parent_one, parent_two, ldap_connect, DelUser

    'number of characters in parent variable e.g. a-coda.com = 10
    parent_length = Len(parent)

    'split front portion of parent variable e.g. a-coda
    parent_one = Left(parent, parent_length - 4)

    'split back portion of parent variable e.g. com
    parent_two = Right(parent, 3)

    'make up LDAP connection string using variables passed to function and
    'parent one and parent two
    ldap_connect = "LDAP://" & host & "/ou=" & ounit & ",dc=" & parent_one &
    ➥ ",dc=" & parent_two

    'create ADSI LDAP object
    Set dso = GetObject("LDAP:")

    'connect to AD using LDAP
    Set Container2 = dso.OpenDSObject(ldap_connect, LDAPLogInName,
    LDAPLogInPassword, 0)

        'format user string
        DelUser = "CN=" & usertogo

        'delete user
        Container2.Delete "User", DelUser

        RemoveMemberLDAP = True

    Set dso = Nothing
    Set Container2 = Nothing

End Function
```

The function takes the name of a Windows 2000 server (and thus Active Directory), the domain name, the OU, the OU login username and password, and the username that you will delete from the OU as its reference. It then deletes the specified user from the specified OU. To start, you declare some variables. Here you declare an Active Directory reference, `IADsContainer`. This variable type is a COM object associated with an Active Directory reference.

```
Dim Container2 As IADsContainer
```

Next you declare an Active Directory reference, `IADsOpenDSObject`. This variable type is a COM object associated with an LDAP object.

```
Dim dso As IADsOpenDSObject
```

Next you split the domain name into two component parts (for example, a-coda.com becomes a-coda and com):

```
parent_length = Len(parent)

parent_one = Left(parent, parent_length - 4)

parent_two = Right(parent, 3)
```

Note that for four-letter top levels (such as a-coda.co.uk), your code is as follows:

```
parent_length = Len(parent)

parent_one = Left(parent, parent_length - 4)

parent_two = Right(parent, 4)
```

Next you create the LDAP connection string:

```
ldap_connect = "LDAP://" & host & "/ou=" & ounit & ",dc=" & parent_one &
➥ ",dc=" & parent_two
```

Next you create an LDAP object. You use that object and the connection string to connect to Active Directory:

```
Set dso = GetObject("LDAP:")

Set Container2 = dso.OpenDSObject(ldap_connect, LDAPLogInName,
LDAPLogInPassword
```

Next you format the username so that it follows LDAP conventions to indicate that the username is a user's common name:

```
DelUser = "CN=" & usertogo
```

Finally, you delete the user, using the formatted username:

```
Container2.Delete "User", DelUser
```

Note that for this function to work, the name you pass to the function and the name listed within the OU must match. A possible upgrade to this function that you could make is to first search for the user, confirm that the user exists (returning an error message if he doesn't), and then delete the user.

PHP Code

To use this function, you add a link to allow users to be deleted when they are listed:

```
print("<TD width=85%>
➡<A HREF=ListMembers_LDAP.php?ou=$ou&delmem=yes&mem=$members[$i]>
➡Delete Member</A></TD>");
```

Here you link back to your PHP script, passing a flag (to indicate that you want to delete) and the name of the user to delete. In your PHP, you see if the delete flag has been raised. You call the delete function of the ADSI COM wrapper if it has.

```
$adsicom = new COM("chapter11.AD");
if ($_REQUEST['delmem'] == "yes") {

$adsicom->RemoveMemberLDAP("emma", "acoda.com", $ou, "terry", "terry", $mem);
}
```

In the script, you first load your ADSI COM wrapper object:

```
$adsicom = new COM("chapter11.AD");
```

Next you check to see if the delete flag has been raised:

```
if ($_REQUEST['delmem'] == "yes") {
```

If it has, you call the RemoveMemberLDAP function to delete the user. You must also pass the Windows 2000 (and hence Active Directory) server name, the domain name, the OU (remember that you pass this in your script's URL), the username and password for a user in the specified OU, and the username of the user you want to delete:

```
$adsicom->RemoveMemberLDAP("emma", "acoda.com", $ou, "terry", "terry", $mem);
```

If you look at the running script (refer to Figure 11.8), you can see that as the usernames are displayed, so too is the option to delete the user. If you click the delete link, the user is deleted from the specified OU. (Note that Windows 2000 protects some users from deletion.) A possible upgrade to the script would be to catch such messages. (As the script currently stands, it displays an ugly error message.)

Using LDAP Over ADSI to Add Users to an Active Directory OU

The final LDAP-over-ADSI function to add to your ADSI COM wrapper is the capability to add users to an Active Directory OU. Here you use a simple HTML form to post user details to the PHP script, add the user, and display the user in your OU.

HTML Code

The HTML form you will use is a simple form that adds the user's first name, last name, and password. It is shown in Listing 11.10.

Listing 11.10   **An HTML Form to Add Users to an Active Directory OU**

```html
<html>
<head>
<title>Untitled Document</title>
<meta http-equiv="Content-Type" content="text/html; charset=iso-8859-1">
</head>

<body bgcolor="#FFFFFF" text="#000000">
<p><font size="4">Add an Active Directory Member </font></p>
<form name="form1" method="post"
➥ action="ListMembers_LDAP.php?postdata=yes&ou=<?php print $ou ?>">
  <table width="100%" border="0" cellspacing="0" cellpadding="0">
    <tr>
      <td width="10%">First Name</td>
      <td width="90%">
        <input type="text" name="fname">
      </td>
    </tr>
    <tr>
      <td width="10%">Last Name</td>
      <td width="90%">
        <input type="text" name="lname">
      </td>
    </tr>
      <tr>
      <td width="10%">Password</td>
      <td width="90%">
        <input type="password" name="pword">
      </td>
    </tr>
  </table>
  <p>
    <input type="submit" name="Submit" value="Submit">
    <input type="reset" name="Submit2" value="Reset">
  </p>
</form>
<p>  </p>
</body>
</html>
```

The form also needs to maintain that the name of your OU is passed back to your script. If it isn't, your script returns the OU not found error message. To do this, I have wrapped the HTML into a PHP script and used a simple PHP script to take the OU from the form's URL and add it to the form's `action` command:

```
<form name="form1" method="post"
➥ action="ListMembers_LDAP.php?postdata=yes&ou=<?php print $ou ?>">
```

Visual Basic Code

After your HTML is created, you can create the function with your COM object to add users to an Active Directory OU, as shown in Listing 11.11.

Listing 11.11 **A Function to Add Users to an Active Directory OU Using LDAP Over ADSI**

```
Public Function AddMemberLDAP(ByRef host As String, ByRef parent As String,
➥ ByRef ounit As String, ByRef LDAPLogInName As String,
➥ ByRef LDAPLogInPassword As String, ByRef Name As Variant,
➥ ByRef LastName As Variant, ByRef Password As String)

    'AD type for AD container
    Dim Container2 As IADsContainer

    'AD type for LDAP
    Dim dso As IADsOpenDSObject
    Dim parent_length, parent_one, parent_two, ldap_connect, DelUser

    'number of characters in parent variable e.g. a-coda.com = 10
    parent_length = Len(parent)

    'split front portion of parent variable e.g. a-coda
    parent_one = Left(parent, parent_length - 4)

    'split back portion of parent variable e.g. com
    parent_two = Right(parent, 3)

    'make up LDAP connection string using variables passed to function and
    'parent one and parent two
    ldap_connect = "LDAP://" & host & "/ou=" & ounit & ",dc=" & parent_one &
➥ ",dc=" & parent_two

    'create ADSI LDAP object
    Set dso = GetObject("LDAP:")

    'connect to AD using LDAP
    Set Container2 = dso.OpenDSObject(ldap_connect, LDAPLogInName,
    LDAPLogInPassword, 0)

        'create user
        Set usr = Container2.Create("user", "cn=" & Name)

        'add user information
        usr.Put "samAccountName", Name & LastName
```

continues

Listing 11.11   **Continued**

```
            usr.Put "givenName", Name
            usr.Put "sn", LastName
            usr.Put "displayName", Name
            usr.Put "userPrincipalName", Name
            'save user to AD
            usr.SetInfo

            'set user password
            usr.SetPassword Password
            'enable user
            usr.AccountDisabled = False
            'update user to AD
            usr.SetInfo

        Set dso = Nothing
        Set Container2 = Nothing

    AddMemberLDAP = True

    End Function
```

The function takes the name of a Windows 2000 server (and thus Active Directory), the domain name, the OU, and the OU login username and password, as well as the first name, last name, and password of the user you will add. It then adds the specified user to the specified OU. To start, you declare some variables. Here you declare an Active Directory reference, `IADsContainer`. This variable type is a COM object associated with an Active Directory reference:

```
    Dim Container2 As IADsContainer
```

Next you declare an Active Directory reference, `IADsOpenDSObject`. This variable type is a COM object associated with an LDAP object:

```
    Dim dso As IADsOpenDSObject
```

Next you split the domain name into two component parts (for example, a-coda.com becomes a-coda and com).

```
    parent_length = Len(parent)

    parent_one = Left(parent, parent_length - 4)

    parent_two = Right(parent, 3)
```

Note that for four-letter top levels (such as a-coda.co.uk), your code is as follows:

```
    parent_length = Len(parent)

    parent_one = Left(parent, parent_length - 4)

    parent_two = Right(parent, 4)
```

Next you create the LDAP connection string:

```
ldap_connect = "LDAP://" & host & "/ou=" & ounit & ",dc=" & parent_one &
➥ ",dc=" & parent_two
```

Next you create an LDAP object. You use that object and the connection string to connect to Active Directory:

```
Set dso = GetObject("LDAP:")

Set Container2 = dso.OpenDSObject(ldap_connect, LDAPLogInName,
LDAPLogInPassword
```

Next you create the user:

```
Set usr = Container2.Create("user", "cn=" & Name)
```

Next you add some resource properties to the user and save the user to Active Directory:

```
usr.Put "samAccountName", Name & LastName
usr.Put "givenName", Name
usr.Put "sn", LastName
usr.Put "displayName", Name
usr.Put "userPrincipalName", Name
usr.SetInfo
```

ADSI reflects resource properties in its IADsUser COM object (which you create when you use the create method of an IADsContainer COM object—in this case, Container2.Create) differently from the way in which Active Directory does. The LDAP syntax mapping to resource properties and ADSI mapping are different. This means that when you use the IADsUser COM object, you must be aware of this change of syntax. (For further information, see http://msdn.microsoft.com/library/en-us/netdir/adsi/mapping_between_iadsuser_properties_and_active_directory_properties.asp.)

Next you set the password for the user:

```
usr.SetPassword Password
```

You must create and save the user to Active Directory *before* you create the password. If you try to set the password before saving the user, you will receive an error.

Next you enable the user:

```
usr.AccountDisabled = False
```

By default, users you create using LDAP over ADSI are disabled. As was done here, you can enable the new user in your code or by using Active Directory GUI tools.

Finally, you save the new information for your user to Active Directory:

```
usr.SetInfo
```

PHP Code

To tie together your HTML form and the `AddMemberLDAP` function of your ADSI COM wrapper object, you modify your PHP script as shown in Listing 11.12.

Listing 11.12 **PHP Code That Uses the HTML Form and the** *AddMemberLDAP* **Function to Add Users to an Active Directory OU**

```
//if add user flag raised
if($_REQUEST['postdata'] == "yes") {

//load ADSI COM wrapper object
$adsicom = new COM("chapter11.AD");

//add new user to OU
$adsicom->AddMemberLDAP("emma", "acoda.com", $ou, "terry", "terry", $fname,
➥ $lname, $pword);

}
```

Here you see if the HTML form was posted to the PHP script by catching the flag from your HTML form:

```
if($_REQUEST['postdata'] == "yes") {
```

If the HTML form was posted to your script, you first load your ADSI COM wrapper object:

```
$adsicom = new COM("chapter11.AD");
```

Finally, you call your `AddMemberLDAP` function, passing the name of a Windows 2000 server (and thus Active Directory), the domain name, the OU, and the OU login username and password, as well as the first name, last name, and password values from your HTML form.

```
$adsicom->AddMemberLDAP("emma", "acoda.com", $ou, "terry", "terry", $fname,
➥ $lname, $pword);
```

If you load the HTML form and add a new user, you will see that a new user has been added.

Summary

This chapter covered the concepts of an X.500 directory service, Active Directory, LDAP, and ADSI and how they relate. We also looked at how you can use PHP's LDAP extension to access Active Directory and how you can use ADSI and COM with PHP to access and administer Active Directory.

IV

Appendices

Creating an ODBC Connection

Tʜɪs ᴀᴘᴘᴇɴᴅɪx sʜows you ʜow ᴛo ᴄʀᴇᴀᴛᴇ an ODBC connection on various Windows platforms. The procedures are slightly different in the first steps, as described in "Section 1." "Section 2" walks you through the rest of the procedure.

Section 1

We start with Windows 9x and then move on to cover Windows 2000.

Windows 9x

Follow these steps to get started:

1. Select Start, Settings, Control Panel.
2. Click ODBC Data Sources (32 bit). You see the dialog box shown in Figure A.1.

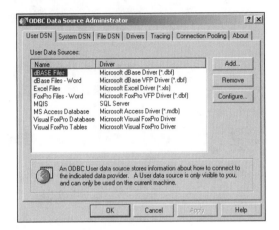

Figure A.1   The ODBC Data Source Administrator dialog box.

3. Continue with "Section 2."

Windows 2000

Follow these steps to get started:

1. Select Start, Settings, Control Panel, Administrative Tools, or select Start, Programs, Administrative Tools.

2. Click Data Sources (ODBC). You see the dialog box shown in Figure A.1.

3. Continue with "Section 2."

Section 2

The following steps apply to both Windows 9x and 2000:

1. Click the System DSN tab.

2. Click the Add button. You see the Create New Data Source dialog box, shown in Figure A.2.

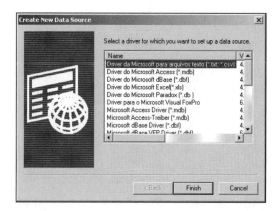

Figure A.2   The Create New Data Source dialog box.

Adding a Microsoft Access DSN

1. From the Create New Data Source dialog box, select Microsoft Access Driver (*.mdb), as shown in Figure A.3.

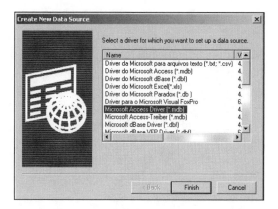

Figure A.3   The Create New Data Source dialog box with Microsoft Access selected.

2. Click the Finish button. You see the ODBC Microsoft Access Setup dialog box, shown in Figure A.4.

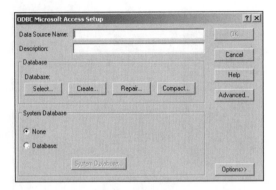

Figure A.4   The ODBC Microsoft Access Setup dialog box.

3. In the Data Source Name field, type the name of the DSN that you will use, such as phpwinaccess. This field is required.

4. In the Description field, you can optionally type a description for the DSN.

5. Click the Select button and choose the path of the Access database that you are creating the DSN up for, such as C:\book\code\phpwin.mdb.

6. Click OK. You see the dialog box shown in Figure A.5.

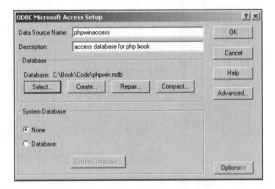

Figure A.5   The ODBC Microsoft Access Setup
dialog box with the required information.

7. Click OK to close the ODBC Microsoft Access Setup dialog box. Your DSN is displayed in the System DSN tab of the ODBC Data Source Administrator dialog box, as shown in Figure A.6.

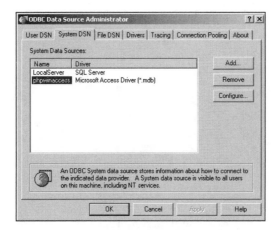

Figure A.6 The ODBC Data Source Administrator
dialog box with the Access DSN added.

Adding a Microsoft SQL Server DSN

1. From the Create New Data Source dialog box, select SQL Server, as
   shown in Figure A.7.

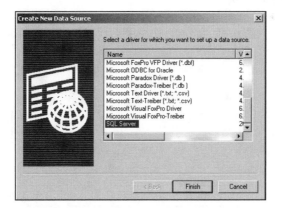

Figure A.7 The Create New Data Source
dialog box with SQL Server selected.

2. Click the Finish button. You see the Create a New Data Source to SQL
   Server dialog box, shown in Figure A.8.

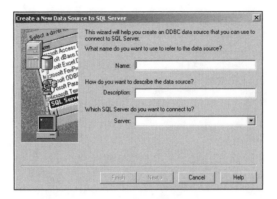

Figure A.8   The Create a New Data Source
to SQL Server dialog box.

3. In the Name field, type the name of the DSN you will use, such as phpwinsqlserver.

4. In the Description field, you can optionally type a description for the DSN.

5. In the Server field, select the name of the SQL database that holds the database you want to make the DSN for. The dialog box should now look like Figure A.9.

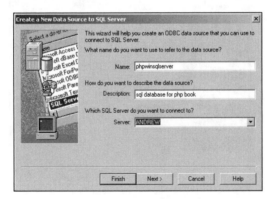

Figure A.9   The SQL Server dialog box with
the required information.

6. Click the Next button. In the dialog box shown in Figure A.10, select With SQL Server authentication using a login ID and password entered by the user. Type your SQL Server login ID and password.

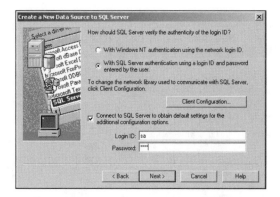

Figure A.10   The SQL Server connection details dialog box.

7. Click the Next button. In the dialog box shown in Figure A.11, change the default database to the database you are setting up the DSN for, such as phpwin.

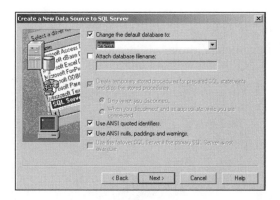

Figure A.11   The SQL Server database selection dialog box.

8. Click the Next button, and then click the Finish button. You see the dialog box shown in Figure A.12.

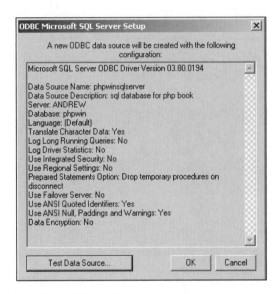

Figure A.12   The ODBC Microsoft SQL Server Setup dialog box.

9. Click the Test Data Source button. You see the SQL Server ODBC Data Source Test dialog box, shown in Figure A.13.

Figure A.13   The successful SQL Server DSN test dialog box.

10. Click OK to close the SQL Server ODBC Data Source Test dialog box.

11. Click OK to close the ODBC Microsoft SQL Server Setup dialog box. Your DSN is displayed in the System DSN tab of the ODBC Data Source Administrator dialog box, as shown in Figure A.14.

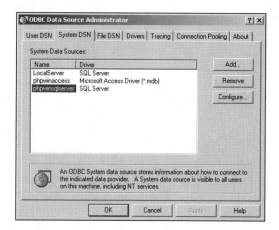

Figure A.14 The ODBC Data Source Administrator dialog box with the SQL Server DSN added.

B

Installing a Web Server

THIS APPENDIX PROVIDES INSTALLATION INSTRUCTIONS FOR the following web
servers:

- Microsoft Internet Information Server (IIS) 4.0
- Microsoft Internet Information Server (IIS) 5.0
- Microsoft Personal Web Server (PWS) 4.0
- Apache
- IMatix Corporation Xitami

Please note that some sort of security issues surround most web servers.
Therefore, before you use any web server in a production environment, you
should first check the vendor's web site for any security information, relevant
security patches, and so on. Also, because this appendix covers setting up a
web server in its default mode only, another good reason to check the vendor's
web site is to find further information on security settings. New Riders
provides a full range of books that focus on security. Visit their web site at
www.newriders.com.

Microsoft Internet Information Server (IIS) 4.0

To install IIS 4 on Windows NT, you must obtain the Windows NT Option Pack from `http://www.microsoft.com/ntserver/nts/downloads/recommended/NT4OptPk/`.

Before you install the Option Pack, be sure that your system meets the following requirements:

- Internet Explorer (IE) 4.01 or above
- Windows NT Service Pack 3 or above

If it does not, both IE 4.01 and NT Service Pack 3 come with the Option Pack. Install them if your are running older versions.

When you launch the Option Pack installer, you see an introduction screen. Click the Next button. You see the End User License Agreement dialog box. Click the Accept button to continue.

If you have a previous version of IIS installed (such as IIS 2 or IIS 3), you see an upgrade dialog box. Click the Upgrade Plus button to continue. If you are not upgrading, you see the Setup dialog box, shown in Figure B.1.

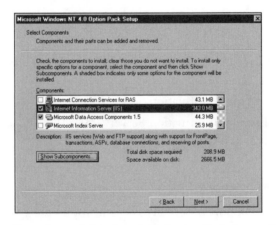

Figure B.1   The Microsoft Windows NT Option Pack Setup dialog box.

Make sure that Internet Information Server (IIS) is selected, and then click the Next button to finish the installation.

Microsoft Internet Information Server (IIS) 5.0

IIS 5 is provided on the Windows 2000 setup disk. You can set up IIS 5 when you install Windows 2000 or afterwards. The information here applies to a post-installation setup.

Select Start, Settings, Control Panel, and choose Add/Remove Programs. In the Add/Remove Programs dialog box, click the Add/Remove Windows Components button. Select Internet Information Services (IIS), as shown in Figure B.2, and click Next to finish the installation. Have the Windows 2000 Server CD on hand, because the installer requires it.

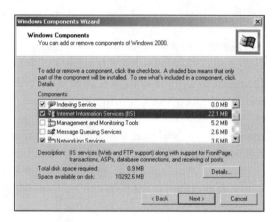

Figure B.2   The Windows Components Wizard dialog box.

Microsoft Personal Web Server (PWS) 4.0

To install PWS on Windows 98, you need to obtain the Windows NT Option Pack from `http://www.microsoft.com/ntserver/nts/downloads/recommended/NT4OptPk/`.

When you launch the Option Pack installer, you see an introduction screen. Click the Next button. You see the End User License Agreement dialog box. Click the Accept button to continue.

Next, you are presented with some setup options (see Figure B.3):

- Minimum: Basic functions; no documentation
- Typical: Basic functions plus documentation and other components
- Custom: All functions with customised choices

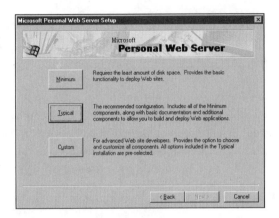

Figure B.3 The Microsoft Personal Web Server Setup dialog box.

For most users, Minimum or Typical is a good choice. However, to ensure that you have the functions you need, the Custom choice is best. Click the Custom button to continue.

The selections presented by default in the Select Components dialog box, shown in Figure B.4, are enough for you to install PWS. However, if you want to customize some selections, you can do so by clicking a selection and then clicking the Show Subcomponents button. When you are happy with your selections, click the Next button to continue.

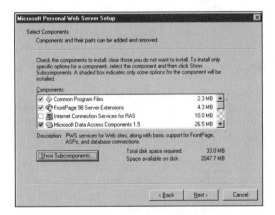

Figure B.4 The Microsoft Personal Web Server setup dialog box with selected options displayed.

Next you see a paths dialog box, as shown in Figure B.5. This dialog box allows you to set the root directory for web pages and other items (depending on the options you selected in the preceding dialog box). The directory for web pages is C:\Inetpub\wwwroot\ by default. It is recommended that you leave this path as the default, because some other software has problems if this path is not the default path.

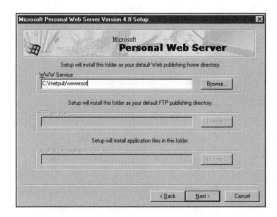

Figure B.5   The Microsoft Personal Web Server Setup paths dialog box.

Click the Next button, and the installation finishes.

Apache

You can download the Apache web server from `http://httpd.apache.org/ dist/httpd/binaries/win32/`. Apache is an open-source web server.

Apache is mirrored on several web sites. If you have trouble downloading Apache from this link, you can download it from one of the mirrors listed on the site.

Installing Apache on Windows requires the Windows Installer. Windows 2000 includes the Installer, but Windows 95/98/NT users need to install it. The link for downloading Installer is available on the Apache download page.

To begin the installation process, double-click the Apache installer. This starts the Apache Installation Wizard. Click the Next button. You see the Apache license agreement. Quickly review the license, and then click the Next button to continue. You see an information page. Click Next to continue.

You see the Server Information dialog box, shown in Figure B.6. Enter your details, and click the Next button to continue.

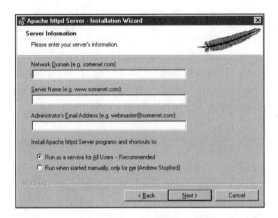

Figure B.6   The Apache setup Server Information dialog box.

Next you see the Setup Type dialog box, shown in Figure B.7. The Custom setting allows you to choose what parts of Apache you want installed. Most users should choose the Complete setting. Click the Next button to continue. You see the Destination Folder dialog box. Here you specify the folder in which Apache will be installed. I recommend that you keep the default setting, but you can change it if you want to. Click the Next button, and the installation finishes.

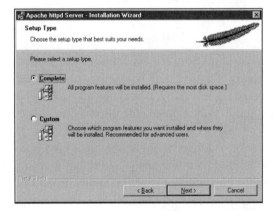

Figure B.7   The Apache Setup Type dialog box.

IMatix Corporation Xitami

Like Apache, the Xitami web server is an open-source web server. It runs on platforms such as Windows, Linux, and OS/2. You can download it from `http://www.imatix.com`.

When you run the installer, you see a welcome dialog box. Click the Next button to continue. You are presented with license information. After you review the licence information, click the Next button to continue.

You see the Select Destination Directory dialog box, shown in Figure B.8. I recommend that you keep the default directory of C:\Xitami, but you can change it if you want. Click the Next button to continue, and the installation finishes.

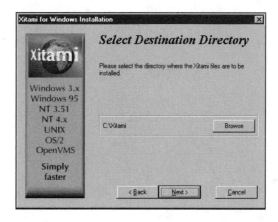

Figure B.8   The Xitami Select Destination Directory dialog box.

Index

S

VOICES THAT MATTER

HOW TO CONTACT US

VISIT OUR WEB SITE

WWW.NEWRIDERS.COM

On our web site, you'll find information about our other books, authors, tables of contents, and book errata. You will also find information about book registration and how to purchase our books, both domestically and internationally.

EMAIL US

Contact us at: **nrfeedback@newriders.com**

- If you have comments or questions about this book
- To report errors that you have found in this book
- If you have a book proposal to submit or are interested in writing for New Riders
- If you are an expert in a computer topic or technology and are interested in being a technical editor who reviews manuscripts for technical accuracy

Contact us at: **nreducation@newriders.com**

- If you are an instructor from an educational institution who wants to preview New Riders books for classroom use. Email should include your name, title, school, department, address, phone number, office days/hours, text in use, and enrollment, along with your request for desk/examination copies and/or additional information.

Contact us at: **nrmedia@newriders.com**

- If you are a member of the media who is interested in reviewing copies of New Riders books. Send your name, mailing address, and email address, along with the name of the publication or web site you work for.

BULK PURCHASES/CORPORATE SALES

The publisher offers discounts on this book when ordered in quantity for bulk purchases and special sales. For sales within the U.S., please contact: Corporate and Government Sales (800) 382-3419 or **corpsales@pearsontechgroup.com**. Outside of the U.S., please contact: International Sales (317) 581-3793 or **international@pearsontechgroup.com**.

WRITE TO US

New Riders Publishing
201 W. 103rd St.
Indianapolis, IN 46290-1097

CALL/FAX US

Toll-free (800) 571-5840
If outside U.S. (317) 581-3500
Ask for New Riders
FAX: (317) 581-4663

New Riders

RELATED NEW RIDERS TITLES

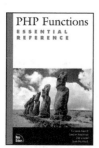

ISBN: 073570970X
768 pages
US$49.99

PHP Functions Essential Reference

Torben Wilson, Zak Greant
Graeme Merrall, Brett
Michlitsch

Co-authored by some of the leading developers in the PHP community, *PHP Functions Essential Reference* is guaranteed to help you write effective code that makes full use of the rich variety of functions available in PHP 4.

ISBN: 0735710201
1152 pages
US$49.99

Inside XML

Steven Holzner

Inside XML is a foundation book that covers both the Microsoft and non-Microsoft approach to XML programming. It covers in detail the hot aspects of XML, such as, DTD's vs. XML schemas, CSS, XSL, XSLT, Xlinks, Xpointers, XHTML, RDF, CDF, parsing XML in Perl and Java, and much more.

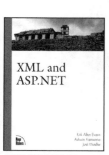

ISBN: 073571200X
848 pages
US$49.99

XML and ASP.NET

Kirk Allen Evans,
Ashwin Kamanna, Joel Mueller

Discover the sheer power and flexibility of the ASP.NET development environment and prepare yourself for the future of web development.

ISBN: 0735709211
800 pages
US$49.99

MySQL

Paul DuBois

MySQL teaches you how to use the tools provided by the MySQL distribution, by covering installation, setup, daily use, security, optimization, maintenance, and trouble-shooting. It also discusses important third-party tools, such as the Perl DBI and Apache/PHP interfaces that provide access to MySQL.

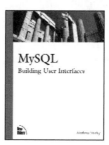

ISBN: 073571049X
656 pages
US$49.99

MySQL: Building User Interfaces

Matthew Stucky

A companion to *MySQL*, this book teaches you to make decisions on how to provide a robust and efficient database solution for any enterprise. The author presents valuable insight from his experience with different companies with varying needs and sizes. This is the only book available that covers GTK+ and database accessibility.

ISBN: 0735709971
416 pages with CD-ROM
US$39.99

Web Application Development with PHP 4.0

Tobias Ratschiller, Till Gerken

Web Application Development with PHP 4.0 explains PHP's advanced syntax including classes, recursive functions, and variables. The authors present software development methodologies and coding conventions, which are a must-know for industry quality products and make developing faster and more productive. Included is coverage on web applications and insight into user and session management, e-commerce systems, XML applications, and WDDX.

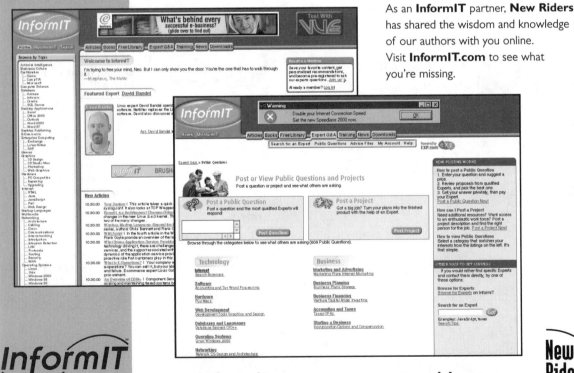

Colophon

Pictured on the cover is a photograph of a Mayan Chac Mool figure in Cancun, Mexico. Chac Mool was considered the 'messenger of the Gods'. This figure always appears holding a receptacle on his lap used to receive Mayan offerings. The original Chac Mool is located in front of the entrance of the Temple of the Warriors in Chichen Itza, Mexico, dating all the way back to 1,000 A.D.

This book was written and edited in Microsoft Word, and laid out in QuarkXPress. The font used for the body text is Bembo and MCPdigital. It was printed on 50# Husky Offset Smooth paper at Von Hoffman Graphics, Inc., in Owensville, Missouri. Prepress consisted of PostScript computer-to-plate technology (filmless process). The cover was printed at Moore Langen Printing in Terre Haute, Indiana, on Carolina, coated on one side.